THE KNITTER'S
BOOK OF WOOL

*The Ultimate Guide to Understanding,
Using, and Loving this Most Fabulous Fiber*

BY CLARA PARKES

POTTER
CRAFT
New York

CONTENTS

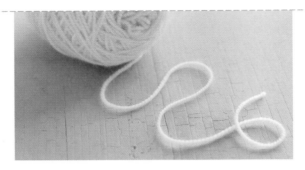

Preface

I have always loved wool—I mean really and truly loved it, like Claude Monet loved his Giverny and Julia Child loved her butter. Discovering a new wool yarn, smelling it, touching it, dreaming of what I can do with it, knitting and washing a swatch and seeing how it transforms . . . those things make me feel complete and fulfilled.

But there would be no wool yarn were it not for the hardworking shepherds who take such pride in their flocks and fleeces. Shepherds sleep little during lambing season, their animals are never far from their thoughts, and they often work two jobs just to keep the farm going.

And there would be no wool yarn were it not for the evervigilant sheepdogs, and guard llamas and donkeys; the shearers who labor under extremely trying conditions; and the mill workers, who care—I mean really care—about each bale of wool that passes through their hands.

To be able to honor this special material and all the people who bring it to us has been like getting to live in the world's largest candy shop after closing time. Over many months I've opened every single jar, sampled each sweet confection on the shelves, and even peeked at the recipes in the back room. Now comes the fun part, when I finally get to unlock the doors, switch the sign to "Open," and share all my discoveries with you.

Introduction

Imagine if all the wine in the world—red and white alike—were mixed together and sold as generic "wine." Think of how many centuries of craftsmanship and flavor would be lost, and how mediocre it would taste compared with how it would taste if the grapes had been kept separate or selectively blended. Such an act would be almost unthinkable in the food world. But in the knitting world, just as much nuance is lost every day when flat, bouncy, long, short, matte, and lustrous fibers from ancient and modern sheep breeds alike are bundled together and sold as generic "wool" yarn.

Contrary to what those yarn labels may suggest, there is no generic, one-size-fits-all wool, just as there is no generic one-size-fits-all sheep. In fact, more than 200 distinct sheep breeds exist today, each growing unique fibers. Sometimes we're given a glimpse of what lies within a wool yarn—usually with the mainstream Merino or perhaps the occasional Shetland or Icelandic wools—but such occasions are rare and represent only the tip of a large and sorely neglected iceberg.

Things are starting to change. Just as the food world is moving away from large-scale monoculture toward locally produced artisanal products, the knitting world is embracing a return to the local and artisanal. Sheep farms, spinneries, and large yarn companies alike are producing new yarns

with words like Bluefaced Leicester, Columbia, Cormo, and Rambouillet on the labels—words that represent actual sheep breeds with diverse kinds of fiber. As each new name appears on our skeins, we need to step back and learn more about what those names actually mean. And that's exactly what I set out to do in this book: translate the vast world of sheep and their wool into the language and context of knitting. The next time you discover a new skein of wool, whether it is breed-specific or not, I want you to have a good idea where it came from, how it's likely to behave, and what you should do with it.

Why? Because sheep can grow different types of fibers that are ideally suited for different kinds of projects. Some are softer than others. Some are slinky, some are crisp and

spongy, some are so rugged and durable you could build a house out of them (and people do). Knowing the distinct personalities of wool fibers ahead of time will help you create a happy marriage between yarn and project.

We begin with the fundamentals: What is wool? What is this magical material made of, how does it get off the sheep, and how is it transformed from a jumbled mass of dirty fluff into a gorgeous yarn that so tempts us at our local yarn store (LYS)?

The answers to these questions prepare us for the next step in our journey: meeting the sheep breeds that provide their fabulous fiber. For the purposes of this book, I've grouped breeds into five high-level categories on the basis of their shared backgrounds and/or fiber characteristics. You'll learn more about how to identify and use the fibers in each category,

and you'll even meet some of each category's most notable wool-growing sheep breeds.

What about the many wool yarns that also have other fibers blended in? We go there, too. You'll learn why certain fibers tend to be mixed with wool, what they add to the yarn, how these qualities may vary depending on the percentage of fibers in the blend, and what *other* fibers can also give you similar results.

And finally, the fun part: we get to grab our needles, cast on, and start playing with these different wools for ourselves. I've assembled a host of patterns that let you experience everything wool has to offer—patterns that let you play with **woolen-** and **worsted-spun** yarns from **finewools** all the way to **longwools**, **primitive breeds**, and generic wool yarns alike. You'll find lace, colorwork, ribbing, and cables; patterns that require attention and others that let you daydream; items to warm head, hands, feet, and body. These patterns will become trusted friends that you can revisit each time you discover a new wool and want to take it for a test drive.

Even if you never seek out a breed-specific yarn in your life, this book will still help you make smarter and happier use of all the wool yarns that you find at your LYS. You may not immediately be able to pick up a skein of wool yarn and know which sheep breed produced the wool—wool graders apprentice for years to gain such knowledge—but you will learn how to look, feel, listen to, and even *smell* a yarn to get hints as to the type of wool it contains, how it was processed and spun, and how you can make it sing on your needles.

Let's begin.

Terms in boldface are defined in the Glossary, page 202.

What Is Wool?

Wool is an extraordinarily ingenious and versatile material that requires no chemistry lab to create, only land, fencing, food, water, and of course a few sheep. It's absorbent, flexible, accommodating, durable, annually renewable, and infinitely varied in how it comes to us. The perfect companion to our knitting endeavors, wool deserves to be every knitter's best friend. It's hard not to sound like an infomercial for wool, but it's also impossible to overstate just how varied and useful a material it is.

Wool fibers welcome being washed, teased apart, pulled into thin strands, twisted together, wrapped around needles, and then worked to form the endless interlocking loops that make up knitted fabric. Wool loves to move—which is convenient since we, the folks who work with it and wear it, also like to move. Cotton fibers may be bent back and forth only about 3,000 times before they break, but a wool fiber can be bent back and forth more than 20,000 times before it even shows signs of breaking. Dry, wool can be stretched up to 30 percent of its length and then return to its original size; wet, those same fibers can be stretched by up to 60 percent with similarly resilient results.

Wool fibers also come with a built-in evaporative cooling and heating system designed to keep sheep warm and dry, but it does an even better job keeping *us* warm and dry. Wool fibers are hygroscopic, which means that they readily absorb ambient moisture and then release it when conditions turn dry again. On any average day, a wool fiber may contain between 10 and 14 percent water, but if the humidity jumps, the fiber can ultimately absorb up to 30 percent of its weight in moisture before it starts to feel wet against your skin. (If you've ever left a plastic bag of wool yarn in a sunny window, you may have noticed a fine layer of condensation gather on the inside of the bag—this is the moisture being pulled out of the fiber.) And as if these moisture-wicking properties weren't enough, wool actually gives off heat as it absorbs moisture (a result of the chemical reaction that occurs between water and wool fiber as the water's hydrogen bonds break down), which explains why you can wear a wool sweater outside on a snowy day and stay toasty warm.

Wool's high internal moisture content is also what keeps the fibers from conducting static electricity. Because static electricity tends to attract fine dirt and dust particles and pull them deep into the fabric, wool is especially popular among allergy sufferers. No static electricity means a low dirt and dust content in your clothes, which means easier breathing.

And although wool's synthetic siblings have a nasty tendency to melt and turn into chemical ooze when exposed to flame (which is not good when that ooze is on your skin), wool fiber does everything possible to extinguish itself. For this very reason, wool has long been used for firemen's blankets, upholstery fabrics, and carpeting in large public buildings; it's also ideally suited for baby clothes and blankets.

Wool has everything going for it. My goal is to help prepare you for all those wonderful new wool yarns emerging in shops and festivals and to help you better understand and enjoy all the generic wool yarns you may already have in your stash.

Anatomy of a Fiber

Wool is a natural protein fiber that begins its life deep in the hair follicles of a sheep's skin. Carbon, hydrogen, oxygen, nitrogen, and sulfur come together to form long polypeptide chains of 19 amino acids that grow out of each follicle and become the shafts of fiber that we see.

As a wool fiber emerges from the follicle, a sebaceous gland coats it with a greasy emollient that both waterproofs the fiber and protects the sheep's skin. The textile industry calls this waxy substance **grease**, and it is removed during washing and often later purified into **lanolin**. Many people prefer to call this material "lanolin" right from the start, because "grease" isn't exactly something you want to hold in your hands.

Whether you call it grease or lanolin, this waxy substance gives yarn a marvelous spicy scent. The more gently and minimally a fiber has been processed, the more distinct that scent can be. Just as lanolin helps waterproof the sheep's coat, a lanolin-rich yarn will also create a remarkably water-repellent garment. In fact, long before the advent of Gore-Tex™, Irish fishermen stayed warm and dry while at sea by wearing "oiled" (i.e., lanolin-rich) Aran wool sweaters. The more processed the fibers, the less lanolin remains. Once wool fibers reach that triple-sifted cake flour state of a fine, highly processed Italian Merino yarn, most traces of lanolin are usually gone.

Sheep also release a small amount of natural perspiration onto the fibers. When it dries, this solution is called **suint**, and it plays a big role in keeping wool fibers clean. This potassium-rich, water-soluble solution actually travels up the fiber shaft toward the outer tip, attracting dirt and directing it away from the skin. Like lanolin, however, suint is also removed when the **fleece** is washed. Fibers need to be clean before they can be processed into yarn.

SCALING THE SURFACE

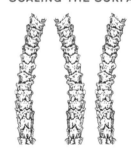

If you look at a wool fiber under a powerful microscope, you'll see that the outer surface is covered with a series of interlocking scales, rather like roof tiles. This outer surface is called the cuticle, and it actually consists of three layers: the epicuticle, exocuticle, and endocuticle. From a knitting perspective, we're interested in those scales. They form a fine but strong protective layer on the fiber surface, helping direct moisture and dirt away from the sheep's body. We have scales on our hair, too. If you rub your fingers along a strand of hair from scalp to the tip, the hair will feel smooth. Rub your fingers backwards, from tip to scalp, and you'll feel

resistance; those are the scales pushing back against your fingers.

Scales play a big role in how a yarn looks and feels because they form the outer surface of the fiber—the surface we touch and off which light reflects. Finer wools, such as Merino and Rambouillet, have extremely small and numerous scales that closely overlap one another. (Picture a stack of nesting flowerpots in which only the rims are visible.) The smaller the scales, the lower chance that even the most sensitive skin will feel them, which translates into a fiber that feels softer. Merino is often marketed as the "no itch" wool because it has such tiny scales—in fact, every inch (2.5cm) of Merino fiber has upwards of 2,000 scales in it.

Moving from finewools to mediumwools, the scales get a bit bigger as the diameter of the fibers also increases. No longer considered "fine," these fibers may have more of a presence when worn against sensitive skin. From medium to longwools, those scales get even bigger and they stop overlapping as much. (Imagine staggered roof tiles instead of those deeply nesting flowerpots.)

Scales and Luster

Scales dictate how light reflects off of the surface of each fiber and, ultimately, how it reflects off the yarn itself. The tinier the scales, the more fragmented their reflection, causing the yarn to appear more matte.

The larger, smoother scales in most longwools (around 700 scales per inch [2.5cm], compared with those 2,000 per inch [2.5cm] in Merino) form a smoother fiber surface with little interruption, causing light to reflect much more brightly. This reflective quality is called **luster**. The smoother the fiber surface, the brighter the reflection and the higher the luster; the more fragmented the fiber surface, the more matte the reflection and the lower the luster.

A high-luster Wensleydale (left) and a low-luster Cormo (right).

The luster in some longwools—fittingly called luster longwools—is so brilliant that it almost rivals silk. Wensleydale is probably the finest, most highly prized fiber in this category, followed by Cotswold, Teeswater, and Leicester Longwool. Less lustrous (or semilustrous) fibers are often called **demiluster** and can include longwools, such as Bluefaced Leicester, as well as a few other special breeds, like Jacob. These terms and numbers are great for late-night trivia games and/or impressing folks at your next fiber festival, but remember always to base your final determination about how a fiber looks or feels based on what *you* see and feel—regardless of how it's been labeled.

Scales and Felt

Scales play another crucial role in wool that many people discover only by mistake. When wool is submerged in warm water, the fiber shaft begins to absorb water and swell. Add soap, and the process occurs even more readily. As each fiber grows, its scales pop out like a row of umbrellas opening. Vigorously rub the fibers together, and all those scales will interlock and tangle irretrievably. When a piece of knitted fabric is subjected to this procedure, the entire fabric shrinks and its surface blurs into the dense, matted material we call **felt**. (You may also encounter the term "fulling,"

which refers to the process of felting knitted garments.) The key thing to know is that felting cannot be undone. You can stretch the fabric out a little by soaking it in warm water with hair conditioner and then forcibly reshaping it. The fabric may give some, but ultimately it will still remain felted.

Not all wools felt as readily as others. It's important to remember that sheep have been bred to serve the textile traditions of the people raising them. Shetland and Icelandic sheep are a perfect example of this cultural intervention. While the breeds are considered close genetic cousins, felt plays a very small role in the Shetland Islands fiber tradition, and Shetland wool does not felt readily. Meanwhile, felt plays a much larger role in the Icelandic textile tradition, and Icelandic wool felts in a heartbeat. We don't know for sure whether the textile tradition evolved to accommodate the materials people had at hand or whether the sheep were bred to accommodate the desired textile tradition, or perhaps a combination of both. But the relationship between sheep breed and textile tradition is ancient.

If enmeshed scales lead to felting, then you might think that fibers with bigger, easier-to-enmesh scales would felt more quickly. But the opposite is true—the more numerous and tightly packed those fine scales, the more umbrellas you have opening and tangling with one another—which is why finewools are so ideal for felting. The fewer the scales and the farther apart they are (which is the case in longwools), the longer you'll have to work to make the fibers felt. Furthermore, most **Down** and Down-type wools won't felt at all either. But be careful: Just because one breed is less likely to felt doesn't mean you should feel safe tossing it in the washing machine. If truly nonfelting yarn is what you need, then stick with yarns that are specifically labeled "machine washable" or "superwash." Also keep in mind that bleaching can erode scales, which is why some bright-white, highly processed wools simply won't felt. When in doubt, knit a swatch and toss it in your washing machine to see how it will felt.

Since scales play a crucial role in felting, then the easiest way to keep wool from felting would be to remove those scales, right? Yes. And that's exactly what early scientists did. The first experiments in the so-called shrinkproofing of wool involved removing the scales from the outside of the fiber. This process is easier than it sounds and has been possible for a long, long time: Simply soak the wool in a caustic soda. Boiling the wool in soap will do the same thing. (It tends to produce a pretty unhappy yarn in the process, so I don't recommend you try this at home.)

Scientists quickly discovered that the scales existed for a reason. Without their protective outer coat, fibers quickly became chalky and brittle. Scientists figured that if they couldn't remove the scales, the next best thing would be to glue them down with a fine polymer resin. That was the standard practice for a long time, but a new enzyme treatment is gaining widespread acceptance today. The enzyme eats away at the outer edges of the scales while leaving the roots of the scales intact, thereby keeping the fiber sealed and protected.

When you see the term "Superwash" on a yarn label, it means that the wool has been processed according to a standard set by the International Wool Secretariat (now The Woolmark Company) in the early 1970s. Other wool yarns processed differently may simply be marketed as "machine washable." For knitters, the difference in processes is usually negligible.

I say "usually" because there is one way that machine-washable yarns can differ from one another, and you can only detect it by swatching. The difference stems from the fact that machine-washable wools no longer have scales that grab onto one another and provide natural friction between fibers. Without that friction, the fibers can slip more easily from one another's grasp, causing your knitted fabric to stretch out of shape—sometimes dramatically. This phenomenon is usually not noticeable while you're knitting. The surprise comes after the first wash, when your previously perfect sleeves are suddenly twice as long. To detect whether or not a machine-washable wool yarn may stretch, it's crucial that you knit a test swatch, *wash* it, and hang it to dry—the hanging part will simulate whatever stretching might occur in a larger piece. Any changes will be revealed, and you'll be glad you checked before spending countless hours on a sweater that becomes a dress after the first wash.

The cortex also dictates a fiber's overall strength, elasticity, and ability to retain dye.

INTO THE CORTEX

Peeling back the scales and venturing deeper into the fiber, we pass through a tiny space called the cell membrane complex, or CMC, which serves as a portal for dye as it heads for the main body of the fiber. After fiber has reached optimal dye saturation, the CMC should be completely devoid of dye.

Immediately past the CMC is the cortex, which occupies the vast majority of space (up to 90 percent) within each wool fiber. The cortex actually consists of two types of cells, the orthocortex and paracortex, which dictate the fiber's **crimp** structure. They wrap around one another helically in such a way that the orthocortex always falls on the outer curve, and the paracortex on the inner curve, of each crimp. Low-crimp fibers tend to have more orthocortex cells, while high-crimp fibers tend to have more paracortex cells. The cortex also dictates a fiber's overall strength, **elasticity**, and ability to retain dye. If this is too much fiber science for you, just remember, "cortex=crimp." Not so hard, right?

MEDULLA IN THE MIDDLE

At the fiber's core we may sometimes find a medulla—a hollow canal or network of hollow tubes filled with air. The trait to grow fibers with substantially developed medullas (often called "medullated fibers") has been largely bred out of the newer finewool breeds, because large medullas result in thick, weak, and wiry fibers that do not take dye well.

Some particularly long, thick, and wiry hairs grow among the softer, downy **undercoat** in **dual-coated** and primitive sheep breeds, such as Shetland and Icelandic. These medullated fibers are called **guard hairs**, and they are usually removed during processing.

Sheep can also grow another fiber called **kemp**, a short, white fiber with a massive medulla, chalky appearance, and prickly disposition. Kemp fibers help the sheep by pulling moisture away from their skin. The wetter the climate, the higher the likelihood for kemp fibers to appear—although the tendency to grow kemp has been carefully bred out of the newer, improved breeds.

The Softness Myth

The quality that matters to most knitters these days is touch. Specifically, *soft* touch. If we want to experience everything wool has to offer, we must begin by adjusting our expectations. In our quest for softness, most of us have been consuming a pretty substantial diet of the yarns in which all the fibers have been blended together into a rather standard, homogenous thing called "wool." Any fiber that doesn't qualify as super-soft has been discarded, and among those wools that have made it into the mix, any unique traits of specific breeds have likely been toned down for the greater good of the blend.

Our hands have been trained to embrace soft and reject everything else. When you start experiencing different breeds on their own, you'll immediately begin to feel a lot of the "everything else"—yarns with greater vibrancy, texture, visual appeal, and what I think of as "crunch." There's an important distinction between crunch (picture a freshly baked loaf of whole-grain bread) and scratch (that same loaf of bread left sitting out on the kitchen counter for a few days). Crunchy yarns are healthy and vibrant, with fibers that have persistence and personality. In a garment they stand their ground, keep you warm, and wear well.

The so-called "scratchy" wools, on the other hand, are often simply a reflection of a sheep's genetic traits. If the sheep originated in a culture that was more interested in meat and milk than in fiber for underwear, then the animals simply weren't bred for softness and their fiber is not suitable for handknitting yarn. Sometimes, like that stale loaf of bread, a yarn can also become scratchy by human intervention—in

VARIETY IS THE SPICE OF LIFE

Nature has its own checks and balances system that relies on genetic variety. Our focus on softness, whiteness, staple length, and strength has put many older breeds at risk of extinction. What remains—highly bred finewool Merinos—has an increasingly limited genetic base lacking untold traits for everything from disease resistance to adaptability to changing climate conditions. As with heirloom versus genetically modified seeds, we risk not knowing what we've lost until it's too late. Knitters can slow the trend by seeking out and supporting other breeds. If we keep going for the white flour, we'll lose the other grains entirely. But if we open our minds and hands to variety, who knows where it may lead us?

which case overzealous processors, and not the animals themselves, are often responsible for the dry, brittle, and lifeless wool yarns you may encounter.

Among those breeds that *are* suitable for handknitting, remember that each breed has its place and purpose among our projects. Not everything needs to be knit in the softest, most delicate wool. In fact, many projects prefer to be made out of something more durable. Take, for example, a sweater you know you'll wear over a turtleneck in winter. Or mittens or a hat that you need to keep you warm. Perhaps a felted doorstop, a tea cozy, or a heavier coat. These kinds of projects long to be made out of hearty, warm wools that are otherwise too robust for next-to-skin wear. In contrast, using superfine baby Merino on such projects would be like using embroidery scissors to cut heavy paper.

At the other end of the spectrum are things like scarves, sleeveless shells, form-fitting sweaters, and baby booties—the kinds of high-touch, low-abrasion garments we want to be as soft as possible because they'll be sitting directly against our bare skin. Finewools such as Merino thrive in these kinds of projects, whereas a sturdier farm wool would be overkill—like using a power saw to cut that same piece of paper.

But the ultimate decision on softness lies in the hands of the beholder. When it comes to touch, each person's perception of crunchy and scratchy varies dramatically. I know some knitters who break out in hives if they touch anything but the finest, purest Merino, whereas others will happily wear socks that could double as pot scrubbers. My advice would be not to discount anything until you actually sit down and work with it for a while. Each new breed brings a new knitting experience. Adjust your expectations and you can start to have fun sampling the nuances of each breed, enjoying the nutrients they bring to your fiber diet. Yes, wools from other

ALLERGIES: WHEN OUR HEART SAYS "YES," BUT OUR SKIN SAYS "NO"

A true allergic response to wool is quite rare, but there's no denying the genuine irritation that a small percentage of people experience when wearing wool. The cause is still up for debate and I am most definitely not a trained dermatologist, but a few theories prevail. First, irritation might be a response to the microscopic scales on the wool fiber, in which case you may want to experiment with finewools such as Merino, which have the tiniest scales. Second, irritation may be a dermatological response to lanolin rather than wool itself. In this case, you may want to try highly processed commercial finewools such as Merino, from which most of the lanolin has been removed. Or you could seek out fibers from breeds that produce a lower quantity of lanolin, such as Shetland or Icelandic. You can also reduce any residual lanolin content in a farm yarn by soaking the skein in hot water with a dab of Dawn dishwashing liquid—being careful to avoid any agitation or extreme temperature changes between the wash and rinse water.

The third theory—one that I've witnessed personally—stems more from the yarn itself than the fibers it contains. Some people respond to materials added to the wool during processing: an oil to tame the fibers during spinning, mordants or dyestuff added during dyeing and not sufficiently rinsed, or even conditioners or fabric softeners that were added after dyeing. Soaking a skein in warm soapy water may get rid of the residual irritant.

breeds may feel different than what you're used to—and that's the whole point.

THE DANCE OF DIAMETER AND SOFTNESS

Over the years, people have come up with many units of measurement to help make the intangible notion of softness, or fineness, more tangible. The problem is that until recently, we relied on our fingers to determine fineness, and nobody could agree on one common measurable unit. Several systems determined a fiber's fineness by the number of hanks you could theoretically spin from 1 pound of clean fiber—one system was based on 300-yard (274-m) hanks, another on 560-yard (512-m) hanks, and yet another on 1,600-yard (1463-m) hanks. Other systems relied on yet more vocabulary and seemingly random numbers, like the Denier and Grex systems, the latter of which includes wraps of 700,000 yards (64008m), 1/7,000-yard (0.0001m) wraplets, and 1/700-pound (0.0648g) grains. Whew!

The advent of high-powered microscopes brought order to the chaos, and the **micron** became the most common international unit of measurement for fiber fineness. One micron is one millionth (0.000001) of a meter, or 1/25,400 of an inch, and it is often represented with the Greek letter mu (μ). You'll see more about micron counts when we reach the breeds section (page 37). For now, just remember that the smaller the fiber diameter, or micron count, the finer the fiber. The higher the micron count, the rougher the fiber.

How do they measure the actual diameter of a fiber, anyway? Perhaps with an extremely tiny measuring tape? Nope. They use electro-optical and image analysis machines, which allow technicians to measure 2,000 fibers from a fleece and generate accurate diameter calculations in a matter of minutes. A newer machine called the Optical Fiber Diameter Analyzer (OFDA) can analyze 4,000 fibers in 30 seconds and includes a portable unit that can be set up right in a **shearing** pen. If you've been to a major fiber festival, gone

to the fleece competition area, and seen people in white lab coats standing next to impressive-looking machines, those people were no doubt measuring the microns of different fleeces.

THE PRICKLE FACTOR

A correlation exists between fiber diameter and skin irritation based on a simple idea: thicker fibers don't bend as easily. And if they don't bend, they poke our skin, activating our pain receptors and causing irritation—the longer the protruding fiber, the greater the likelihood of irritation. From the sensation of "prickle" or "itch" was born the term "prickle factor."

According to an Australian study[*], males are less sensitive overall to skin prickle than women, and prickle sensitivity may decrease with age—possibly because skin hardens as it ages. The study also shows that our sensitivity increases in warmer weather.

The study concludes that woven fabrics are less prickly than knitted ones, but more important, it suggests that comfortable next-to-skin wear is best obtained from fabric with a mean micron count of 21 or less, and that contains no more than 5 percent of fibers with a micron count of 30 or greater. Remember, this is just *next-to-skin* wear we're talking about—the addition of any fabric barrier between other fibers and your skin (say, a turtleneck or T-shirt) eliminates all prickle factor.

[*] Released by Australia's Textile and Fibre Technology Research Program of the Commonwealth Scientific and Industrial Research Organisation

A perfectly preserved fine, even, and well-defined crimp pattern in unwashed Cormo locks.

While the micron reigns supreme in the handspinning world, the older systems haven't completely gone away. The **Bradford count** system—also called the English worsted yarn count system or **spinning count**—is still widely used. A truly subjective measure of fineness, the Bradford count is based on the number of 560-yard (512-m) hanks theoretically spun from 1 pound (2.2kg) of clean wool **roving**, and the resulting number has an "s" after it. The idea behind the Bradford count system is that the finer the wool, the more fibers per pound, which means that more yarn can be spun from that pound of fiber. The rougher the wool, the thicker each fiber, and the fewer fibers per pound, which means less yarn can be spun from that pound of fiber. For example, a fine Merino might be graded anywhere from 80s to 64s, meaning one could spin between 80 and 64 hanks of yarn, each with 560 yards (512m), from 1 pound (2.2kg) of clean fiber. Much of the standard generic wool on the market falls in the 62s to 56s range.

Developed before technology existed to evaluate fiber diameter, the Bradford count system was based partly on the notion that there was a direct correlation between a fiber's fineness and its crimp pattern, a theory that has since been disproved. Rarely, if ever, were fibers actually spun at their optimal Bradford count; it is mostly a theoretical measure.

To ground this theory in reality and make it more objective, the U.S. Department of Agriculture (USDA) has assigned specific micron ranges to those Bradford wool grades, resulting in the USDA wool grades. These numbers get more precise. The average fiber diameter of an 80s wool, for example, is 17.70–19.14 microns, while that of a 56s wool corresponds to an average fiber diameter of 26.40–27.84 microns. But even these numbers still refuse to be pinned down too precisely—the USDA rating allows for a standard fiber diameter deviation of 7.59 microns within any fleece.

Most of us probably won't be measuring our yarn down to the tenth of a micron anytime soon. But understanding the language of softness, as interpreted through the Bradford and USDA wool count systems, can help us set appropriate expectations for how a particular kind of wool is going to feel and what it is most eager to become. Every wool has an ideal purpose, and not every purpose can be met by the same wool. That's what makes wool so much fun.

Every wool has an **ideal purpose,** *and not every purpose can be met by the same wool. That's what makes wool* **so much fun.**

Creating with Crimp

Some people grow straight hair, others grow curly—and the variety between the two extremes is nearly infinite. The same is true with sheep, and the natural curl pattern in wool, called crimp, has a huge impact on our knitting experience. The finest wool fibers tend to have the most crimps packed into each fiber, zigzagging their way evenly along the length of the fiber at rates of 14–30 crimps per inch (2.5cm). Moving from finewools to mediumwools, the crimps get larger and the waves more pronounced, decreasing to 8 or even fewer crimps per inch (2.5cm). By the time we reach the longwools, the waves have become large ringlets with a beautiful curl at the tip rather like soft-serve ice cream.

Crimp doesn't always show up as a zigzag, wave, or large curly ringlet, either; it can also be a chaotic jumble that moves in a corkscrew fashion and in fine side-to-side waves. These traits are most often found in what are called Down and Down-type wools. The springy fibers tend to be a little heartier than their tidily crimped finewool counterparts, but their unusual crimp gives them the ability to add bulk and **loft** to other yarns, rather like iceberg lettuce can be used to add bulk and crunch to a salad.

Crimp dictates not only how fibers look but also how they interact with one another in yarn. The fewer crimps in the fiber, the less the fibers will resist lying flat against one another, resulting in a smooth, dense yarn with great luster and drape. The more crimps in the fiber, the more the fibers will push away from one another, creating a lofty, springy yarn.

Crimp also plays a role in a yarn's warmth because it affects the amount of air that can be trapped between neighboring

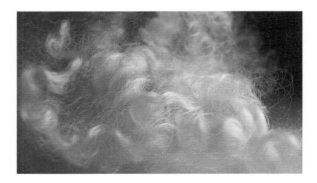

Crimp can be deceiving. The curly locks of this luster longwool may look lofty here, but they will produce a dense and fluid yarn when spun.

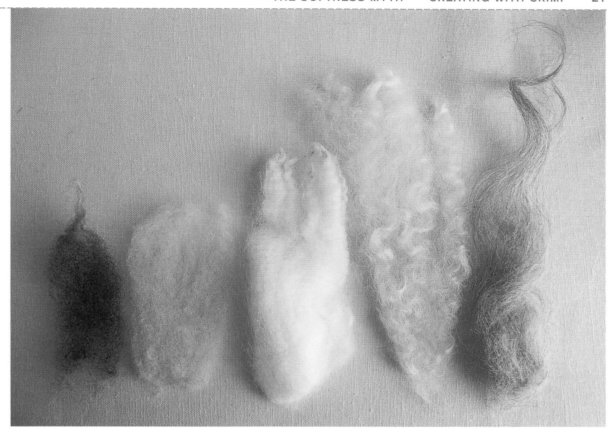

A cross-section of breeds and their natural crimp structures. From left to right: Jacob (dual-coated), Rambouillet (finewool), Corriedale (mediumwool), Teeswater (longwool), and Navajo–Churro (dual-coated).

fibers. The finer and higher the crimp, the more still air will be trapped between the fibers, and the more insulating the fabric will be. But the lower the crimp, the flatter the fibers will lie together and the denser, less insulating the fabric will be.

Handspinners are taught to "spin to the crimp," meaning to spin a yarn so that its plies mimic the wool's natural crimp structure. Although we can't specify the crimps per inch (2.5cm) in commercial yarns, we can use our understanding of the breed's natural crimp pattern to determine whether a breed-specific yarn has been spun the best way for its characteristics. The sample lock photos in the breeds section (page 37) and opposite will help you get a sense of the different crimp structures that exist.

Mills do play with crimp a little bit, spinning flatter or loftier yarns as need dictates, but the fibers will ultimately always dictate what is and isn't possible. It takes an airy wool to make an airy yarn and a long smooth wool to make a long smooth yarn. The most harmonious results come when fiber and twist work with, instead of against, each other.

From Pasture to Pullover—
Turning Wool into Yarn

2

Now that we know what's in a sheep's coat, we can turn our attention to the next step: getting that furry coat off the animal, cleaning it up, and turning it into beautiful yarn. How does that happen, anyway? And can variations in how it's done really produce different results in your knitting? Yes—and we'll find out how in this chapter.

First, a little language lesson. A sheep's coat is called a fleece, and a cluster of fibers growing adjacent to one another on a fleece is called a **lock**. The process of removing a sheep's fleece is called shearing and usually is done once a year, although some breeds grow such long fibers that the sheep can be shorn twice a year. In flocks, shearing is generally timed to occur before lambing season, which is when the ewes are due to deliver their lambs. (Farmers monitor breeding closely so that they know exactly when to expect the lambs, making all this scheduling much easier than it could be otherwise.) Shearing also is timed to coincide with the arrival of warmer weather, because the sheep will be without insulation for several weeks until their coats begin to grow back.

A skilled shearer can remove an entire fleece in two to three minutes—maneuvering both a squirming animal and sharp electric blades in graceful moves that are mesmerizing to watch. The shearer makes precise strokes with the blade so that the fleece is preserved in the exact arrangement in which it grew on the sheep's back. The natural crimp and lanolin help hold all the fibers together even after they've been removed from the sheep, allowing you to spread out a properly shorn fleece and see the full outline of the animal's body, from rump to neck.

Because of a severe shortage of skilled shearers in the United States, some farmers with smaller flocks have had to learn how to shear sheep themselves. Depending on the flock size, some farmers may even invest in their own electric shears or simply use an old-fashioned pair of shearing scissors. They have the advantage of a more leisurely schedule and intimate knowledge of each animal. If they know what they're doing, they can do a beautiful job; if they don't, you probably won't want their yarn—because how fibers are cut makes a huge difference in the final yarn.

In an ideal world, each fiber gets snipped and pulled away from the skin with its neighboring fibers. But sometimes, a shearer misses a spot and needs to pass the shears over it again. Even skilled shearers are forced to do this on occasion. Any fibers that were already cut once but not yet pulled away from the skin are left with what are called second cuts.

Twice-cut fibers tend to be much, much shorter than the rest of the fleece, sometimes measuring just ¼ inch (6mm). These cuts congregate at the base of the fiber, and if they aren't removed before processing, they can have the same effect on your yarn as tissues in a full load of laundry: The short fibers clump together in little pills, called **neps**.

Perfectly healthy, well-shorn fibers—especially finewools—also can get neppy if they are processed too roughly prior to spinning. The finer the fiber, the gentler the processing needs to be so that the fibers don't break. Lofty woolen-spun yarns are more accommodating to neps than smooth yarns, because the fibers tend to be all jumbled already. But even when safely tucked in the jumble of woolen-spun yarns, neps lack the staple length to stay anchored in the yarn and will likely rise to the fabric surface as pills.

Neps can be removed before spinning through a process called **combing**. Removed neps—which are then called **noils**—often are saved and sold for use in other types of textiles. As helpful as combing can be, however, it adds to production costs, subtracts quite a bit of usable fiber, and isn't appropriate for all kinds of fibers, so not every fiber producer chooses to do it. Sometimes a yarn is so marvelous that you're willing to overlook the neps or pluck them out as you go along. But the bottom line is that if you see little pill-like clumps in your yarn, know that more will likely follow.

People haven't always needed to shear sheep to remove their coats. The earliest sheep—those scraggly little guys that tempted our ancestors thousands of years ago—naturally shed their fibers during molting season. When the sheep began to molt, shepherds and their families would sit down with the animal and simply pluck off its wool by hand, a practice called **rooing**. Today, many of the primitive breeds you'll read about later still molt, but the trait has been almost completely bred out of the newer and improved breeds. Those animals will simply keep growing and growing and growing more fiber until it's removed. The best modern example of this is Shrek, the Merino **ram** in New Zealand that had evaded shearing for six years. By the time he was caught in 2004, his fleece was 15 inches (38cm) long, weighed 59 pounds (27kg), and took some 25 minutes for former world blade-shearing champion Peter Casserly to remove.

PRESTO SHEAR-O!

Merino sheep farmers have another shearing option at their disposal, one that involves no shearing whatsoever. Instead, the sheep are injected with a protein that naturally causes a break in their fiber within 7 to 10 days. The sheep are outfitted with a mesh bag that they wear for 28 days—enough extra time for the sheep to start growing a new coat. When the mesh netting is finally pulled off, the entire fleece underneath comes off with it.

The process, commonly referred to as biological shearing and natural wool harvesting, is used primarily on Merino-based sheep breeds in Australia and New Zealand. Farmers who use biological shearing see the practice as a time and stress saver, but the process does have its opponents. Some people are concerned not only about the long-term effects of such injections on animals but also on the livelihoods of the shearers whose jobs the procedure could replace.

Some modern breeds present more challenges for the shearer than others do. Merino and Cormo sheep, for example, have naturally deep folds in their skin. Breeders love the additional square footage for growing fibers, but shearers dread these folds because they present greater opportunities for nicks and second cuts. Large Merino farm operations have the benefit of swift and skilled shearing teams that know exactly how to handle these folds. But small finewool farms lacking the luxury of a skilled shearer may inadvertently see more neps in their yarn, and this is why.

Skirting and Sorting

After a fleece has been shorn, it is spread out so the nastiest of the nasty bits can be removed in a process called skirting. These unwanted pieces—plant matter, second cuts, and manure tags—tend to be around the outer edges of the fleece: the neck, the belly, and the area around the tail.

Then the fleece is ready for sorting. Because one sheep can grow several types of fiber, each with its own micron range, a fleece generally is sorted by areas of the sheep's body. The finest, softest fibers grow around the shoulders, with the next-softest fibers growing along the upper portion of each side of the body. The fibers on the back, rump, and tops of the hind legs tend to be slightly rougher and much more durable. If the difference between fibers is dramatic, a farmer may sort fleeces so that the finest fibers can be sold at a premium. In large flocks, however, this step can be too time consuming, so fleeces will be sold pretty much whole.

Next, the fleece is graded according to characteristics like fineness, brightness, staple length, and strength and then bundled with similar fleeces in giant bales for sale. Sheep farms that don't produce their own yarn will sell raw fibers directly to a dealer or broker or to a wool pool, where they are consolidated and auctioned off in larger lots to commercial producers. More than 100 such wool pools exist across the United States. Some growers—especially those in New Mexico and Texas—send their wool to warehouses that market and sell fibers on consignment.

THE COMMERCIAL CLASS SYSTEM

Wool pools and warehouses are vital tools for the commercial wool industry, but they often come at the expense of breed awareness. The international commercial yarn market doesn't deal in breeds at all; it deals in giant bales of wool sourced from around the world. The fibers in those bales share a

VIRGIN WOOL

In your yarn adventures, you may come across a skein that proudly advertises its fiber content as 100% Virgin Wool. This quaint marketing term harks back to the days when people sold their old knits and woven goods to shoddy mills, where they were shredded and resold in blankets, comforters, and even yarn. Manufacturers needed a way to promote the fact that the wool in their product had never ventured forth into the textile world before, so they coined the term Virgin Wool. In today's commercial yarn market, I know of almost no yarns that aren't considered virgin—yet the term still appears periodically on labels.

similar fineness, brightness, staple length, and strength, but not always the same breed. Sometimes they do, sometimes they do not, and often nobody knows—which is how your favorite generic wool yarn may actually contain fibers from several sheep breeds.

The only exception is Merino wool, which sells at a premium and is always sorted separately. Otherwise, the commercial wool market sees wool through the eyes of its own class system: fine white, regular white, crossbred black face, or carpet white. After you learn how these classes are defined, you'll understand why the breed-specific artisan yarns are so important to knitters.

▶ **Fine white** represents wool fibers of 22 or fewer microns, usually from Merino, Rambouillet, Cormo, Targhee, and some Columbia sheep. These are the finest fibers and they always sell at a premium.

▸ **Regular white** represents wool fibers of 22–26 microns, likely from Columbia and sometimes Targhee, Rambouillet, and Merino sheep. These fibers usually go into the more affordable mainstream wool yarns. (Note: The previous two classes are the only ones that the commercial textile market considers marketable. Because most of our mainstream hand-knitting yarns come from commercial textile mills, the wool used is most often fine white or regular white. Which leaves quite a few sheep breeds out in the dust.)

▸ **Crossbred black face** (white fleece with any colored fibers in it) represents wool fibers of 26–30 microns, from sheep that tend to be crosses between meat sheep breeds (such as Suffolk, Dorset, or Hampshire) and finewool sheep (like Merino).

▸ **Carpet white** includes any wool fibers of 30–40 microns. Period. If you look at the many breeds described in this book, you'll see that quite a few of them fall within this category—including perhaps the best known, Romney. Minus what the artisan mills and microspinneries use, most of these fibers are sold, as the name suggests, to the carpet manufacturing industry.

Because colored fibers cannot be easily bleached and dyed, which is how the international textiles market prefers its materials, they tend to be put in mixed bales and are sold to developing nations—regardless of which breed produced the fiber or how soft it may be.

If fine white and regular white are the only real categories used by the commercial yarn industry, then what happens to all the other marvelous sheep breeds—the Romneys, Blue-faced Leicesters, Cotswolds, and Icelandics—of the world? And what about the fibers that may qualify as fine white or regular white but that we never hear about?

THE GEOGRAPHY OF COMMERCIAL WOOL

If you're commissioning a wool yarn from a mill in the United States, chances are you'll hear the terms "territory," "range," and "fleece" used in reference to the available wools. The commercial wool market has divided up the country into different areas of wool production. Large ranches in the west—especially in Texas, South Dakota, the Rocky Mountains, and the Pacific Coast—grow what they call territory or range wool ("territory" and "range" relating to the land where the animals graze). In the states east of the Mississippi and Missouri Rivers, small farms grow what is simply called fleece wool.

Fortunately for both knitters and the farmers of these niche breeds, a few forward-thinking artisan mills recognize the beauty and marketability of these fibers and are willing to work with smaller quantities per run, and you'll see many examples of their work later in the discussions of the specific breeds (Chapter 3) and in the patterns (Chapter 5). As more artisan mills and microspinneries enter the market, yarn from even more niche breeds will find their way into our knitting baskets.

Rub-a-Dub-Dub: Scouring Fleece

Our skirted, sorted, and graded bales of wool may have journeyed far from the farm by now, but the fleeces themselves are still coated in lanolin and suint, and they still have dirt and dust, twigs, and other bits of random farmyard debris tucked among their fibers. All of this material must be removed and the fibers washed before the fleece can be turned into anything vaguely resembling yarn.

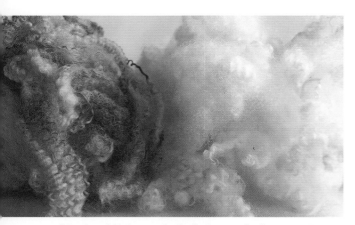

Bluefaced Leicester locks before and after scouring.

The process of washing raw fleece is called **scouring**, and it's a little trickier than just dumping a fleece in a machine and turning the knob to "wash." Suint is water-soluble and can be removed easily, but the waxy secretion we call lanolin requires more work to eliminate. Effective scouring is tricky because it involves removing a fiber's protective coat without damaging the unprotected fiber underneath.

The standard scouring procedure involves putting fleeces in giant tubs of detergent-laced hot water. The fibers are gently agitated ("gently" is the key word with felt-prone finewools) and then squeezed through rollers into a second tub, and a third, and sometimes even a fourth, until most of the grease has been removed.

Wastewater is often collected and further processed to extract and purify the grease, which can then be sold to the cosmetics industry as lanolin. Finewool breeds such as Merino are notoriously high lanolin producers and can lose

up to 40 percent or more of the original fleece's weight with scouring. Other breeds, such as Shetland, grow such clean fleeces that the fibers can sometimes be spun without any scouring at all. (Don't worry, all the commercial yarns you can buy in your LYS have been at least minimally washed.)

Environmental concerns about the chemical detergents and solvents used in commercial scouring, not to mention the sludge and waste they can leave behind, have led some mills to develop more earth-friendly processes. Green Mountain Spinnery, for example, uses only vegetable-based soaps and oils for its Greenspun processing, and Marr Haven Farm (whose yarn is used in the Allegan Cardigan on page 146) uses only soap, water, and salt for scouring. The gentler the scouring process, the more lanolin remains in the fibers—and the greater the water repellency and scent of lanolin in the resulting yarn.

> *The gentler the scouring process, the more lanolin remains in the fibers— and the greater the water repellency and the scent of lanolin in the resulting yarn.*

Scouring may take care of the suint and lanolin, but random twigs, burrs, and other vegetable matter still need to be removed. Here a second process, called carbonization, comes in to play. The wool fibers are soaked in a sulfuric acid solution, dried, and then baked. Any vegetable matter turns to carbon dust and falls out.

Again, concerns about the ecological impact of these chemicals, as well as their effect on the resulting fiber, have led some processors to experiment with other methods for removing vegetable matter. One technique involves running the fibers under heavy rollers, crushing the plant matter into small pieces that fall out easily during **carding**, which is the next step in the process.

Many of the stereotypical "farm" wools have a telltale rich lanolin fragrance and more twigs in them because they come from smaller mills with gentler, less rigorous scouring processes. The first wash or two will eliminate the strongest of that farmyard essence, leaving behind a mellow, full-bodied wool yarn. Bigger mills that mass-produce Merino and generic wool yarns for larger companies often scour the fibers much more rigorously. Usually they do a fine job, but a yarn that feels brittle, dry, or lifeless on the skein may have been scoured too harshly. The drying and damaging effect on the wool fibers is similar to what would happen if you washed your hair with laundry detergent. Although you cannot reverse any damage done to the fibers, you can reintroduce some moisture by washing the yarn and adding hair conditioner to the rinse. Or, you can simply avoid the yarn and choose one that feels better in your hands.

BOTHERING WITH BREAKS

If you study a single wool fiber under a powerful microscope, you'll notice that the fiber's diameter is inconsistent. Sometimes it's thicker, sometimes thinner. While some variation is natural, if a fiber gets too thin, it may break during processing. You can check the soundness of a fleece yourself by taking out a lock of fiber, holding one end in each hand, and giving the lock a few vigorous tugs. A healthy fleece will make a high-pitched "ping" noise. A fleece with thin areas will make a dull noise accompanied by the light static sound of fibers breaking. Spinners call these thin areas "breaks" even if the fibers may not have actually broken yet.

Whether the spinning happens in a commercial mill or in your own living room, removing those broken fibers adds an additional step that increases production costs and subtracts fiber from the yarn. But if not removed, those shorter fibers can turn into puffy pills (neps) in the finished yarn. Even when they don't turn into neps during processing, these shorter fibers can cause your finished garment to pill and wear much more quickly than it should.

What causes these variations in thickness? Sheep grow wool at an average rate of one inch (2.5cm) every two months, and everything that happens to the animal during those two months will be reflected in that growth. Most changes in fiber diameter are brought about by food. As the lush spring pastures dry out and the sheep's diet is supplemented with grain and hay, the fiber can grow thin. If a lamb is moved from mother's milk to grass too quickly, thinning can also occur then. Shepherds often time the annual shearing to coincide with this natural diet-based "break" in the fiber. This way, the thinner areas stay near the ends and are less likely to cause problems during processing and spinning.

Fiber diameter also can fluctuate when an animal comes under other kinds of stress, like illness, pregnancy, extreme heat or drought, or changes in environmental conditions. Many smaller specialty breeders won't even take their finest animals to crowded fiber festivals for this same reason: The stress of the noise and people and other animals may cause a break in the sheep's fleece.

Personally, I prefer the minimally processed wools because they tend to retain more of their natural oils, giving the yarn a livelier feel. Plus, they keep me one step closer to the source, letting me experience many of the smaller breeds that the big mills won't yet touch. If this quality puts you off, stick with the more highly processed wool yarns, but know that you'll miss out on many breeds in the process.

Spin City

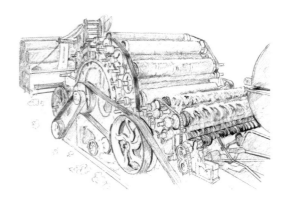

After the fibers have been cleaned, it's time to get them ready for spinning. The first step is to open up the locks and separate all the fibers so that each can be pulled and twisted on its own, in a process called carding. Clean fibers are fed into a carder, a massive machine that has a series of large, fierce-looking cylinders covered with fine metal teeth. Each cylinder rotates at a different speed, causing the teeth to grab the fibers off the previous cylinder and lead them onto the next, opening up the clumps and teasing apart the fibers as they go. As the clumps open and fibers separate, remaining bits of vegetable matter fall out. A wide blanket of blended fibers spills from the other end of the carder. Handspinners call this fiber blanket **roving**, but mills call it **sliver** (pronounced "sly-ver") or slubbing. It's usually split into several narrower ribbons of fiber and fed into tall bins to await the next step: spinning.

Mills have two real choices here. They can spin a woolen yarn straight from that sliver, producing an airy yarn with a fuzzy, jumbled surface. Or they can further tidy up the fibers and spin a tighter, more orderly worsted-spun yarn. Each spinning technique has its reasons for existing, its benefits and its drawbacks, all of which you can learn about in much greater detail in my previous book, *The Knitter's Book of Yarn* (Potter Craft 2007). Here I focus on those two spinning techniques as they relate specifically to wool.

SPINNING WOOLEN

The oldest and easiest path from fiber to yarn is to spin directly from the carded sliver—producing a lofty, jumbled, old-fashioned-looking yarn we call woolen or woolen-spun. The carding machine organizes the fibers to a certain degree, but they still may lie in all sorts of directions, including perpendicular to the direction of the yarn.

Remember, it takes an airy fiber to make an airy yarn. This is why the woolen spinning process lends itself best to fibers that are 2½ inches (6.5cm) or shorter and that have a high degree of natural crimp.

All that built-in crimp gives woolen-spun yarns a marvelous elasticity and a willingness to forgive any irregular tension you may have in your stitches. It also gives you greater flexibility with gauge—you can go up or down a needle size (or two) to get the gauge required in a pattern without having to worry that the fabric will be too loose or tight. The fibers simply expand or contract to fill whatever space you give them.

This same expansion and contraction is especially noticeable after you wash your woolen-spun garment for the first time. The fibers relax, stretch their legs, and explore their new neighborhood, often shifting and resettling in a process we call **blooming**. The final fabric has a much more cohesive, "finished" look and feel. The tendency to bloom is what

TWIST AND TOUCH: THE WOOLEN SIDE

Our experience of a yarn is greatly affected by the number of fibers that touch our skin. This makes our experience of a woolen-spun yarn—with all those loose ends sticking out—highly dependent on the grade of fibers that it contains. If the fibers come primarily from softer finewool breeds, such as the Elsa Wool Company Cormo yarn used in the Sweet Fern Mitts (page 96), you'll feel a buttery softness against your skin. If the fibers are from mediumwool, Down, or Down-type breeds, such as the Rowan Scottish Tweed yarn used in the Allegan Cardigan (page 146), you may feel a little more crunch depending on your skin sensitivity and comfort level. On the flipside, however, that crunchier yarn may create a stronger and warmer garment.

Elsa Wool Company Cormo spun woolen (left) and worsted (right).

makes woolen-spun yarns so exciting, because the magic occurs at the very end of the creative process.

Nearly 90 percent of most woolen-spun yarn is actually composed of air, not fiber. All that air gives you an incredibly insulating but potentially vulnerable material, because short fibers provide less reinforcement along the length of the yarn. For this reason, woolen-spun yarns tend to be composed of two or three plies to help hold the fibers together. But even with multiple plies for protection, the loose ends that give woolen yarns their telltale fuzzy halo also can join together and form pills relatively easily.

From a knitting perspective, woolen-spun wool yarns are ideal for projects you want to have lots of loft without being too heavy, as well as projects that won't see undue abrasion

or wear and tear. Woolen-spun yarns tend to render textured stitchwork with a subdued, mossy overtone that extends to colorwork as well.

SPINNING WORSTED

The second path from fiber to yarn involves the worsted-spinning process, which produces a smoother, stronger yarn by bringing total order to fibers before spinning. Mills do this by literally pulling the carded sliver through a series of fine metal combs so that the fibers are all aligned in the same direction and any short or irregular fibers are removed. The difference between carding and combing wool fibers is much like the difference between brushing and combing your own hair: Brushing creates general order with a little frizz left for good measure, while combing aligns every hair into smooth submission. In wool yarn, combing best lends itself to longer, smoother fibers—ideally 3 inches (7.5cm) or longer—that naturally enjoy lying flat against one another.

Once combed, the fibers are then drawn out and twisted together, creating a yarn we call worsted or worsted-spun.

WORSTED VS. WORSTED: KNOW YOUR CONTEXT

Be careful when you see the word "worsted," because it also describes a specific thickness of yarn—regardless of whether that yarn was spun woolen or worsted. Worsted-spun yarns exist in almost every weight, but worsted-*weight* yarns always knit up at approximately 16–20 stitches per 4 inches (10cm).

Worsted-spun yarns are often made from loosely spun individual plies that are then tightly twisted together for structure. Thus, worsted-spun yarns tend to be much smoother than woolen-spun yarns, with less bounce or jumble. The resulting knitted fabric can be brighter, with crisper stitch definition, which is especially beautiful in intricate colorwork patterns such as the Risti Mittens (page 100) or the Frida Pillow (page 183). With less fuzz and bounce to conceal any flubs, worsted-spun yarns give us less flexibility in gauge and needle size before the fabric will look too tight or too loose. And because all the fiber ends are smoothed and tucked in tightly before spinning, worsted-spun yarns bloom less in the wash and also see less pilling with wear.

With all those fibers lying closely against one another, little still air gets trapped in between them (on average, a worsted-spun yarn is only 70 percent air). Worsted-spun yarns thus can be a little cooler than their well-insulating woolen-spun counterparts, although the degree to which this is true also depends on how much crimp is in the fibers and how thick the yarn is.

The Charms of Color

Among all fibers, natural and synthetic alike, wool is said to have the highest capacity to absorb and retain dyes. For thousands of years, people have experimented with ways to apply permanent color to wool. We used natural materials for those early attempts—twigs and berries and bugs and such—but today chemical and synthetic dyes do most of the work for us.

Wool is amphoteric, which means that it can absorb large quantities of both acids and alkalis. Many of the dyes used on wool fibers today are based on an acidic solution and are thus called acid dyes. Thanks to the incredibly strong bond that occurs between a dye molecule and fiber, we can wash our woolens over and over again without their colors ever fading.

Worsted-spun yarns give bright, beautiful definition to colorwork patterns.

Dye can be applied to wool fibers at several stages along the production process. Wool fibers dyed before spinning are "dyed in the wool" or "fleece dyed." This technique offers a wealth of creative options because the dyed fibers can then be further blended together to create heathered hues. Layering colors on top of one another produces a yarn of great visual depth and complexity, with colors that can shift dramatically depending on the light. You'll see this effect most often in woolen-spun yarns, such as those used for the Allegan Cardigan (page 146).

Dyeing completely unprocessed fibers can be risky, though, because it can inadvertently damage the fibers and make them harder to process. It is also considered more costly because it involves dyeing everything, including neps and other materials that may be later removed and discarded before spinning.

Wool is said to have the highest capacity to absorb and retain dyes.

TWIST AND TOUCH: THE WORSTED SIDE

If loose ends contribute to how a yarn feels against your skin, then you could immediately assume that worsted-spun yarns—with fewer ends sticking out—have a clear softness advantage over their woolen cousins. But the truth is that worsted-spun yarns aren't always softer than woolen-spun ones. You can have a horribly scratchy worsted-spun yarn made from a mediumwool fiber, and a delightfully soft woolen-spun yarn made from a finewool fiber. Softness depends on the grade of fibers used in the yarn and the tightness of the yarn's twist and ply—as well as, of course, your own sense of touch.

Wool fibers are sometimes dyed after they've been carded, combed, and pulled out into thin ribbons of fiber. This "top dyeing" process (so named because the wool is called combed **top** at this stage) allows mills to have much larger dye lots than if they were dyeing individual skeins. Any irregularities in the dye are smoothed out during the final preparation before spinning, resulting in a cohesive and uniform color. Different colors of dyed top also can be blended together before spinning to produce a heathered effect.

And finally, wool fibers can be "yarn dyed," which is exactly what it sounds like. Dye is applied directly to yarn that is otherwise spun and ready to go. This method allows mills to make one nonstop production run and then split up the yarns for dyeing, whereas each color in a dyed-in-the-wool or fleece-dyed yarn needs to be set up and spun separately.

Hand-dyed color in the Windjammer Socks, page 110.

Kettle-dyed color in the Mama Bear Pullover, page 126.

There are as many ways to apply dye to yarn as there are ink to paper or paint to canvas. It can be done with varying degrees of sophistication and subtlety, from painting the dye by hand (which you can see in the Windjammer socks on page 110 and Falling Waters Shawl on page 168) to dropping skeins into giant bubbling kettles of dye (which is how the Mama Bear Pullover, page 126, got its color) to winding the yarn onto special bobbins and sealing them in a giant metal contraption that looks like a 1950s-era UFO. Each process produces varying results, from multicolored painterly precision to slightly semisolid to completely solid through-and-through colors. Wool yarns can have pretty much any color manifestation under the sun, especially when you add hand-dyeing and hand-painting to the mix.

Wool 101: Quick Tips for Reading a Generic Wool Yarn

You've found a yarn you like, and the label says "100% Wool." Now what? We usually go by feel alone, taking the yarn in our hands, rubbing it against our cheek, neck, or anywhere else we trust as a barometer for our sense of touch. But we need not stop there. Here are some ways to read that yarn and get a sense of how it might behave.

Look. Hold the skein up to the light. What do you see? Is it just a blur, or do the fibers reflect light back with a brilliant shine? Remember that this reflective quality will carry through to the knitted fabric. Also remember the relationship between luster and softness. With a few exceptions, the finer and softer wools tend to have a low luster—although worsted spinning can add a hint of luster to most fibers.

Shake. Take the skein in one hand and give it a good shake. Does it hold still, or does it wobble to and fro like a big chunk of JELL-O™? In skeins or hanks that haven't been twisted too tight, the shake test can give you a hint about how this yarn will drape in the finished garment. If it moves on the skein, it's going to move in a knitted fabric. If it stays firm, like a well-cooked piece of steak, then it will likely have more loft and bulk than slink or drape when knit up.

Tug. Separate a length of yarn from the skein—with practice you can do this without messing up the rest of the skein and losing your LYS privileges. Hold it relaxed between your hands, then tug it. How much length do you gain? Does the yarn grow thin as you pull it, or does it remain unchanged? Woolen-spun yarns tend to have much more bounce than worsted-spun yarns, thinning slightly when tugged. This translates into a more elastic knitting and wearing experience. Worsted-spun yarns, on the other hand, tend to be less elastic and produce a more durable fabric.

Smell. That's right, stick your nose deep into the skein and give it a nice long sniff. (If you're among knitters, nobody will raise an eyebrow. I promise.) What do you smell? Are your nostrils immediately filled with the pungent spicy aroma of lanolin, or can you detect just a gentle hint? Does the yarn smell like nothing at all, or like the plastic bags or cardboard box in which it was shipped? If it's a hand-dyed yarn, do you smell the vinegar-rich essence of a fresh dye job, or perhaps the floral notes of synthetic perfume added during the washing? All these scents will give you a hint of how the yarn was processed; the less lanolin you smell, the more thoroughly scoured and processed the fibers were. The more lanolin you smell, the gentler the processing, the more natural oils remain in the fibers, and the closer to the sheep this yarn is. For those of you who aren't as crazy about the smell of lanolin as I am, rest assured that some of that lanolin fragrance will come out with the first wash, as will any residual vinegar or synthetic perfume.

Twist. Pull a short length of yarn from the skein and untwist it between your fingers. How is it made? How many plies are in this yarn, and how tightly were they spun or plied together? In *The Knitter's Book of Yarn*, I wrote about twist and ply in much greater detail than we have room to do here. But the fundamental thing to remember is that twist is energy. The more twist in your yarn, and the more individual plies that are twisted together, the more strength and resilience that yarn will have. Too much twist and your yarn will behave like piano wire; too little twist and it'll fall apart like tissue. Longer fibers don't need as much twist to hold together, while shorter fibers do.

Mills work overtime to try and find a happy medium that suits the needs and characteristics of the fibers while producing a desirable yarn. Most of the time they succeed, but sometimes they don't. Because unmarked wool yarns give us very little indication of what breed they contain, we have no way of knowing whether the fibers were spun in the optimal manner. Over time, however, your hands will develop a greater ability to instinctively detect happy yarns and reject unhappy ones. Until then, I urge you to swatch, swatch, and swatch some more—each stitch will teach you a new lesson.

Meet the Breeds

So far, we've talked about wool in fairly general terms—where it comes from, how it gets off the sheep, and how it's cleaned up and spun into yarn. This foundation prepares us for what comes next, which dictates more than anything else how a wool yarn will look, feel, and behave: the breed of sheep that grew the fiber.

Breed Categories

I've already mentioned that more than 200 distinct breeds of sheep exist in the world today. Not all produce wool ideally suited to hand-knitting, and not all breeds can be easily found at fiber festivals, farms, or yarn stores. For this reason, I've narrowed the field to five general types of wool-bearing sheep breeds, sorted by fiber characteristics and backgrounds. These breed categories are only guidelines; you'll see several sheep breeds that straddle the micron range of two categories.

▸ First are the finewools, whose fineness averages 25 or fewer microns. These are the wools you can sleep in, the ones to be used for baby blankets or scarves, summer shawls, sweaters, and any other garment that will come into direct and frequent contact with your skin. You want them to be soft, even if it means they'll wear out more quickly than heavier-weight wools. The grandfather of all finewools is Merino, and all of the other breeds in this category have some Merino ancestry.

▸ Next are the **mediumwools**. Their larger fiber diameters (averaging 24–31 microns) make these wools slightly stronger than finewools yet still comfortably wearable. They like to be used in durable everyday sweaters as well as mittens, mitts, hats, socks, and the like.

▸ Then we have the Down and Down-type wools, which come from short-wool sheep that originated in the Downs of England or from sheep that originated elsewhere but share the same characteristics. The fibers—24–34 microns on average—are exceptionally lofty and springy, with a crimp that runs in wavelets and corkscrews in all directions. Down and Down-type wools feel bouncy and crisp, and they are often used as filler in wool yarns because they give lightweight bulk to the finished product.

▸ From here we progress to the **longwools**, which come from a distinct category of sheep that evolved on the fertile grassy lowlands and coastal plains of Britain. Their long, curly locks are almost always spun worsted to create smooth, fluid yarns with exceptional drape and durability. Their appearance ranges from luster (bright and silky) to demiluster (i.e., more subdued and pearlescent). Softness varies quite dramatically among longwools, from 24 to 41 microns. The finer fibers can be exquisitely soft and suitable for shawls, blankets, socks, and even sweaters—but the rougher end of the spectrum is better left for hand-wovens and the textile industry.

▸ Finally, we reach the oldest and most intriguing breed category, the **primitive** and dual-coated sheep. Most of these animals have been our companions, virtually unchanged through any kind of modern breeding programs, for more than a thousand years. These animals grow complex coats that can differ in length, texture, fineness, and even color within the very same fleece. Fiber fineness and project suitability vary more widely with these breeds than with any other, depending partly on the animal and partly on the way in which the fibers are processed. The breed descriptions (beginning page 43) explain these differences in more detail.

In discussing the different sheep breeds, I'd hoped to provide a tidy summary of how each breed is typically spun. But the truth is much more nuanced. First, if some of these animals can grow as many as five different types of fiber on the same fleece, and if each animal's fiber is slightly different from the next, we couldn't possibly expect all of these fibers to be ideally spun the same way. They can't. Second—and perhaps more important—most wool has been spun throughout history in whatever way the nearest commercial mill was configured to spin it, regardless of how that particular fiber may have *wanted* to be spun. I once saw two knitters almost come to blows over whether "true" Shetland lace was knit from one- or two-ply yarn. The truth is that it was likely knit from whatever yarn the closest mill provided to knitters. And in many ways, this is still true—our creativity is fueled by whatever materials we have closest at hand.

The Criteria

Although sweeping generalizations are nearly impossible to make, I do outline a few common facts about the different sheep breeds—and that's where each description starts. You'll find the average fineness, staple length, crimp, and luster for that breed as well as the projects for which it is well suited. I also note whether or not the fiber felts easily. To help you make the best use of this information, let's quickly review these categories and how they translate into knitting terms.

FINENESS

The average fiber diameter for each breed is listed in microns on the basis of breed association standards, the American Sheep Industry Association, the British Wool Marketing Board, and Australian Wool Innovation Limited. Remember that these micron counts are averages and that the actual fineness of a breed can vary dramatically from animal to animal, farm to farm, climate to climate, and country to country. Don't assume that because a yarn came from a finewool breed it is extremely soft; and don't discount a yarn from a medium or longwool as "too scratchy" until you've actually touched it. The extreme variety that exists is part of what makes wool such an enchanting material.

STAPLE LENGTH

Given in inches and centimeters, staple length is the average length of fiber growth on the animal, usually per year. From a knitting perspective, staple indicates the average length of fiber that goes into your yarn. Fibers best suited to the woolen spinning process tend to be 2½ inches (6.5cm) or shorter, whereas fibers 3 inches (7.5cm) or longer tend to do better in smoother worsted-spun yarns. You can't make a woolen-spun yarn from a long, smooth fiber, and you can't make a worsted-spun yarn—not easily, anyway—from a short crimpy fiber. The longer the fiber, the more durable the yarn tends to be and the less susceptible it will be to pilling; although how the yarn was spun will also impact its performance.

CRIMP

Crimp refers to the type of natural curl that occurs in each fleece. Along with fineness, crimp has a major influence on how yarn feels and behaves. The finer the crimp, the more bouncy and elastic the fiber tends to be, and the more tightly it can be plied without losing this bounce; the larger and more open the crimp, the more loosely it can be spun and plied, and the more fluid and smooth the fiber can be when spun into yarn. Crimp is often categorized as distinct (an

CATEGORY	BREED	FINENESS (in microns)
FINEWOOL	CVM	22–25 microns
	Cormo	17–23
	Merino	17–22
	Polwarth	22–25
	◄ **Rambouillet**	**19–23**
	Romeldale	22–25
	Targhee	21–25
MEDIUMWOOL	California Red	28–31
	Columbia	24–31
	Corriedale	25–31
	◄ **Finnish Landrace (Finn)**	**24–31**
	Montadale	25–30
	Tunis	24–29
DOWN AND DOWN-TYPE WOOL	Cheviot	27–33
	Clun Forest	28–33
	Dorset Down	26–29
	Dorset Horn and Poll Dorset	27–33
	Oxford	28–34
	Ryeland	26–32
	◄ **Shropshire**	**25–33**
	Southdown	24–29
	Suffolk	26–33
LONGWOOL	Bluefaced Leicester	24–28
	Border Leicester	30–38
	Coopworth	35–39
	Cotswold	34–40
	Leicester Longwool	32–38
	Lincoln	34–41
	◄ **Perendale**	**29–35**
	Romney	32–39
	Teeswater	30–36
	Wensleydale	33–35
DUAL-COATED AND PRIMITIVE	Icelandic	19–30
	Jacob	27–35
	Navajo–Churro	18–47
	◄ **Scottish Blackface**	**28–38+**
	Shetland	12–40

even pattern of waves or curls visible throughout the lock) and indistinct (general jumbled chaos). The crimp I describe is the breed association standard; what you discover at farms and festivals may be very different depending on the traits for which those particular farmers chose to breed their sheep. Also be aware that in some breeds, multiple crimp patterns can appear on the same animal.

LUSTER

Luster describes how fiber reflects light. High-luster wools have a natural silky shine that sometimes rises to an almost artificial-looking gloss. As I've mentioned, most high-luster wools are called luster longwools (so named because their staple is—you guessed it—long). Low luster is not necessarily a bad thing, however. Most finewools, including Merino and Cormo, are considered low luster. Instead of gloss, these fibers have a bright, almost pearlescent sheen. You'll often see Merino blended with higher-luster fibers (such as silk, Tencel®, or mohair) to give a yarn more sheen while still letting you enjoy the benefits of a softer, higher-crimp wool. Wools with less luster (demiluster) can include some longwools as well as other breeds. In contrast, Down and Down-type wools tend to maintain a fairly blank expression when exposed to light. No sheen reflects back from their corkscrew-crimped fibers.

*High-luster wools have a **natural silky shine** that sometimes rises to an almost artifical-looking gloss.*

Knowing a breed's general luster can be helpful when you're searching for a wool yarn that will really "pop" in a project or, conversely, take a back seat and let the stitches tell the story.

SUITABLE FOR

This is one of the more subjective areas of this book. My goal was to give you a general framework from which to launch your own experiments. But wool comes from living animals— and the variety within a single breed can be extreme—so what I say here is based very much on averages. The reality of what you feel in your own hands may vary depending on the grade of fibers and how they were prepared and spun. Use my recommendations as guidelines only, and always— *always*—let your hands be your ultimate guide.

Next-to-Skin Wear

These are the fibers that most people will be able to wear directly against their skin without feeling any irritation. Choose yarns from the next-to-skin category when knitting for babies and small children. As the babies become children who can wear turtlenecks under their sweaters, you can slowly introduce other grades of fiber and see how they react. The wearing of my grandma's allegedly "scratchy" hand-knit sweaters was a rite of passage in my family, a sort of anti-itch immunization for life. The sooner you expose children to different types of wools, the broader your yarn choices will be later. If never weaned from the supersoft, they'll never want anything else.

Other garments that fall in this category include scarves, shawls, wraps, cowls, turtlenecks, nightshirts, tights, and form-fitting sweaters you'd want to wear directly next to the skin. Socks made with yarn from these breeds will be soft and comfortable, but they may not wear as well as their midrange counterparts. Finewool sock yarns often include nylon for reinforcement and usually are composed of several tightly spun plies to help protect against abrasion.

Midrange Garments

This category represents the gray area between "too soft" and "too scratchy" that each person will define for him- or herself. It is the workhorse of garment categories, including everything from cardigans and pullovers to hats, socks, blankets, and shawls. These fibers would suit Goldilocks: not too rough, not too soft, but just right. They get you where you need to go in relative comfort without much fuss or fanfare. And best of all, these fibers provide options: a sweater under which you don't *always* need to wear a long-sleeved shirt, durable socks that won't double as Brillo pads. If you aren't too sensitive to wool and enjoy variety, the midrange category will be your loyal friend.

Outerwear to Rugged Outerwear

Occasionally you'll hear me recommend yarn from certain breeds for outerwear and rugged outerwear. These terms describe the kinds of garments that likely will be worn, as the term suggests, over another garment or possibly against areas of skin less sensitive than the head and neck. These projects need to be sturdy and not prone to immediate pilling: a warm sweater you wear over a long-sleeved T-shirt or turtleneck; hats, mittens, and gloves you reach for on a particularly chilly day; a scarf you wrap around the turned-up collar of your winter coat; or booties you slip on over a pair of socks before trudging downstairs in the morning to make your first cup of tea.

This outerwear concept extends to accessories, such as bags and tea cozies, which can be perfect project choices for "crunchier" fibers. As I've said, there is a wool breed for every purpose—especially where outerwear is concerned.

The Sweet Fern Mitts (page 96) are ideal for breeds all the way along the suitability spectrum from next-to-skin to midrange and outerwear. The loftier the fibers, the happier the results.

FELTING QUALITIES

This category can be interpreted in two ways. On the one hand, it can tell you how nervous you should be when washing a garment made out of this fiber. But on the other hand, it can tell you how long you need to keep it in the washing machine before it'll actually begin to felt. It all depends on your intentions. Some wools will, in the words of spinning and fiber luminary Judith MacKenzie McCuin, "felt if you walk across them." Others would need a stampede of wild elephants before any signs of felting will appear.

Finewools

The finest of the bunch, these wools are soft enough to wear to bed each night. *I define finewools here as having an average fineness of 21–25 microns (or finer). Every breed in this category was obtained, at some point in its ancestry, through* **cross-breeding** *with a Merino sheep.*

CALIFORNIA VARIEGATED MUTANT (CVM)

The multicolored variant of the Romeldale sheep (page 48), the CVM was developed by Glen Eidman after he discovered a multicolored **ewe** lamb in his Romeldale flock. He was intrigued because the Romeldale breed usually does not produce multiple colors. When a similar-patterned ram was born a few years later, Eidman decided to cross the two and see if he could replicate the patterning. Over the next 15 years, he diligently continued to selectively breed subsequent generations until he had developed what is now known as the California Variegated Mutant. Unlike so many other sheep breeds that were developed for food and foraging as much as for fiber, Eidman created the CVM with handspinners in mind. Upon his retirement in 1982, he dispersed his entire flock of approximately 75 sheep to other farms across California, and the breed continues to grow.

The fine, long-staple CVM fleece has a well-defined crimp that is uniform across the body and can grow in a multitude of colors ranging from white to gray, brown, moorit (reddish brown), and black. The feel of the fiber is both springy and buttery. Unlike other sheep breeds, the CVM grows subsequently softer fleece over time, and the fleece darkens during the animal's first year (whereas in other breeds, the fleece tends to lighten). The pleasant touch, elastic hand, and intriguing color variety make the CVM particularly popular among handspinners. It can be spun woolen or worsted, depending on the staple length and the spinner's objectives (loftier for softness and warmth, tighter for greater durability). CVM is still rare in the commercial yarn world.

CVM FACTS

FINENESS
22–25 microns

STAPLE LENGTH
3–6 inches (7.5–15cm)

CRIMP
Well-defined and uniform from base to tip

LUSTER
Bright and shiny

SUITABLE FOR
Next-to-Skin Wear

FELTING QUALITIES
Moderate

CONTACT
National CVM Conservancy
www.nationalcvmconservancy.com

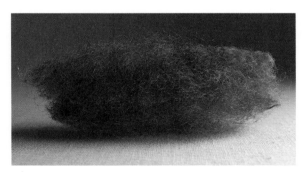

A washed CVM lock.

CORMO

The Cormo comes from Tasmania, Australia, where a farmer named Ian Downie crossbred Corriedale rams (page 51) with 1,200 of his Superfine Saxon Merino ewes (page 45) in the early 1960s. His goal was to produce a more fertile sheep with a larger frame and higher fleece production, and the result was this cross-breed fittingly called Cormo (because of its Corriedale and Merino parents). Valued as much for its meat as for its soft, dense fleece, the breed was introduced to the United States in 1976 and has become well established.

The fibers grow in highly uniform quality from head to tail, with 90 percent of the fleece varying by just 2 microns. Cormo is extremely soft, warm, and pleasant to the touch, with a balance of loft and elasticity most comparable to Merino but with a more moist, velvety feel, or **hand**, as it's often called.

Cormo is equally beautiful spun worsted or woolen. Commercial mills find it a bit challenging to spin; the high crimp and short staple length make maintaining even tension somewhat of a challenge. If you find a Cormo yarn that's somewhat lumpy, this is why. However, the fiber's natural loft and crimp will help absorb these lumps so that they won't be as visible in the finished knitted fabric.

CORMO FACTS

FINENESS
17–23 microns

STAPLE LENGTH
2½–4 inches (6.5–10cm)

CRIMP
Fine, even, well-defined

LUSTER
Low

SUITABLE FOR
Next-to-Skin Wear

FELTING QUALITIES
Excellent

CONTACT
Cormo Sheep Conservation Registry
www.cormosheep.org

American Cormo Sheep Association
www.cormosheep.com

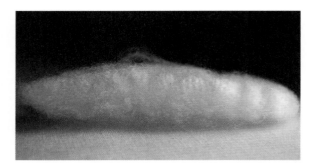

A washed Cormo lock.

Cormo yarn.

MERINO

Trace the lineage of pretty much any finewool breed on the planet and you'll find Merino genes. Now the most numerous sheep breed in the world, Merino sheep were introduced into Spain from North Africa by the Moors. By the 1400s, the highly prized fiber from the Merino sheep had elevated Spain to the top of the European wool market—a position it maintained for centuries. Raw Merino fiber was often exported by Spain to other countries for processing, but the actual Merino breeding stock was closely guarded, and *its* export was punishable by death. The Spanish did, however, take Merino sheep with them wherever they went, which is why strains of Merino exist in nearly every corner of the world. Only as the Spanish empire began to fall in the late 1700s did "official" Merino breeding stock begin to reach other countries, which is when breeding improvement programs—based on Merino genes—really began.

When you see the word Merino on a yarn label, the fiber could actually come from one of several different strains of sheep. The most common in Australia is the Peppin, named after the Peppin brothers, who established the breed at their sheep station near Wanganella in the mid-1800s. As with many breed developments, the brothers' goal was to develop a sheep that would better thrive in the local climate. Also from Australia are the highly fertile Booroola Merino, the hornless **Polled** Merino, and the Saxon Merino, from which comes the finest, most highly prized Merino fiber. A small sheep, the Saxon Merino thrives in southern Australia and can grow fibers that are 17.5 microns or finer. The Delaine Merino thrives across the United States. It's a direct descendant of the Spanish Merinos and has a smoother body than the Peppin, with fewer wrinkles and thus an easier-to-shear fleece.

Most people consider Merino wool the only option if they want the softest of the soft; it is an extremely soft, fine fiber. So fine, in fact, that the average Merino fleece has 60,000–75,000 fibers growing per square inch (2.5cm^2). As with other finewool breeds, Merino sheep have an extremely high amount of lanolin to protect all those fine fibers, usually 40 percent or more of the total fleece weight.

Be aware, however, that not all Merino yarns are equally soft. The range between 17 and 22 microns is fairly significant, especially for a luxury fiber that tends to be sold at a premium price. Look for words like fine (18.6–19.5 microns, according to the Australian Wool Corporation), superfine (15–18.5 microns), or even ultrafine (11.5–15 microns) on the label, but again, let your fingers be your ultimate guide.

High tensile strength helps Merino fibers overcome their relatively short staple length. The fiber is versatile in spinning, with a well-developed crimp that is quite suitable for woolen spinning but also performs beautifully and more enduringly when spun in a smooth worsted fashion. Merino can happily go from laceweight to bulky. The shorter staple length *does* make Merino more susceptible to abrasion and pilling, which is why many sock yarns often contain a small amount of nylon and are spun and plied more tightly to increase durability.

In the 1990s, a process called Optim™ was developed to make Merino fibers even softer and more appealing to the fashion industry. It involved twisting, stretching, and permanently setting the fibers, often reducing the fiber diameter by as many as 3–4 microns. Stretching the fiber causes the crimps to smooth out and the scales to separate, giving the fiber a much smoother, more lustrous appearance that closely resembles silk.

MERINO **FACTS**

FINENESS
17–22 microns

STAPLE LENGTH
2½–4 inches (6.5–10cm)

CRIMP
High, fine, and even

LUSTER
Low with an almost pearlescent sheen

SUITABLE FOR
Next-to-Skin Wear

FELTING QUALITIES
Very high

CONTACT
American Delaine & Merino Record Association
www.admra.org

Australian Association of Stud Merino Breeders
www.merinos.com.au

A washed Merino lock.

Merino yarn.

POLWARTH

Another Australian innovation established in 1880, the Polwarth is essentially 75 percent Saxon Merino and 25 percent Lincoln (page 66). It's a dual-purpose breed, valued as much for its meat as for its fiber, and it tends to thrive under diverse conditions, including damp climates where Merinos typically don't do so well. The Polwarth produces a truly lovely fleece that rivals Merino in softness and has a marvelous crimp and good elasticity. The addition of Lincoln genes gives the fiber a hint more length, strength, and luster with an enhanced drape that performs beautifully in shawls. Polwarth usually is spun worsted and in multiple-ply form. In South America, the breed is known as Ideal.

POLWARTH **FACTS**

FINENESS
22–25 microns

STAPLE LENGTH
4–5½ inches (10–14cm)

CRIMP
Clear, well defined

LUSTER
Low but with a subtle sheen

SUITABLE FOR
Next-to-Skin Wear

FELTING QUALITIES
High

CONTACT
Polwarth Sheepbreeders' Association of Australia
www.polwarth.com.au

A washed Polwarth lock.

RAMBOUILLET

After enjoying a monopoly on the fine Merino wool market for some 600 years, Spain began to allow the export of Merino animals to a few select countries by the late 1700s, and that's where the Rambouillet got its start. In 1786, Louis XVI received 366 Royal Escurial Merino from Spain and installed them at his Royal Farm in Rambouillet, France. Although Louis perished during the French Revolution, the sheep were protected, and the breed continued to evolve in France and later in Germany and the United States. Today, the Rambouillet is the foundation of most of the range flocks in the western United States.

The Rambouillet is the largest animal of the finewool breeds. Its fiber has a wonderfully plump hand, thanks to its springy crimp. The shorter fibers create beautiful yarn when left jumbled and spun woolen, but longer Rambouillet wool also can make an exceptional laceweight yarn if spun worsted and plied tightly to mimic the breed's natural crimp structure.

RAMBOUILLET **FACTS**

FINENESS
19–23 microns

STAPLE LENGTH
2–4 inches (5–10cm)

CRIMP
Very fine, even, and well defined

LUSTER
Low

SUITABLE FOR
Next-to-Skin Wear

FELTING QUALITIES
Exceptional

CONTACT
American Rambouillet Sheep Breeders Association
www.rambouilletsheep.org

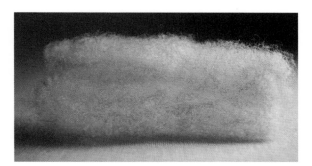

A washed Rambouillet lock.

ROMELDALE

In 1915, a man named A. T. Spencer attended the Pan-American exposition in San Francisco and was so smitten with a group of New Zealand Romney rams (page 68) on display that he bought the whole mob and brought them back to his ranch. There he diligently bred them with his flock of Rambouillet ewes with the hope of improving the fleece staple and length, and thus the Romeldale breed began. In the 1940s and '50s, the J. K. Sexton family and their partners continued the breeding and helped fine-tune the Romeldale breed. Beginning in the 1960s, one of the partners—Glen Eidman—continued the fine-tuning to produce a multicolored variant called the California Variegated Mutant (CVM). With the exception of fleece color, the Romeldale and CVM are essentially identical.

Romeldale fleece is extremely soft, elastic, and pleasant to the touch, sharing all the qualities of the CVM but with solid coloring. Available primarily in fleece form for handspinners, Romeldale can be spun woolen or worsted depending on the staple length and the spinner's objectives.

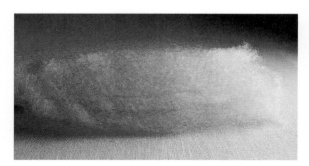

A washed Romeldale lock.

ROMELDALE **FACTS**

FINENESS
22–25 microns

STAPLE LENGTH
3–6 inches (7.5–15cm)

CRIMP
Well defined and uniform from base to tip

LUSTER
Bright and shiny

SUITABLE FOR
Next-to-Skin Wear

FELTING QUALITIES
Moderate

CONTACT
American Romeldale/CVM Registry
www.nationalcvmconservancy.com/arcr.htm

ADDITIONAL READING

Many more sheep exist than you'll read about in this book, and they're all waiting for you to meet them. If you'd like to learn more about the other breeds, I highly recommend Nola and Jane Fournier's book, *In Sheep's Clothing*, as well as the encyclopedic sheep reference book that Carol Ekarius and Deborah Robson have just completed for Storey Publishing.

TARGHEE

One of the more recently established breeds, the Targhee was developed by the U.S. Sheep Experiment Station in Dubois, Idaho, in 1926. The goal was to develop the "ideal sheep" based on three-quarters finewool and one-quarter longwool blood. They bred 9 Rambouillet rams with 210 ewes, themselves crossbreeds of Rambouillet, Lincoln, and Corriedale (page 51). By the late 1940s, some Columbia genes (page 51) were added to the mix.

The resulting large animal grows a fine, dense, and uniform fleece whose magnificent high crimp gives any knitted fabric a plush, elastic quality reminiscent of well-yeasted bread dough. Targhee can be spun woolen or worsted; try yarns prepared both ways and see which you like best.

Targhee yarn.

TARGHEE **FACTS**

FINENESS
21–25 microns

STAPLE LENGTH
3–5 inches (7.5–12.5cm)

CRIMP
Fine, dense, and relatively indistinct

LUSTER
Relatively low but with an opalescent quality

SUITABLE FOR
Next-to-Skin Wear

FELTING QUALITIES
High

CONTACT
U.S. Targhee Sheep Association
www.ustargheesheep.org

A washed Targhee lock.

Mediumwools

Bumping up the fiber diameter to a slightly thicker range of 24–31 microns, we begin to see many more breeds that might otherwise be overlooked in the mainstream quest for super soft. The sheep in this category are often the result of crossbreeding between a finewool and a longwool breed. Because you won't often find these fibers in their own custom yarns, I've listed only a few breed highlights to whet your appetite. Literally dozens more breeds like these exist, each with its own compelling story.

CALIFORNIA RED

Sometimes the best innovations are the exact opposite of what you'd intended. In the early 1970s, a man named Dr. Glen Spurlock wanted to create a quality meat breed that didn't grow wool, so he crossbred Tunis (page 54) and Barbados sheep. The resulting hybrid animal—which produced plenty of wool—wasn't what he expected, so he gladly let Aime and Paulette Soulier purchase some animals and take them to their farm in Winters, California. Gradually and with more selective breeding, the California Red was created.

An exceptionally beautiful sheep, the California Red gets its name from its unusual coloring: short, smooth chestnut-colored hair grows on its head and legs, while its fleece (cinnamon-colored in young lambs, gradually lightening to beige and oatmeal with age) is peppered with hairs in shades ranging from gold to raspberry. Some California Reds also have a "mane" of auburn fibers around the neck.

Although the contrasting fibers can be removed through combing, most handspinners prefer to leave them in and simply card the fibers together. Coveted by handspinners, weavers, and knitters, this fiber is not yet widely available as commercial yarn, but I hope to see at least one artisan yarn available in this fiber soon.

CALIFORNIA RED **FACTS**

FINENESS
28–31 microns

STAPLE LENGTH
3–6 inches (7.5–15cm)

CRIMP
Well developed and indeterminate

LUSTER
Low

SUITABLE FOR
Midrange Garments

FELTING QUALITIES
Low

CONTACT
California Red Sheep Registry, Inc.
www.caredsheep.com

A washed California Red lock.

California Red yarn.

COLUMBIA FACTS

FINENESS
24–31 microns

STAPLE LENGTH
3½–5 inches (9–12.5cm)

CRIMP
High and indeterminate

LUSTER
Low

SUITABLE FOR
Next-to-Skin Wear, Midrange Garments, and Outerwear, depending on the fiber grade

FELTING QUALITIES
Good

CONTACT
Columbia Sheep Breeders' Association
www.columbiasheep.org

COLUMBIA

Developed in the United States through breeding that began in 1912, the Columbia is the result of crossing Rambouillet ewes with Lincoln longwool rams (page 66). The goal was to produce a hearty sheep that was large enough for meat production, grew a dense and heavy fleece, and could serve as a true breeding type for the western ranges of the United States.

Columbia is a robust, all-purpose wool that does equally well spun woolen and worsted and at various weights. The fineness of the fleeces among Columbia sheep varies quite a bit, meaning that some Columbia yarns will be soft enough for comfortable wear next to the skin; most are ideal for midrange to outerwear projects where you want volume, substance, and a soft hand with a faintly crunchy finish.

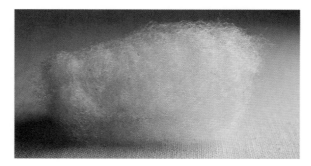

A washed Columbia lock.

CORRIEDALE

In the 1860s, the manager of the Corriedale Estate at Otaga in the South Island of New Zealand began working on a new ideal dual-purpose breed. Like many shepherds before and since, James Little wanted to create a sheep that could deliver maximum value across two markets: a heavy and high-quality fleece for the fiber market, and, when the time came, a sizeable carcass for the meat market. He bred Merino ewes with English Lincoln Longwool rams (page 66), then inbred subsequent generations. Simultaneous breeding projects in New Zealand also included Leicester rams (page 65). The result of both projects is the Corriedale breed, named in 1902. Corriedales were brought to the United States in 1914 and have since become the second most numerous sheep breed in the world (Merino ranks first).

The Corriedale produces a bulky, uniform fleece with an inviting hand that falls somewhere between finewool and longwool, rather like the breed itself. Beginning handspinners love Corriedale because of its pronounced crimp, generous staple length, and ease of handling. Corriedale makes a smooth and extremely durable worsted yarn but it can also be spun into a loftier, more elastic woolen yarn—and both incarnations are particularly forgiving for beginning knitters.

CORRIEDALE **FACTS**

FINENESS
25–31 microns

STAPLE LENGTH
3½–6 inches (9–15cm)

CRIMP
Well defined with a distinct zigzag pattern

LUSTER
Medium

SUITABLE FOR
Midrange Garments, Outerwear, and Rugged Outerwear, depending on the fiber grade

FELTING QUALITIES
Very good

CONTACT
American Corriedale Association, Inc.
www.americancorriedale.com

Corriedale yarn.

FINNISH LANDRACE (FINN)

The Finnish Landrace, called Finnsheep or Finn among its many fans, originated in Finland. It thrived there for centuries before being introduced into North America in the late 1960s.

The Finn is one of my personal favorites because of its unusual combination of length and high, fine crimp. The average staple is 3–6 inches (7.5–15cm), but the animal can grow as many as 14 inches (35.5cm) of fiber per year. Along with its Shetland and Icelandic cousins, the Finn belongs to the Northern European Short-Tailed group of sheep.

Finn fiber grows clean on the animal, with a relatively low amount of lanolin. It also survives commercial processing well, creating a yarn that is both soft and springy *and* strong and resilient. The wool from Finn lambs can be soft enough for baby wear, whereas most other Finn fiber falls in the semifine category and is suitable for midrange knitwear. It is an exceptional fiber for felting.

A washed Corriedale lock.

FINN **FACTS**

FINENESS
24–31 microns

STAPLE LENGTH
3–6 inches (7.5–15cm)

CRIMP
High

LUSTER
Medium

SUITABLE FOR
Next-to-Skin Wear and Midrange Garments, depending on fiber grade

FELTING QUALITIES
Excellent

CONTACT
American Finnsheep Breeders Association
www.finnsheep.org

A washed Finn lock.

Finn yarn.

MONTADALE

Another result of the quest for the "perfect" sheep, the Montadale was created by E. H. Mattingly, a commercial lamb buyer in Kentucky. He decided to blend the large frame and quality fleece production of the Columbia breed with the hearty, vigorous, and good meat-producing characteristics of the Cheviot (page 55). He began his experiments in 1932 and quickly became convinced that he was on the right track. By 1945, after much more breeding, crossbreeding, and **linebreeding** (i.e., the breeding together of successive generations), the Montadale Sheep Breeders Association was formed.

The Montadale produces a bright, dense, uniform fleece with an open hand, a long staple, and a high crimp accompanied by a slightly crisp feel. Its generous staple length lends itself to durable and lofty worsted-spun yarns that are ideal for lightweight yet well-wearing outerwear.

MONTADALE **FACTS**

FINENESS
25–30 microns

STAPLE LENGTH
3–5 inches (7.5–12.5cm)

CRIMP
High and indistinct

LUSTER
Very low

SUITABLE FOR
Midrange Garments and Outerwear, depending on fiber grade

FELTING QUALITIES
Modest

CONTACT
Montadale Sheep Breeders Association
www.montadales.com

A washed Montadale lock.

TUNIS

One of the best all-purpose sheep breeds, the Tunis is also one of the oldest indigenous breeds in the United States. It began with the 1799 gift of Middle Eastern fat-tailed sheep from Tunisia. Under the care of Judge Richard Peters in Pennsylvania, the sheep were selectively bred with other sheep that had been brought from Europe, primarily Leicester Longwools (page 65) and Southdowns (page 60). The Tunis breed emerged, and even Thomas Jefferson insisted that he preferred his large Tunis flock over Merino for meat and wool production. Today, the Tunis is valued for its ability to thrive in diverse climates, including hot and humid ones.

Tunis sheep grow a beautiful, semilustrous mediumwool fleece with peach overtones that often lighten to a bright ivory after scouring. Lambs are born with a reddish color that fades as the animal matures. Thanks to its even balance of crimp and staple length, Tunis fiber performs equally well spun woolen or worsted.

TUNIS **FACTS**
FINENESS 24–29 microns
STAPLE LENGTH 4–6 inches (10–15cm)
CRIMP Medium and mostly indistinct
LUSTER Low but with faint overtones
SUITABLE FOR Next-to-Skin Wear and Midrange Garments, depending on fiber grade
FELTING QUALITIES Low to modest
CONTACT National Tunis Sheep Registry, Inc. www.tunissheep.org

A washed Tunis lock.

Down and Down-Type Wools

Down sheep are native shortwool breeds *that get their name from the Downs of southeast England—Southdown, Hampshire, Oxford, Shropshire, and the like—where they originated. Down-type wools* have similar characteristics but come from other regions. *As with mediumwools, Down and Down-type wools often are raised as much for their meat as for their fiber, if not more so. Their fineness averages 24–34 microns, right on the cusp of what may feel scratchy to some.*

Unlike mediumwools, which try to maintain some connection with the finewools, Down and Down-type wools are a category apart. From shortwool sheep, these fibers have a high spiral crimp that is unusual for fibers in their micron range. The combination of high crimp and a thicker fiber diameter helps the yarn stay lofty and open, maintaining a higher amount of trapped air and, consequently, creating a warmer fabric. For this reason, Down and Down-type wools are excellent options for hats, mittens, sweaters, and any other garment where warmth matters more than next-to-skin softness.

Consider Down and Down-type breeds rather like the iceberg lettuces of the fiber world: They're all about adding bulk and crunch to yarn, not so much about fineness and uniformity of crimp. There's crimp alright, but it goes in wavelets and corkscrews in every direction. You've probably already knit with some of these breeds without ever knowing it, because they're often anonymously blended into generic wool yarns.

CHEVIOT

Since the late 1300s, the Cheviot Hills between England and Scotland have been home to this hardy little white sheep. It thrives in barren, windswept conditions where Merino would fear to tread. The Cheviot was introduced in the United States in 1838 and in Australia 100 years later. Breeding in the United States has resulted in a much larger animal than the original Cheviots, prompting the establishment of the American Miniature Cheviot Registry to preserve the breed's original diminutive size.

The bright white Cheviot fiber is dense and strong, with a long staple and helical crimp that makes it particularly springy, especially when carded and spun woolen. Although the fiber is used mostly in the carpet and woven tweed industries, finer grades of Cheviot fiber are also enjoyed by handspinners and are suitable for handknitting yarns.

CHEVIOT **FACTS**

FINENESS
27–33 microns

STAPLE LENGTH
3–5 inches (7.5–12.5cm)

CRIMP
High and indeterminate with helical shape

LUSTER
Very low

SUITABLE FOR
Midrange Garments and Outerwear, depending on fiber grade

FELTING QUALITIES
Low

CONTACT
Cheviot Sheep Society
www.cheviotsheep.org

American Cheviot Sheep Society
www.cheviots.org

A washed Cheviot lock.

CLUN FOREST

The Clun Forest takes its name from the market town of Clun in southwest Shropshire, where the breed took hold in the lowlands region's wild, desolate marshes. Although not officially standardized until 1925, some say that the Clun Forest breed is a descendant of the sheep that pastoral and seminomadic shepherds raised in this area of England some 1,000 years ago. Whatever its origins, the breed today has evolved greatly—especially in the last 200 years.

The dark brown faces and legs of these hornless sheep are a stark contrast to their dense and springy white fleece. The fiber itself is downy shortwool, which means a high but jumbled crimp, low luster, and medium to short staple length. Clun Forest fiber is happiest when spun woolen.

Clun Forest yarn.

CLUN FOREST **FACTS**
FINENESS
28–33 microns
STAPLE LENGTH
2½–4 inches (6.5–10cm)
CRIMP
High and indeterminate
LUSTER
Low
SUITABLE FOR
Midrange Garments and Outerwear, depending on fiber grade
FELTING QUALITIES
Low
CONTACT
North American Clun Forest Association www.clunforestsheep.org

DORSET DOWN

Originating in the Downs of England, the Dorset Down produces a highly springy and robust fleece with a medium fineness. Sometimes considered a little too crunchy on its own, Dorset Down fiber is often added to blends for elasticity, crispness, and an overall enhanced body. The shorter fibers make an especially ideal addition to woolen-spun yarn blends because they are lofty and light, increasing bulk without increasing weight; the longer fibers can also be spun worsted and make an ideal yarn for socks.

DORSET DOWN **FACTS**

FINENESS
26–29 microns

STAPLE LENGTH
2–3 inches (5–7.5cm)

CRIMP
High and indistinct

LUSTER
Low

SUITABLE FOR
Midrange Garments and Outerwear,
depending on fiber grade

FELTING QUALITIES
Very low

CONTACT
Dorset Down Sheep Breeders' Association
www.dorsetdownsheep.org.uk

Dorset Down yarn.

DORSET HORN AND POLL DORSET

Legend has it that the Dorset Horn—a well-established breed from the United Kingdom—was the result of inbreeding between shipwrecked Merinos from the Spanish Armadas in 1588 and the native horned sheep of Wales. Regardless of whether this story is true, the Dorset Horn has become the most common white-faced sheep breed in the United States.

The all-white sheep produces a brilliant white fleece with a slightly longer staple length than the brown-faced Dorset Down. A high and indistinct crimp provides lightweight loft and a hint of crunch to any yarn blend, and the fiber can be spun woolen or worsted depending on intent—worsted for strength, woolen for lightweight warmth.

The hornless Poll Dorset is the result of a genetic mutation observed among the purebred Dorset Horn flock at North Carolina State College in the 1950s. Excepting the lack of horns, the Poll Dorset otherwise exhibits the same fleece characteristics as the Dorset Horn.

A washed Poll Dorset lock.

DORSET HORN + POLL DORSET **FACTS**

FINENESS
27–33 microns

STAPLE LENGTH
2½–4 inches (6.5–10cm)

CRIMP
High and indistinct

LUSTER
Low

SUITABLE FOR
Midrange Garments and Outerwear,
depending on fiber grade

FELTING QUALITIES
Very low

CONTACT
Continental Dorset Club
dorsets.homestead.com

OXFORD

The largest and heaviest of the Down breeds, the Oxford Down originated in Oxford County, England, beginning in 1830. It resulted from the crossing of older Cotswold (page 64) and Hampshire strains at a time when those two breeds were in transition. Some livestock historians suggest that this shortwool breed also was influenced by a small amount of Southdown blood (page 60) early in its development. The breed remained in flux through the early 1800s, but by 1851 it was recognized by its current name. Today, the Oxford Down is primarily raised for meat, but its fiber is highly prized among handspinners for its loft and ease of spinning.

A decidedly poofy fiber, Oxford Down is a medium-grade wool with great indeterminate crimp that produces an exceptionally lofty and warm yet lightweight fabric, especially when spun woolen.

OXFORD **FACTS**

FINENESS
28–34 microns

STAPLE LENGTH
3–5 inches (7.5–12.5cm)

CRIMP
High and indistinct

LUSTER
Low

SUITABLE FOR
Midrange Garments and Outerwear,
depending on fiber grade

FELTING QUALITIES
Modest

CONTACT
Oxford Down Sheep Breeders' Association
www.oxforddownsheep.org.uk

American Oxford Sheep Association
www.americanoxfords.org

RYELAND

One of the oldest recognized sheep breeds in the United Kingdom, the Ryeland comes from Herefordshire, where the Monks of Leominster had them graze on the tops of recently sprouted rye to make the plants grow more vigorously—hence the name Ryeland.

Ryeland yarn.

Long ago, this wooly-faced semicompact sheep was the only British breed that came close to rivaling Merino in softness. Breeding has changed this, but the Ryeland sheep still grows one of the softest fleeces in the Down-type category. The fiber has a deep, dense staple yet feels light and springy to the touch. It makes a strong, resilient yarn that produces highly durable garments, especially when spun worsted.

RYELAND **FACTS**

FINENESS
26–32 microns

STAPLE LENGTH
3–4 inches (7.5–10cm)

CRIMP
Rounded and somewhat indistinct

LUSTER
Low to medium

SUITABLE FOR
Midrange Garments and Outerwear, depending on fiber grade

FELTING QUALITIES
Medium

CONTACT
Ryeland Flock Book Society
www.ryelandfbs.com

SHROPSHIRE

Bred to thrive in England's Shropshire and Staffordshire hills, the Shropshire is called Britain's "oldest pedigree breed." It is believed to have evolved via crossbreeding between native shortwool heath sheep and Cotswolds (page 64), Southdowns (page 60), and possibly Leicesters (page 65) in the early 1800s. It was first imported into the United States in 1855.

The Shropshire produces a typical Down fleece whose relatively fine, dense fibers have exceptional crimp. It is frequently used for generic woolen-spun hand-knitting yarn, although it also can fare well when spun worsted.

SHROPSHIRE **FACTS**

FINENESS
25–33 microns

STAPLE LENGTH
3–4 inches (7.5–10cm)

CRIMP
Well developed but indistinct

LUSTER
Low

SUITABLE FOR
Midrange Garments and Outerwear, depending on fiber grade

FELTING QUALITIES
Low

CONTACT
Shropshire Sheep Breeders' Association
www.shropshire-sheep.co.uk

American Shropshire Registry Association
www.shropshires.org

SOUTHDOWN

The Southdown is the original Down breed from which so many others were developed. It owes its success to an enterprising man named John Ellman, who was as  brilliant a breeder as he was a marketer and promoter of his animals. Starting in the late eighteenth century, Ellman began selectively improving the native shortwool sheep in the hills of Sussex, England. Over time, a distinct breed type began to emerge, dubbed Southdown.

One of the finest wools of all the British breeds, Southdown fiber is short and springy, soft and bouncy, with a surprisingly strong underlying disposition. The British Wool Marketing Board insists that Southdown is the ideal wool for underwear because it is soft, elastic, and insulating. Regardless of whether you'd like to go *that* far, it is definitely one of the most pleasantly springy and soft Down fibers.

Over time, the breed has evolved to produce a much larger carcass for meat production. In 1990, small flocks of "original" small Southdowns were discovered and relabeled Olde English Babydoll Miniature Sheep, often simply called Babydoll Southdowns. Other than their shorter frame, they are very similar to the standard Southdowns.

SOUTHDOWN **FACTS**

FINENESS
24–29 microns

STAPLE LENGTH
2–3 inches (5–7.5cm)

CRIMP
High and indistinct

LUSTER
Very low

SUITABLE FOR
Next-to-Skin Wear and Midrange Garments, depending on fiber grade

FELTING QUALITIES
Very low

CONTACT
Southdown Sheep Society
www.southdownsheepsociety.co.uk

American Southdown Breeders' Association
www.southdownsheep.org/sdownfamily

A washed Southdown lock.

Southdown yarn.

SUFFOLK

The result of crossbreeding Southdown rams and Norfolk Horn ewes with the intent of improving both breeds, the Suffolk was recognized as a pure breed in 1810 and first

imported into the United States in 1888. Primarily recognized as a meat breed, the Suffolk produces a dense, full-bodied, and springy Down-type fleece. Spun worsted, it creates a warm and robust yarn that is ideal for midrange garments and, micron count permitting, excellent socks.

SUFFOLK **FACTS**

FINENESS
26–33 microns

STAPLE LENGTH
2½–3½ inches (6.5–9cm)

CRIMP
High and somewhat distinct

LUSTER
Very low

SUITABLE FOR
Midrange Garments and Outerwear, depending on fiber grade

FELTING QUALITIES
Low

CONTACT
Suffolk Sheep Society
www.suffolksheep.org

United Suffolk Sheep Association
www.u-s-s-a.org

Suffolk yarn.

Longwools

Although most of the breeds discussed thus far were established with the help of Merino genes, longwool sheep are a distinctly British creation that originated in the fertile grassy lowlands and coastal plains of Britain. As the name suggests, longwool sheep grow long locks of curly fiber that often gather together into large beautiful ringlets. The fiber tends to be medium to coarse, with an average fineness of 24–41 microns and a luster that runs from brilliant (luster longwools) to moderate (demiluster). All longwool fibers dye beautifully.

The longer fibers—averaging 5–12 inches (12.5–30.5cm)—beg to be spun worsted. They lie together much more densely than their shorter, springier counterparts, providing fewer open pockets to trap air and keep the wearer warm. What you lose in insulation, however, you gain in incredible strength and a fluid, well-draping fabric.

A few breed highlights follow to whet your appetite. As with the other categories, there are dozens more breeds where these came from, each with its own characteristics and history.

BLUEFACED LEICESTER

First things first: No, these sheep don't *really* have blue faces. They get their name from the short white hairs growing over their black-skinned heads. In certain light, the color really does look blue.

One of many descendants of Robert Bakewell's Leicester Longwool (page 65), the Bluefaced Leicester originated near Hexham in Northumberland County, England, in the early 1900s. It was imported into Canada in the 1970s and soon made its way to the United States, where the breed continues to find success among artisan fiber farms.

Bluefaced Leicester fiber represents an ideal compromise among longwools: just the right amount of length, a crimp with open but smaller curls, a fine fiber diameter, and a silky demiluster with exquisite drape. This means you can use Bluefaced Leicester for just about anything, from socks and sweaters to beautifully draping lace shawls. The fiber also takes dye brilliantly—a good thing, because Bluefaced Leicester yarn has recently become a staple of many hand-dyers' yarn offerings.

BLUEFACED LEICESTER **FACTS**

FINENESS
24–28 microns

STAPLE LENGTH
3–6 inches (7.5–15cm)

CRIMP
Small curls

LUSTER
Demiluster

SUITABLE FOR
Next-to-Skin Wear to Midrange Garments, depending on fiber grade

FELTING QUALITIES
Moderate

CONTACT
Bluefaced Leicester Sheep Breeders Association
www.blueleicester.co.uk

Bluefaced Leicester Breeders Association
www.bflba.com

A washed Bluefaced Leicester lock.

Bluefaced Leicester yarn.

BORDER LEICESTER

Another descendant of Robert Bakewell's Leicester Longwool (page 65), the Border Leicester was developed by two of Bakewell's friends, George and Matthew Culley, in 1767. From their farm in Fenton, Northumberland, they bred Bakewell's improved rams with Cheviot ewes. Some livestock historians argue that Teeswater blood (page 69) was also added to the mix. Regardless, the Border Leicester was firmly established in England by the 1850s.

Border Leicester fleece is similar in fineness to Leicester Longwool (both of which are generally less soft than Bluefaced Leicester) but with a slightly shorter, loftier staple. Semilustrous curls cascade from the animal in pencil-sized locks that are relatively free of lanolin. The fiber dyes beautifully and can be used to produce extremely well-wearing outerwear.

BORDER LEICESTER **FACTS**
FINENESS
30–38 microns
STAPLE LENGTH
6–10 inches (15–25.5cm)
CRIMP
Well defined in slender locks
LUSTER
High
SUITABLE FOR
Outerwear and Rugged Outerwear, depending on fiber grade
FELTING QUALITIES
Modest
CONTACT
Border Leicester Sheep Breeders www.borderleicester.com
American Border Leicester Association www.ablasheep.org

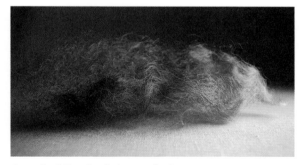

A washed Border Leicester lock.

COOPWORTH

A relatively recent addition to the sheep world, the Coopworth was developed in the 1950s and '60s at Lincoln College in Canterbury, New Zealand, under the direction of Ian Coop. Border Leicester rams were crossbred with Romney ewes (page 68) in the hopes of creating a more prolific, adaptable, and easy-care sheep. In 1968, the breed was officially recorded in New Zealand and given the name Coopworth in recognition of Mr. Coop's efforts.

A favorite among handspinners, Coopworth sheep produce a sturdy medium-grade fleece that boasts bright luster and an even, well-bodied crimp from base to tip. Fiber qualities can vary widely depending on the animal, so don't be surprised to find a Coopworth yarn that behaves much more like Border Leicester or Romney, its parent breeds.

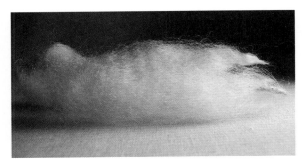

A washed Coopworth lock.

Coopworth yarn.

COOPWORTH **FACTS**

FINENESS
35–39 microns

STAPLE LENGTH
6–8 inches (15–20.5cm)

CRIMP
Well defined and uniform from base to tip

LUSTER
Bright and shiny

SUITABLE FOR
Rugged Outerwear

FELTING QUALITIES
Good

CONTACT
Coopworth Sheep Society of New Zealand
www.coopworth.org.nz

American Coopworth Registry
americancoopworthregistry.org

COTSWOLD

One of the oldest known sheep breeds, the Cotswolds are allegedly descendants of longwool sheep introduced into England by the Romans in the 1st century A.D. Thriving in the hills around Gloucestershire and Oxfordshire, the Cotswold breed was improved in the late 1700s and early 1800s with the addition of some Leicester Longwool blood.

Often referred to as "the Cotswold Lion" because of the incredible economic power it gave the British empire, Cotswold sheep produced *the* fine wool of England for centuries. Jesuit robes and nun's habits were made from it, and churches and manor houses were built from its fortunes in the Cotswolds area. Even today, the Lord Chancellor sits on a bale of Cotswold fiber in the U.K. Parliament to remind him from where England's strength comes. By 1879, the Cotswold also was the most popular breed in the United States—until Merino eventually took its place.

A true luster longwool, Cotswold fiber has several nicknames, including "the poor man's mohair" and "the golden fleece." It is exceptionally strong and lustrous, with a firm hand that can have a silky feel, especially among the finer grades. Although the fibers tend to be spun worsted, some grades of Cotswold are bouncy and robust enough to be spun woolen. Either way, Cotswold wool will produce an extremely durable garment with fluid drape and a brilliant luster.

A washed Cotswold lock.

COTSWOLD **FACTS**

FINENESS
34–40 microns

STAPLE LENGTH
7–12 inches (18–30.5cm)

CRIMP
Naturally wavy curls

LUSTER
High and silky

SUITABLE FOR
Outerwear and Rugged Outerwear

FELTING QUALITIES
Modest

CONTACT
Cotswold Sheep Society
www.cotswoldsheep.org.uk

Cotswold Breeders Association
www.cotswoldbreedersassociation.org

Cotswold yarn.

LEICESTER LONGWOOL

The Leicester Longwool is the triumph of Robert Bakewell, an eighteenth-century English farmer who pioneered modern selective breeding techniques and whose work has influenced everyone from Charles Darwin to Gregor Mendel. From his farm in Leicestershire, Bakewell selectively bred multiple generations of Old Leicester sheep to create an improved breed that matured for slaughter more quickly. That animal was called the Dishley Leicester, and the Leicester Longwool (also called English Leicester) is its direct descendant. Most other longwool breeds have been improved with Leicester Longwool blood at some point in history. Both George Washington and Thomas Jefferson imported Leicester rams from England to improve their own flocks.

The long and extremely lustrous fleece grows off the animal in curly ringlets that cascade down in well-defined locks. The fiber takes in dye eagerly and reflects back the color with a silky brilliance. The fleece has a soft **handle** and a consistent length and fineness from head to tail—a desirable trait because it gives the farmer more marketable fiber after shearing. Always spun worsted, Leicester Longwool fiber creates a firm yet fluid yarn with a halo reminiscent of mohair. Finer grades can make long-wearing socks and magnificent lace shawls with splendid luster and drape. Medium-grade fibers are best suited for rugged and long-lasting outerwear, while the rougher-grade fiber is best suited for the carpet and textile industry.

A washed Leicester Longwool lock.

Leicester Longwool yarn.

LEICESTER LONGWOOL **FACTS**

FINENESS
32–38 microns

STAPLE LENGTH
5–14 inches (12.5–35.5cm)

CRIMP
Medium with well-defined curls

LUSTER
High and silky

SUITABLE FOR
Midrange Garments, Outerwear, and Rugged Outerwear, depending on fiber grade

FELTING QUALITIES
Poor

CONTACT
Leicester Longwool Sheepbreeders' Association (U.K.)
www.leicesterlongwoolsheepassociation.co.uk

Leicester Longwool Sheep Breeders Association (U.S.)
www.leicesterlongwool.org

LINCOLN

Another byproduct of Robert Bakewell's Leicester Longwool breeding work, the Lincoln Longwool was created in Lincolnshire, England, in the late 1700s by crossing Old Lincoln and Bakewell's Leicester Longwool sheep. The goal was to improve the Old Lincoln breed to produce a better meat carcass and finer wool. Some 100 years later, the improved Lincoln was used to develop other breeds, including the Corriedale, Polwarth, and Columbia and, in subsequent breeding generations, Montadale and Targhee.

The foundation of any hand-spinner's flock, the Lincoln grows a large, heavy fleece of smooth, lustrous, and extremely strong fibers. It's often used in mohair blends and other wool blends to add tensile strength and luster.

Most Lincoln fiber is considered too rough to be used alone in hand-knitting yarns. Consider using a laceweight Lincoln yarn for a lace "outer" shawl to be worn over other clothes; the strong and lustrous Lincoln fibers hold open the space around them, highlighting lacework beautifully.

LINCOLN FACTS

FINENESS
34–41 microns

STAPLE LENGTH
8–15 inches (20.5–38cm)

CRIMP
Well-defined curls

LUSTER
High

SUITABLE FOR
Rugged Outerwear

FELTING QUALITIES
Very good

CONTACT
National Lincoln Sheep Breeders Association
www.lincolnsheep.org

A washed Lincoln lock.

PERENDALE

This easy-care sheep breed was developed at Massey University in New Zealand in the 1950s. The goal was to help establish a breed that would thrive in the cold, rainy areas of New Zealand's hill country and produce both quality lambs and wool. Under the direction of Sir Geoffrey Peren, a professor at the university, Cheviot rams were crossed with Romney ewes (page 68). Success came swiftly, and the resulting animal was named the Perendale in honor of its creator. By 1959, the Perendale Sheep Society of New Zealand was formed.

The Perendale sheep has a medium frame that grows a bright, medium-wool fleece with all the best qualities of Romney and Cheviot: crisp springy fibers, high loft, good staple length, and low luster. Its springiness makes the fiber ideal for those garments that need to be warm and durable without being too heavy. Because of its resilience, Perendale wool also is popular for carpets.

PERENDALE FACTS

FINENESS
29–35 microns

STAPLE LENGTH
4–6 inches (10–15cm)

CRIMP
High and clear

LUSTER
Low

SUITABLE FOR
Midrange Garments, Outerwear, and Rugged Outerwear, depending on fiber grade

FELTING QUALITIES
Medium

CONTACT
Perendale Sheep Society of New Zealand
www.perendalenz.com

A washed Perendale lock.

Perendale yarn.

ROMNEY

Since the thirteenth century, this hearty breed has called the cold and damp marshy areas of Kent and Sussex, in southeast England, home. The introduction of Leicester Longwool blood in the nineteenth century helped the Romney become the truly adaptable, highly valued dual-purpose breed that it is today. The Romney's ability to thrive in exposed and isolated climates has made it the predominant breed in both New Zealand and the Falkland Islands. Romneys have been used to help build other breeds, including Coopworth, California Variegated Mutant, Perendale, and Romeldale.

Romneys were first imported into the United States in 1904 and quickly gained in popularity, to the point that, today, they are considered a national breed. The American Romney has both English and, more recently, New Zealand bloodlines.

The Romney sheep may be adaptable, but its fiber is even more so. Romney fiber has more crimp than most longwools, helping it spin worsted *or* woolen in weights ranging from lace to bulky. And its demiluster qualities translate into hearty, earthy-looking yarn that is matched by an equally hearty, earthy feel. Although the rough grades of fiber may have some scratch to them, the medium and fine grades are robust, with only a hint of crunch.

Primarily used by the rug and carpet industry, Romney also is popular among handspinners because of its eagerness to spin. An increase in Romney-based artisanal yarns available from farms and festivals also means that we see more Romney in our knitting baskets.

ROMNEY **FACTS**

FINENESS
32–39 microns

STAPLE LENGTH
5–8 inches (12.5–10cm)

CRIMP
Definite and uniform from base to tip

LUSTER
Good

SUITABLE FOR
Midrange Garments, Outerwear, and Rugged Outerwear, depending on fiber grade

FELTING QUALITIES
Very good

CONTACT
Romney Sheep Breeders Society
www.romneysheepuk.com

American Romney Breeders Association
www.americanromney.org

A washed Romney lock.

Romney yarn.

depending on the grade of fibers used: The younger the animal, the softer and more silky the fibers and yarn; the older the animal, the more rugged and long-wearing the yarn.

TEESWATER FACTS
FINENESS 30–36 microns
STAPLE LENGTH 6–12 inches (15–30.5cm)
CRIMP Large and open curls
LUSTER Very high
SUITABLE FOR Outerwear and Rugged Outerwear, depending on fiber grade
FELTING QUALITIES Modest
CONTACT Teeswater Sheep Breeders Association Limited www.teeswater-sheep.co.uk

TEESWATER

For more than 200 years, farmers in northern England have raised Teeswater sheep in Teesdale, County Durham. The breed produces a true luster longwool fleece that hangs freely in long, curly locks.

Teeswater fiber withstands processing well, retaining its luster and its silky hand. When woven, it produces a smooth, well-wearing fabric with a pearly finish. In the hand-knitting world, a small amount of Teeswater is sometimes added to short-staple wools to give a yarn strength and sheen. On its own, the fiber has a distinct presence that varies sharply

A washed Teeswater lock.

WENSLEYDALE

Many breeds described in this chapter can be traced back to one person, but the Wensleydale can be traced back to one *sheep*. His name was Blue Cap, and he was the result of a union between a Muggs (a now-extinct longwool breed similar to today's Teeswater) ewe and one of Robert Bakewell's Dishley Leicester rams. Blue Cap was born in 1839 in North Yorkshire, England, and so perfect were his majestic size, exquisite wool, and unusual dark skin that the breed standards were decided right then and there. In 1876, after careful breeding of Blue Cap's descendants, the new breed was officially dubbed Wensleydale.

Today's Wensleydale is arguably the largest of the longwools, and it produces the finest and most valuable high-luster longwool on the market. Wensleydale fiber has the same micron count from nose to tail, with a staple length averaging 8–12 inches (20.5–30.5cm). Some animals can even grow as many as 30 inches (76cm) of fiber each year, which is why some Wensleydales are shorn twice a year.

Wensleydale fiber usually is spun worsted to retain its luster and give a fluid drape to knitted fabric. The tighter the fiber is spun, the stronger and more durable the yarn, but the less huggable it becomes; the looser the spin, the softer the yarn. Because of its length and luster, Wensleydale fiber often is blended with mohair and used for cloth and upholstery fabrics.

WENSLEYDALE FACTS

FINENESS
33–35 microns

STAPLE LENGTH
8–12 inches (20.5–30.5cm)

CRIMP
Open curly ringlets

LUSTER
Highest of the luster longwools

SUITABLE FOR
Outerwear and Rugged Outerwear, depending on fiber grade

FELTING QUALITIES
Modest

CONTACT
Wensleydale Longwool Sheep Breeders' Association
www.wensleydale-sheep.com

A washed Wensleydale lock.

Wensleydale yarn.

Dual-Coated and Primitives

All of these breeds trace their lineage back to early Bronze Age sheep, *but some evolved into distinct breed characteristics more recently than others. The Vikings made* a practice of leaving sheep on the islands *they passed to provide food in case of later shipwrecks—a practice that the Spanish explorers continued. Left alone to breed with one another or with any indigenous sheep in the area, those animals evolved and* adapted to thrive in varying climates *and serve the textile needs of the local people. Likewise, Spanish explorers brought Churra sheep to Mexico in 1494, and those animals that thrived under Navajo care became the Navajo–Churro.*

These early sheep gave us milk, meat, leather, and fiber. We used their fleeces for everything from underwear and sewing thread to rope and even sails for our ships. Sheep readily met our needs by producing intricate fleeces that often had up to five distinct fiber types growing together, each perfectly suited for a different use.

As modern civilization evolved, we began to rely less on these sheep to serve our every need. We had the luxury of breeding more for what we wanted and breeding out the traits that were no longer useful to us. Slowly our attention turned away from these rugged little animals and toward larger, faster-maturing, meat-laden sheep that would grow consistently crimpy, fine, bright white fleece. And that's when primitive breeds began to pass into the quiet background of the modern textile industry.

For knitters, primitive breeds present both an opportunity and a challenge. These fibers have a rich history as well as distinct colors and textures that lend an entirely different dimension to our projects. But availability and quality are issues.

Spinners can process their own fleeces and separate out the different fibers, reserving only the softest for clothing. And they will be soft indeed—the finest undercoat fibers of the Shetland sheep can be as soft as cashmere. But sorting fibers takes time and care, something that commercial processors aren't as able to reproduce on a large, mechanized scale. A broader range of fiber grades can get mixed up in the same yarn, making many of the commercial yarns made from these fibers feel harsher than they could be. As a result, some dual-coated and primitive breeds have an unnecessarily bad reputation.

All the breeds in this category share a few traits that set them apart from the other breed categories. First, the sheep grow double coats that contain a mix of long, sturdy outer hairs and short, soft, insulating undercoat. They also can have some wiry white kemp intermingled among the fibers.

Second, these sheep tend to grow a variety of natural colors beyond white—perhaps a relic from when these sheep lived in the wild and needed to camouflage themselves. The modern breeding emphasis on staple length, softness, and continuous growth without shedding has eliminated the color genes in many other breeds, but it remains intact in the dual-coated and primitive breeds.

From a commercial standpoint, the natural colors of these breeds—fewer bright whites for dyeing—restrict the kinds of yarns a commercial mill can make. Creatively speaking, however, the natural colors enhance what we can do with the yarn without the fibers ever having to hit a dye pot. The

Reflecting Pools Bag (page 186) is a perfect illustration of the beauty that can be achieved right off the sheep's back, using five natural shades to complete a delicate Fair Isle colorwork pattern. Having natural colors at our disposal is also helpful because primitive breed fibers lack the well-developed dye receptors (or sites, as they're called) of the modern breeds, making them more challenging to dye.

In this section, I focus on the primitive and dual-coated breeds that you're most likely to find at fiber festivals and on the shelves of your LYS. Many more such breeds exist and await your discovery. Most of the breeds discussed here are splendidly suited for outerwear—nice thick rugged sweaters, coats, hats, mittens, and such. And when you wear these fibers, you'll be wearing a piece of human history.

ICELANDIC

 Brought to Iceland by the Viking settlers some 1,100 years ago, the Icelandic sheep is one of the world's oldest and purest breeds. It is part of the Northern European Short-Tailed group of sheep, whose cousins include the Shetland (page 75) and Finn.

Only a few attempts were made to improve the breed through crossbreeding, and the results were so disastrous that all the crossbred animals were culled and the importation of any sheep to Iceland was declared illegal. As a result, Icelandic sheep today have the same genetic makeup they did 1,100 years ago. They are bright, feisty, and independent, with few modern flocking instincts.

Icelandic sheep often are shorn twice a year. The first shearing occurs in late winter for rams and spring for pregnant and lactating ewes, at which time a natural break occurs in the animal's wool. The second shearing usually takes place in the fall before the animals move from pasture to hay for the winter. Fleeces from fall shearings tend to go for a premium because they have the finest, cleanest fibers.

Unlike other primitive sheep breeds, both coats on the Icelandic sheep are considered wool and almost always are kept together in commercially spun yarns. The fine undercoat is made of short, irregularly crimped fibers called thel, which can be extremely soft and luxurious when spun on their own. The second coat of longer, wavy, more lustrous fibers is called the tog. In finer grades of fleece, it behaves similarly to mohair; rougher grades are better suited to rope and rugs.

When blended together, the tog acts as reinforcement to hold open the yarn and allow the thel fibers to bloom within, but it can also cause the yarn to feel more rugged. The thel and tog can be different colors, which can add another element of exquisite subtlety to yarn, whether left natural or overdyed with another color. The traditional Lopi-style Icelandic yarn is a loosely twisted bulky worsted single containing both thel and tog.

ICELANDIC **FACTS**

FINENESS
Undercoat (thel): 19–22 microns
Outercoat (tog): 27–30 microns

STAPLE LENGTH
Thel: 2–3 inches (5–7.5cm)
Tog: 6–8 inches (15–20cm)

CRIMP
Thel: fine and irregular; tog: smooth, large waves

LUSTER
Medium to high, depending on whether both thel and tog are present

SUITABLE FOR
Midrange Garments, Outerwear, and Rugged Outerwear, depending on the fiber grade

FELTING QUALITIES
Magnificent

CONTACT
Icelandic Sheep Breeders of North America
www.isbona.com

A washed Icelandic lock.

Icelandic yarn.

JACOB

This spotted and multiple-horned sheep breed made its way to England in the seventeenth century, most likely from North Africa via Spain as a variant of the Spanish Churra. Thanks to the efforts of landscape architect Lancelot "Capability" Brown, Jacobs became a common sight in the grand parks, manors, and estates of England by the eighteenth century. They were given the name Jacob as a nod to the Old Testament story of Jacob and his spotted sheep.

Although the Jacob rose to prominence as an ornamental novelty animal, it also produces an intriguing fleece that is commonly used in hand-knitting yarn. The animal grows a randomly spotted coat of white and a black that sometimes strays to brown or a lighter color called lilac. Each color patch can have its own micron count, length, and crimp pattern. The colors are either sorted and spun separately or blended together to create a light gray tweed yarn. Jacob fleece is generally open with a soft, springy handle. This medium-grade fiber enjoys being spun woolen and used for any lightweight yet lofty garment where warmth and durability matter more than next-to-skin softness.

JACOB FACTS

FINENESS
27–35 microns

STAPLE LENGTH
4–7 inches (10–18cm)

CRIMP
Medium

LUSTER
Demiluster

SUITABLE FOR
Outerwear and Rugged Outerwear, depending on fiber grade

FELTING QUALITIES
Good

CONTACT
Jacob Sheep Breeders Association
www.jsba.org

Washed Jacob locks.

Jacob yarn.

NAVAJO-CHURRO

A direct descendant of the Churra sheep brought to Mexico in 1494 by Spanish explorers, the Navajo–Churro breed is a story of survival against nearly all odds—from a massive slaughter by the U.S. Army in 1863 to drought and government-imposed stock reductions in the 1930s. The sheep that thrived and evolved under Navajo care is now called the Navajo–Churro, and it differs only slightly from the early Churra. Hardy and adaptable, the Navajo–Churro grows a dual-coated fleece with a long hair outercoat and a finewool undercoat. The fibers grow in a multitude of colors ranging from white to tan, black, brown, gray, and spotted.

Navajo–Churro sheep were bred to meet both the meat and textile needs of the Navajo people, who focused on producing a strong, colorful, durable, and lustrous wool that would be ideal for weaving. Today's Navajo–Churro fiber is still best suited for woven rugs, saddle blankets, bags, and rugged outerwear. But the finer grades of undercoat fibers also can be separated and spun woolen to produce a warm, lofty, and relatively soft yarn for midrange garments. While this fiber is primarily for hand-weavers, there's a movement afoot to breed the animal for a softer, more "knittable" fiber.

NAVAJO–CHURRO **FACTS**

FINENESS
Undercoat: 18–30 microns
Outercoat: 30–47 microns

STAPLE LENGTH
Undercoat: 3–6 inches (7.5–15cm)
Outercoat: 6–8 inches (15–20.5cm)

CRIMP
Low, with curly tips

LUSTER
Moderate

SUITABLE FOR
Midrange Garments, Outerwear, and Rugged Outerwear, depending on the fiber grade

FELTING QUALITIES
Medium

CONTACT
Navajo–Churro Sheep Association
www.navajo-churrosheep.com

A washed Navajo–Churro lock.

SCOTTISH BLACKFACE

Little is known about the origins of this breed except that it most likely evolved from the native, short-wooled sheep that roamed the mountains and hills between England and Scotland. By 1503, James IV of Scotland had established a flock of 5,000 Scottish Blackface sheep in Ettrick Forest. Today, the breed continues to play an important role in the Scottish textile industry, accounting for nearly 40 percent of all Scottish wool production.

To help it thrive in the rugged mountain and hill regions, the Scottish Blackface grows a true double coat, with a particularly long, coarse outercoat that conceals a much finer undercoat. Most of the coarser grades of fiber are sent to Italy, where they are used to stuff mattresses. The finer grades are highly valued in the fine carpet industry because of their durability and resistance to compression (a result of their robust fiber diameter and crimp structure). Finer grades also are used in the woven Harris Tweed fabrics and a handful of artisan yarns.

A washed Scottish Blackface lock.

SCOTTISH BLACKFACE **FACTS**

FINENESS
28–38+ microns

STAPLE LENGTH
10–14 inches (25.5–35.5cm)

CRIMP
Low

LUSTER
Low

SUITABLE FOR
Undercoat: Outerwear and Rugged Outerwear, depending on fiber grade

FELTING QUALITIES
Good

CONTACT
Blackface Sheep Breeders' Association
www.scottish-blackface.co.uk

Scottish Blackface Breeders Guild
www.ramshornstudio.com/blackface_breeders
_guild.htm

SHETLAND

Like their Icelandic cousins, Shetland sheep most likely were deposited on the rocky, windswept islands between Scotland and Norway by Viking settlers more than

1,000 years ago. They are part of the Northern European Short-Tailed group of sheep, whose cousins include Finns and Icelandics.

Geographic isolation helped maintain the genetic purity of the breed until the Shetland woolen industry reached its peak, at which point the quest for more valuable bright white fiber caused breeders to eliminate many of the colored variants. Today, only 11 main colors and 30 markings remain, many of which still bear their original names like *mioget*, *musket*, *moorit*, *blaegit*, *fleckit*, and *sholmit*.

Shetland sheep have an alert and nimble disposition. Having accompanied humans since the Bronze Age, they are rather comfortable around people. But whereas their improved-breed counterparts have been bred to trust and follow sheepdogs, Shetland sheep instinctively consider sheepdogs predators and run away from them. Put a sheepdog in with a flock of Shetlands, and by the end of the day you'll have one very depressed dog—and a flock of Shetlands on the opposite end of the field.

The quality and behavior of Shetland fiber can vary dramatically from region to region and flock to flock. One animal can grow as many as five different types of fiber, the suitability of which ranges from underwear to socks, sweaters, and rope. The finest wool comes from around the neck area and can make an extraordinarily fine, soft yarn—especially in lace weight. Those fibers were traditionally reserved for Shetland lace wedding ring shawls, enormous works of art that were so fine that they could pass through the inside of a wedding ring.

Shetland wool usually is spun woolen so that the short, crimpy fibers can spread out—or "bloom"—and make themselves at home. It produces a warm, cohesive, and well-wearing fabric. In colorwork, woolen-spun Shetland wool creates the beautiful, heathered effect for which the Fair Isle colorwork tradition is so well known. The fiber's tendency to bloom is especially handy in concealing colors that are being carried along the back of the work. And as an added benefit, the fibers stay put so nicely that if you drop a stitch, it'll stay right where you left it.

SHETLAND **FACTS**	
FINENESS	Undercoat: 12–20 microns Outercoat: 30–40 microns
STAPLE LENGTH	2–4½ inches (5–11cm)
CRIMP	Undercoat: fine; outercoat: smoother than the undercoat, often with a curl at the tip
LUSTER	Low
SUITABLE FOR	Next-to-Skin Wear, Midrange Garments, and Outerwear, depending on fiber grade
FELTING QUALITIES	Moderate
CONTACT	Shetland Sheep Society www.users.zetnet.co.uk/ssbg North American Shetland Sheepbreeders Association www.shetland-sheep.org

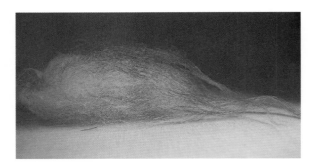

A washed Shetland lock.

Shetland yarn.

FLEECE-FRIENDLY FIBER FESTIVALS

Ready to meet the breeds for yourself? Check your calendar, pack your bags, and head to the nearest sheep and wool festival. That's the ultimate place to meet up with small-scale sheep farmers and get your hands on artisan fibers, fleeces, and yarns. The following is a select list of well-established festivals that are known for their fiber offerings. For a current and more complete list of events around the world, go to www.knittersreview.com and click on "Events."

If there's a breed you really want to meet, contact the breed association listed within each breed description. They'll help put you in touch with the nearest farm.

APRIL

Connecticut Sheep and Wool Festival, Vernon, CT (www.ctsheep.org)

MAY

Maryland Sheep and Wool Festival, West Friendship, MD (www.sheepandwool.org)

New Hampshire Sheep and Wool Festival, Contoocook, NH (www.yankeeshepherd.org)

Massachusetts Sheep and Woolcraft Fair, Cummington, MA (www.masheepwool.org)

JUNE

Maine Fiber Frolic, Windsor, ME (www.fiberfrolic.com)

Hoosier Hills Fiberarts Festival, Franklin, IN (www.hhfiberfest.com)

Iowa Sheep and Wool Festival, Adel, IA (www.iowasheep.com)

Estes Park Wool Market, Estes Park, CO (www.estesnet.com/events/woolmarket.htm)

Black Sheep Gathering, Eugene, OR (www.blacksheepgathering.org)

Woolfest, Cockermouth, Cumbria, England (www.woolfest.co.uk)

JULY

Australian Sheep and Wool Show, Bendigo, Victoria, Australia (www.sheepshow.com)

AUGUST

Michigan Fiber Festival, Allegan, MI (www.michiganfiberfestival.info)

World Sheep and Fiber Arts Festival, Bethel, MO (www.worldsheepfest.com)

SEPTEMBER

Wisconsin Sheep and Wool Festival, Jefferson, WI (www.wisconsinsheepandwoolfestival.com)

Vermont Sheep and Wool Festival, Tunbridge, VT (www.vermontsheep.org)

Finger Lakes Fiber Arts Festival, Hemlock, NY (www.gvhg.org/fest.html)

Common Ground Country Fair, Unity, ME (www.mofga.org)

Oregon Flock and Fiber Festival, Canby, OR (www.flockandfiberfestival.com)

OCTOBER

Wool Festival at Taos, Taos, NM (www.taoswoolfestival.org)

Lambtown Festival, Dixon, CA (www.lambtown.com)

Fall Fiber Festival of Virginia, Montpelier Estate, VA (www.fallfiberfestival.org)

New York State Sheep and Wool Festival, Rhinebeck, NY (www.sheepandwool.com)

Southeastern Animal Fiber Fair, Fletcher, NC (www.saffsite.org)

4

Plays Well with Others

As magnificent as wool can be on its own, most of us don't live by pure wool yarns alone. Wool is a physically and creatively versatile ingredient that loves to be blended with other fibers for different effects. The choice to blend can be a product of aesthetic intent, but yarn companies often are driven by financial, functional, and logistical demands as well. From a consumer perspective, wool blends truly let us have our cake and eat it too.

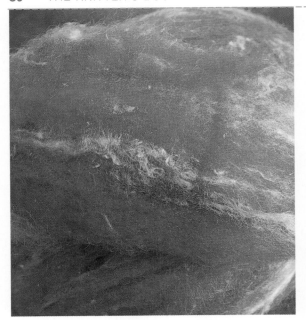

Dyed wool and silk fibers blend together during carding to produce a gently variegated roving and, ultimately, yarn.

Blending for Luster and Drape

As you've probably noticed by now, the silkiest, most lustrous wools tend not to be the softest or most commonly available. And the softest, finest wools tend *not* to have the silkiest luster or drape. So how do the yarn companies make yarns that are soft but also have shimmer and drape? When in doubt, they usually start with a soft wool (such as Merino) and blend it with an equally soft but fluid, high-sheen, non-wool fiber.

SILK

The most common choice for such blends is silk, and we have a phenomenal number of silk/wool blends—especially silk and Merino—to show for it. These two fibers together give you the best of both worlds: a soft, plump, and squishy wool and a smooth, lustrous silk. Also a warm fiber, silk complements the insulating qualities of wool. But it's a smooth fiber with no crimp, lending excellent drape to help anchor otherwise lofty fabrics.

Blending 30 percent silk with 70 percent wool gives shimmery overtones and a lightly enhanced drape to the Falling Waters Shawl (page 168).

A lot of the yarn's behavior can depend on how much silk has been added to the mix. Silk is a fine, lightweight fiber, which means that a little bit goes a long way. To help illustrate this, I chose silk/wool blends for two special projects in this book. The yarn used in Jane Cochran's Falling Waters Shawl (page 168) has a foundation of 70 percent wool to which 30 percent silk was added. The wool still clearly dominates

An even mix of 50 percent silk and 50 percent Merino brings more luster, drape, and ethereal elegance to the knitted fabric in the Tibetan Clouds Beaded Stole (page 173).

the mix, creating a plump and robust fabric, yet there's no denying the shimmer lurking right beneath the surface, especially when the fabric is held up to the light. The silk also gives additional weight to the shawl, helping it drape luxuriously around your shoulders.

In Sivia Harding's Tibetan Clouds Beaded Stole (page 173), the yarn blend is an even mix of silk and wool, and you can see a far more substantial luster and drape. And yet the Merino is never far behind, pulling the fabric together and helping the yarn hug your needles and, eventually, your shoulders. The higher silk content is appropriate for this project because it enhances the lace openwork patterning.

MOHAIR AND ALPACA

Silk isn't the only high-luster possibility. Mohair has extraordinary shimmer and a relaxed, fluid, low-crimp drape

that benefits from the openness and elasticity of wool. Any wool/mohair blend made from kid or baby kid mohair will be extremely soft and luxurious. The older the angora goat (from which mohair comes), the rougher the fiber becomes. Just a hint of mohair was added to organic Columbia wool in the yarn used for the Comfy Cardigan (page 138). Mohair adds a touch of luster where the Columbia fibers are lacking and also helps to ground the otherwise lofty yarn.

Suri alpaca is another warm, shimmery, well-draping fiber that enjoys being blended with wool yarn. It grows off the animal in long lustrous locks. (Note: Suri is the less common of the two alpaca types—the other being huacaya—so be sure to look for it by name.)

CELLULOSIC FIBERS

What if you're seeking a mix that still has shimmer and drape but is cooler and more breathable? Regenerated cellulose to the rescue. With an even brighter, crisper shine than silk, lyocell is made from the regenerated cellulose in wood pulp and is primarily marketed to knitters by its trade name Tencel®. The fiber also has extraordinary tensile strength, making Merino/Tencel a popular blend for sock yarns.

Another source of warm-weather shimmer comes from SeaCell®, made from 95 percent lyocell and 5 percent seaweed. The yarn I chose for version A of Ilga Leja's Leafy Glen Shell (page 152) is a blend of 70 percent Merino and 30 percent SeaCell. The high Merino content keeps the fabric lofty, supple, and squeezable, while the SeaCell adds a marvelous shine to highlight the lace and give the fabric a cooler feel, appropriate for a sleeveless top.

And then there's bamboo fiber, which is made from regenerated cellulose in bamboo stalks. Another high-sheen fiber, bamboo adds softness and comfort to the mix, as well as internal evaporative cooling behavior that is especially appealing to knitters in warm climates.

The addition of 30 percent SeaCell in Fleece Artist Sea Wool gives the yarn more shimmer and a cooler body for summer, fitting for the Leafy Glen Shell (page 152).

Note that all of these fibers generally dictate a worsted spin, although the raw grade of silk *can* be carded and spun woolen. Worsted-spun yarns tend to be more smooth, compact, and long wearing. But as long as Merino or another high-crimp finewool holds the majority percentage in the blend, you'll still end up with a fairly lofty yarn that holds its shape. When the wool percentage dips below 50 percent, however, the resulting yarn will take on more of the traits of the other ingredients, usually losing a great deal of bounce and elasticity in the process.

Blending for Halo

All yarns are heavenly to me, but that's not the kind of halo I'm referring to here. I'm talking about what happens when crimpy and jumbled wool fibers are loosely spun in the woolen style. The fibers are held under tension while spinning, but as soon as they're allowed to relax (usually after a garment has been knitted and then washed in warm water for the first time), their fine little ends spring out from

captivity and form a fuzzy halo that renders the knitted fabric truly plump and cohesive, not to mention *warm*. The fact that this transformation occurs at the end of the project lends a delicious sense of anticipation to the entire process.

When a yarn is spun worsted, however, the fibers are tightly combed to uniform lengths and then their ends firmly tucked into the yarn, which means that washing will result in less relaxation and bloom. The yarn will have a crisper stitch definition and may wear longer, but that sense of plump succulence and extra warmth will be lacking.

ANGORA AND ALPACA

Yarn companies can still achieve a lovely halo in worsted yarns by blending wool with extremely fine fibers whose

Just 10 percent angora and 30 percent baby alpaca give a gentle halo to the wool blend in the Flicka Hat (page 92) without distracting from the delicate colorwork patterning.

innate halo cannot be tamed by any amount of worsted spinning. And nothing says "halo" like angora, which comes from the angora rabbit. As with silk, angora is such a fine fiber that only a small amount—percentagewise—is needed to see results. The worsted-spun yarn used to knit Shelia January's Flicka Hat (page 92), for example, has only 10 percent angora, yet there's no denying the presence of a halo. Angora becomes dense fairly quickly, however, and it tends to overpower any other fibers in a mix when it passes beyond the 50 percent mark.

The other fiber contributing to the halo in Shelia's Flicka Hat is baby alpaca, of which the yarn has 30 percent. Until the last decade or so, alpaca was considered primarily a long, smooth, dense, and extremely warm fiber with little elasticity. But breeders have been working to create animals that grow a finer, crimpier, more cashmere-like fiber that adds a deliciously quiet and somewhat slippery halo to any yarn. These fibers come from the more common huacaya alpaca, and the finest, crimpiest ones come from the youngest animals. To get the most possible halo in an alpaca/wool blend, look for the words "baby alpaca" or "royal baby alpaca" on the label.

Adding qiviut and silk gives an already fine Merino a luxurious halo and a hint of shimmer in version A of the Prairie Rose Lace Shawl (page 162).

CASHMERE, QIVIUT, AND AMERICAN BISON

As marvelous as angora and alpaca are, my vote for the most ethereal bloom would have to go to the downy undercoats of the cashmere goat, the arctic musk ox, and the American bison. Because all three animals typically live exclusively outdoors in remote areas with brutally cold winters, they need downy undercoats to stay warm. And if you've ever seen an arctic musk ox in the winter, you'll know that the fibers are doing their job: Snow falls on the animals' backs and just sits there without melting.

In the spring, these hardy animals naturally shed their coats. The fibers are collected and painstakingly separated from the longer, pointy guard hairs in a process called dehairing. In the case of the undomesticated American bison, most commercial fibers are collected from the hides of bison that have been slaughtered for the meat market.

All of these fibers are extremely fine—the undercoat of the arctic musk ox, called qiviut, averages 10–13 microns; that of the cashmere goat, 16 microns; and that of the American bison, 12–29 microns—with a springy but highly irregular crimp. Blended with wool, these fibers immediately soften the surface of any yarn and increase its insulating power exponentially. These blends are also economically helpful because cashmere, qiviut, and bison fibers can be costly on their own. Blends aren't just about economic compromise, though; the wool actually enhances these fibers. On their own, most downy undercoat fibers are extraordinarily soft but fairly lightweight. The addition of wool or another heavier fiber (such as silk or bamboo) helps anchor the fibers and give them more substance.

You can see this symbiotic relationship in version A of the Prairie Rose Lace Shawl (page 162), which is knit from a yarn containing 45 percent qiviut, 45 percent extra fine Merino, and 10 percent silk. (Careful, the mere mention of those three fibers in the same sentence may cause dizziness.) The Merino and silk help anchor the flyaway qiviut fibers and give the shawl drape, the silk helps highlight the open lace pattern, and the qiviut—despite the fact that this yarn has been spun in a nice tight worsted fashion—lends a mysterious mistiness to the fabric surface.

In addition to anchoring otherwise short and fairly delicate down fibers, wool also gives them greater strength for use in all sorts of projects—even socks. Need proof? The Windjammer Socks (page 110) are knit from a tightly spun blend of 80 percent superwash Merino, 10 percent cashmere, and 10 percent nylon.

MOHAIR

Some of the finest grades of mohair (such as kid and baby kid) also can add halo, although the fiber's longer staple length can limit the amount of bloom. For this reason, mills often spin mohair as a bouclé yarn and then run it through a brushing machine to snip the loops and force the fibers to bloom.

Blending for Warm-Weather Comfort

A common misconception is that wool is too warm for summer wear. Although this might be true in the hottest, most tropical regions of the world, it's not necessarily true elsewhere. With a little creative blending, wool can be entirely appropriate for comfortable summer wear.

The most common blend for comfort is wool and cotton, a fiber that comes with its own internal evaporative cooling

The 30 percent linen in Louet MerLin is immediately apparent in the open, airy fabric of version B of the Leafy Glen Shell (page 152).

system. A soft and relatively smooth, low-crimp fiber, cotton can sometimes become dense and inelastic on its own, which is why a lot of mills get creative with their spinning and plying to add volume and bounce. Wool adds that volume and bounce naturally, while still letting you enjoy all the cooling and comfort benefits of cotton.

Another well-known warm-weather fiber is linen, a long, sturdy fiber derived from the stalk of the flax plant. Although it's hard to believe that this firm, extremely durable material could have anything to do with the soft, succulent fibers grown by sheep, it definitely can. The key issues with linen are that it isn't soft to the touch initially, and it doesn't have any bounce or elasticity. Many knitters miss the fact that linen does, with wear, soften and become more lustrous. And if blended with a hearty percentage of wool, the yarn might even have a hint of bounce to it. Some yarn companies blend wool and linen together intimately before spinning, but the fibers also can be spun separately and plied together. The latter process was used to make the 70 percent Merino, 30 percent linen yarn used in version B of Ilga Leja's Leafy Glen Shell (page 152).

And finally, no discussion of evaporative cooling is complete without mentioning bamboo. Bamboo fibers have microscopic holes along their surface. These tiny vents aid in the rapid absorption and evaporation of any ambient moisture, making the fiber extremely comfortable and breathable against your skin. Bamboo also brings luster and drape to the table, so keep this characteristic in mind as you study the yarn labels of any wool/bamboo blend. If you want more bounce, look for yarns with a higher percentage of wool. If you prefer drape and better cooling qualities, choose a blend that is predominantly bamboo.

Blending for Strength

Most commercial mills use the finest wool fibers for their hand-knitting yarns—fibers that may feel soft to the touch but lack substantial tensile strength or abrasion resistance. Sometimes a mill will blend these finewool fibers with a small amount of sturdier wool from breeds that have greater tensile strength and usually longer staple length. But some softness is lost in the process. Here's where synthetic fibers come in handy.

One of the most durable and commonly used manufactured fibers for wool blends is nylon, a synthetic fiber-forming polyamide created by a DuPont research team in 1935.

Strong enough to replace Japanese silk in World War II parachutes and fine enough to create women's stockings, nylon also can substantially reinforce any wool. You only need 10–25 percent nylon to do the trick. At higher percentages, nylon's low moisture uptake can make fabric clammy and uncomfortable against the skin—an especially undesirable trait in perspiration-prone garments like socks. The yarn in the luxurious Windjammer Socks (page 110), contains only 10 percent nylon and is quite sturdy.

Although not as strong as nylon, acrylic fiber also can add strength, elasticity, and moisture-wicking properties to wool blends. Superfine synthetic fiber less than 1 denier thick is called microfiber, and it adds great strength and softness to blends. (The denier is a textile term used only to define the fineness of silk, rayon, and nylon fibers. It represents the fiber's mass in grams per 9,000 meters. All you need to know here is that 1 denier is really, really fine.)

Natural fibers that add strength to wool blends also tend to be the fibers that bring luster and drape into the mix. Silk, bamboo, and Tencel are among the most useful in this category.

Blends play a vital role not only in the wool market but also in our own knitting baskets. They help us achieve our creative goals without great sacrifice. Blending fibers is like mixing ingredients in a kitchen. Each tablespoon added or subtracted further changes the chemistry of the recipe—and the results. Understanding the subtleties of this chemistry can make us smarter cooks, able to confidently choose the ideal yarns for whatever our hearts desire.

Patterns

5

William Shakespeare wrote, "Joy's soul lies in the doing." Those words ring especially true in knitting, where the fun is truly in the *doing.* The real pleasure comes when we pick up our needles, choose a yarn, and cast on—which is how we've arrived at this chapter.

To help you experience the joy of wool to its fullest, I've enlisted the help of designers who love wool as much as I do. Together we've prepared a large buffet of tasty samples for you. We have hearty ribs and cables, delicate lace, and subtly textured stockinette to cover you from head to toe. There's everything from next-to-skin scarves and sweaters to rugged outerwear and hearty home projects, in skill levels that span from beginner to experienced.

SKILL LEVELS EXPLAINED

Knitters are intelligent people. We can look at a project and feel pretty confident about whether we're up to the task. But sometimes photographs are misleading, especially if they make a project look harder than it really is. That's why I added a skill level rating to each project. The rating is based on standards set forth by the Craft Yarn Council of America (CYCA). It is only a general guideline. We learn best by doing, and I encourage you to choose projects that will challenge you to the next skill level.

EASY:
These kinds of projects use basic stitches, repetitive stitch patterns, simple color changes, and simple shaping and finishing techniques. They are perfect for taking to knitting groups because they don't require as much concentration as the intermediate and experienced projects.

INTERMEDIATE:
The bread-and-butter category for most knitters, these projects have a variety of stitches, such as basic cables and lace. They may use double-pointed needles or knitting in the round techniques, shaping, and finishing.

EXPERIENCED:
These projects use so-called "advanced" techniques and stitches, such as short rows, intricate lace patterns, and numerous color changes. I always have at least one such project going; I work on it when I'm at home and can sit quietly and concentrate. I love the feeling of pride and accomplishment that the finished project gives me.

We conceived these projects with specific fiber characteristics and design goals in mind, since, as I already mentioned, every kind of wool has an ideal purpose and not every purpose can—or should—be met by the same wool. The projects are shown in some of the most beautiful, appropriate, and reasonably available yarns I could find. Does this mean your project will self-destruct if you use any other yarn? Not at all. I expect you to choose from among the yarns that are interesting and available to you, and to be confident in your substitution. For that reason, these projects were also designed for absolute yarn flexibility. Each pattern includes yarn notes explaining the fiber qualities, and sometimes specific breeds you may want to consider when matching yarn to project.

Each time you knit these projects in a different yarn, your experience will be slightly different, too. Swatch and experiment. You may be surprised, amazed, or betrayed—but you'll always learn from the experience. Let these patterns become old trusted friends that you can refer to again and again each time you discover a new skein of wool. I want you to experience just how versatile wool can be, and these projects will start you on that journey.

Hill Country Hat

Designed by Clara Parkes

We begin with a very easy, low-yardage unisex hat pattern you can knit with any bulky wool yarn. I encourage you to play with different breeds, delicate and rugged alike, and to try both woolen- and worsted-spun yarns—each will produce varied yet equally warm and attractive results and will help your hands become better acquainted with the different possibilities of wool.

I like to think that this hat, with its thick ribbing and alternating knit and purl stitches, would be perfect for an autumn stroll through the English hill country where so many cherished sheep breeds originated, including the Bluefaced Leicester and Suffolk, whose wool is used in versions A (pictured above) and B (page 90) of this project.

SKILL LEVEL
Easy

SIZE
One size fits most

FINISHED MEASUREMENTS
Circumference (relaxed): 20" (51cm)
The hat will stretch to accommodate most heads.

YARN
120 yd (109m) of bulky-weight yarn: 1 skein
Rowan Purelife British Sheep Breeds Collection,
100% wool, 3½ oz (100g), 120 yd (110m);
hat A (above): color 950 Bluefaced Leicester,
hat B (page 90): color 952 Steel Grey Suffolk

NEEDLES
Set of 5 size 10½ (6.5mm) double-pointed needles,
or size to obtain gauge

NOTIONS
Tapestry needle

GAUGE
16 stitches and 20 rows = 4" (10cm) in Hills and
Valleys Pattern

Stitch guide

Hills and Valleys Pattern

Round 1: * (K1, p1) 6 times, (p1, k1) 4 times; repeat from * to the end of the round.

Rounds 2 and 4: Knit around.

Round 3: * K1, p1; repeat from * to the end of the round.

Crown

Cast on 8 stitches, leaving a 6" (15cm) tail. Arrange the stitches so 2 stitches are on each of the 4 needles. Join to work in the round.

Round 1: Kfb each stitch—16 stitches.

Round 2 and all even-numbered rounds: * K1, p1; repeat from * to the end of the round.

Round 3: * K1, kfb; repeat from * to the end of the round—24 stitches.

Round 5: * K2, kfb; repeat from * to the end of the round—32 stitches.

Round 7: * K3, kfb; repeat from * to the end of the round—40 stitches.

Round 9: * K4, kfb; repeat from * to the end of the round—48 stitches.

Round 11: * K5, kfb; repeat from * to the end of the round—56 stitches.

Round 13: * K6, kfb; repeat from * to the end of the round—64 stitches.

Round 15: * K7, kfb; repeat from * to the end of the round—72 stitches.

Round 17: * K8, kfb; repeat from * to the end of the round—80 stitches.

Round 18: * K1, p1; repeat from * to the end of the round.

Round 19: Knit around.

Sides

Work Hills and Valleys Pattern 3 times, or until the hat is approximately 2" (5cm) short of the desired finished length, ending with round 4 of the pattern.

Brim

Next round: * K1, p1; repeat from * to the end of the round.

Repeat this round until the brim measures 2" (5cm). Bind off loosely.

Thread the cast-on tail through a tapestry needle and use it to close up the top of the hat. Weave in remaining ends.

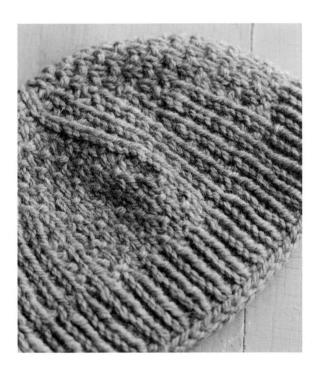

Flicka Hat   Designed by Shelia January

Inspired by the Bohus style of colorwork developed in Sweden in the 1930s in the Bohus Stickning workshop, and taking its name from the Swedish word for "girl," this hat was designed with halo in mind. That halo could come from a traditional woolen-spun wool yarn (such as Jamieson & Smith) or from a worsted-spun yarn to which other halo-friendly fibers have been added, such as the wool/baby alpaca/angora blend shown here.

The Bohus style of stranded colorwork differs from many others in that more than two colors can be used in each row, and purl stitches are used on the right side of the knitting to create color "bumps" that are part of the design. The ideal yarn for this project has a fine gauge and a gentle halo to help obscure individual stitches and present a uniform, painterly picture.

SKILL LEVEL
Intermediate

SIZE
Women's S/M (L/XL)

FINISHED MEASUREMENTS
Circumference (relaxed): 19¼ (21¼)" (49 [54]cm)
The fabric will stretch by a few inches if necessary.

YARN
200 yd (183m) of sportweight yarn: Classic Elite Yarns Fresco, 60% wool, 30% baby alpaca, 10% angora, 1¾ oz (50g), 164 yd (150m), 2 skeins color 5304 Sugar Blue (MC), 1 skein each 5320 Ashley Blue (A), 5381 Fair Green (B), and 5356 Delft Blue (C)

NEEDLES
Size 2 (2.75mm) and size 3 (3.25mm) 16" (40cm) circular needles, or size to obtain gauge
Set of 4 size 3 (3.25mm) double-pointed needles

NOTIONS
Stitch markers
Tapestry needle

GAUGE
30 stitches and 32 rows = 4" (10cm) in color pattern on larger needles

Notes

▸ *Each square of the chart represents 1 stitch and indicates the color in which the stitch is to be worked.*

▸ *Boxes marked with ⊡ on the chart indicate stitches to be purled; empty boxes indicate stitches to be knit.*

▸ *Carry colors not in use loosely along the wrong side of the work. Do not weave in the stranded yarns.*

▸ *Break off colors not in use for more than 1 row, then rejoin them when they are needed again.*

Stitch guide

Cdd (centered double decrease): Slip the next 2 stitches together as if you were going to knit them together. Knit the next stitch. Pass the 2 slipped stitches over the stitch just knit.

Brim

Using MC and the smaller circular needle, cast on 144 (160) stitches. Join to work in the round, being careful not to twist the stitches around the needle. Place a stitch marker on the needle to indicate the beginning of the round.

Round 1: * K1, p1; repeat from * to the end of the round. Repeat this round until the piece measures 1" (2.5cm).

Next 3 rounds: Knit.

Change to larger needles.

Next round: Knit.

Begin working pattern from Flicka Hat Chart. The pattern is repeated 18 (20) times around the hat.

When row 26 of chart is complete, continue with MC only, and knit every round until the hat measures 7" (18cm) from the beginning.

Next round: * K34 (24), k2tog; repeat from * to last 0 (4) stitches, k0 (4)—140 (154) stitches remain.

Next round: Knit.

Crown

Round 1: K9 (10), * cdd, k17 (19); repeat from * 5 times more, cdd, k8 (9)—126 (140) stitches remain.

Round 2 and all even-numbered rounds: Knit.

Round 3: K8 (9), * cdd, k15 (17); repeat from * 5 times more, cdd, k7 (8)—112 (126) stitches remain.

Round 5: K7 (8), * cdd, k13 (15); repeat from * 5 times more, cdd, k6 (7)—98 (112) stitches remain.

Change to double-pointed needles.

Round 7: K6 (7), * cdd, k11 (13); repeat from * 5 times more, cdd, k5 (6)—84 (98) stitches remain.

Round 9: K5 (6), * cdd, k9 (11); repeat from * 5 times more, cdd, k4 (5)—70 (84) stitches remain.

Round 11: K4 (5), * cdd, k7 (9); repeat from * 5 times more, cdd, k3 (4)—56 (70) stitches remain.

Round 13: K3 (4), * cdd, k5 (7); repeat from * 5 times more, cdd, k2 (3)—42 (56) stitches remain.

Round 15: K2 (3), * cdd, k3 (5); repeat from * 5 times more, cdd, k1 (2)—28 (42) stitches remain.

Round 17: K1 (2), *cdd, k1 (3); repeat from * 5 times more, cdd, k0 (1)—14 (28) stitches remain.

Size L/XL only

Round 19: K1, * cdd, k1; repeat from * 5 times more, cdd—14 stitches remain.

Both sizes

Final round: K2tog 7 times—7 stitches remain. Break yarn, leaving a 6" (15cm) tail. Thread the tail through a tapestry needle and draw it through the remaining stitches. Pull tight, and fasten off. Weave in ends.

Block hat gently by soaking it in warm water, blotting it dry, and shaping it on a form covered with a towel or another absorbent material.

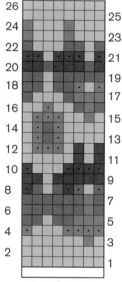

Flicka Hat Chart

COLOR AND STITCH KEY

☐ = MC

■ = A

■ = B

■ = C

⊡ = P on RS with designated color

8-st Repeat

Sweet Fern Mitts

Designed by Clara Parkes

I made several prototypes of these fingerless mitts in smooth, worsted-spun yarns, but they just didn't look right. These mitts are at their happiest when worked in a hearty, woolen-spun two- or three-ply farm yarn. The woolen spinning helps the fibers bloom into place with their first wash, creating a plump and cohesive fabric that will keep your hands toasty warm. The multiple plies give greater durability and extra dimension to the ribbing and cables. And the low yardage—a mere 120 yards (110m)—makes this project perfect for sampling single skeins from different farms and sheep breeds.

Depending on your personal comfort level, these mitts would be just as well suited to any of the mediumwools, Down wools, and Down-type wools. Mitts A (pictured at left) shows the mitts in a crisp and springy, Down-like commercial yarn that's most likely from an old variety of short-wooled Alpine sheep. But the mitts also perform beautifully in finewools, such as the succulent Cormo from Elsa Wool Company (mitts B, shown above), as well as any of the loftier dual-coated or primitive breeds. The ribbing and cables look especially three-dimensional in multiple-ply yarns.

The mitts get their name from the sweet ferns that grow throughout my back field. Their sweet fragrance is, to me, the epitome of summer in Maine. And their distinct long, wavy leaves are reflected in the cable motif along the center top of each mitt.

SKILL LEVEL
Intermediate

SIZE
Women's M

FINISHED MEASUREMENTS
Hand circumference (relaxed): 6½" (16.5cm)
Length (cuff to fingertip): 7" (18cm)
The ribbing makes for a flexible fit. These mitts will
comfortably accommodate an 8" (20.5cm) hand.

YARN
120 yd (110m) of worsted-weight yarn:
Mitts A (page 96): 2 skeins Schoeller & Stahl
Edelweiss, 100% wool, 1¾ oz (50g), 109 yd
(100m), color Light Rose Heather

Mitts B (page 97): 1 skein Elsa Wool Company
Woolen-Spun Worsted-Weight, 100% Cormo
wool, 4 oz (114g), 237 yd (217m), color Medium
Gray ④ MEDIUM

NEEDLES
Set of 4 size 5 (3.75mm) double-pointed needles,
or size to obtain gauge

NOTIONS
Cable needle
Tapestry needle

GAUGE
24 stitches and 28 rows = 4" (10cm) in k2, p2 rib
pattern

Stitch guide

M1R (make 1 right): Make a right-leaning increase
by picking up the bar between stitches from back
to front and knitting into the front of the picked-up
stitch.

M1L (make 1 left): Make a left-leaning increase
by picking up the bar between stitches from front
to back and knitting into the back of the picked-up
stitch.

Right mitt

Cuff

Cast on 41 stitches. Arrange the stitches on 3 needles,
and join to work in the round.

Round 1: (K2, p2) twice, kfb, k2, kfb, (p2, k2) twice,
p1, (k2, p2) 5 times.

Round 2: (K2, p2) twice, kfb, k4, kfb, (p2, k2) twice,
p1, (k2, p2) 5 times—45 stitches.

Round 3: (K2, p2) twice, work pattern from Sweet Fern
Cable Chart over next 10 stitches, k2, p2, k2, p1, (k2,
p2) 5 times.

Continue in ribbing and Sweet Fern Cable pattern as
established until 6 cable twists have been made—24
rounds.

Thumb gusset

Round 25 (row 3 of chart): Work 20 stitches in pattern
as established, place marker, M1R, p1, M1L, place
marker, work in ribbing to the end of the round—45
stitches.

Rounds 26–28: Work 20 stitches in pattern as
established, slip marker, k1, p1, k1, slip marker, work in
ribbing to the end of the round.

Round 29 (Increase Round): Work in pattern to marker,
slip marker, M1R, knit to center stitch, p1, knit to marker,
M1L, slip marker, work in ribbing to the end of the
round—49 stitches.

Rounds 30–38: Continue in pattern as established,
working Increase Round every other round 4 times
more—57 stitches.

Round 39: Work in pattern to marker, remove marker,
place next 13 stitches on a holder, cast on 1 stitch
to bridge the gap, work in pattern to the end of the

round—45 stitches. In the next round, purl that new stitch to reestablish the rib pattern.

Rounds 40–48: Work in pattern as established.

Round 49: (K2, p2) twice, k2, ssk, k2tog, k2, (p2, k2) twice, p1, (k2, p2) 5 times—43 stitches.

Round 50: (K2, p2) twice, k1, ssk, k2tog, k1, (p2, k2) twice, p1, (k2, p2) 5 times—41 stitches.

Bind off loosely.

Work thumb as instructed below.

Left mitt

Cuff

Cast on 41 stitches. Arrange the stitches on 3 needles, and join to work in the round.

Round 1: (K2, p2) twice, kfb, k2, kfb, p2, (k2, p2) 6 times, k2, p1.

Round 2: (K2, p2) twice, kfb, k4, kfb, p2, (k2, p2) 6 times, k2, p1—45 stitches.

Round 3: (K2, p2) twice, work pattern from Sweet Fern Cable Chart over next 10 stitches, (k2, p2) 6 times, k2, p1.

Continue in ribbing and Sweet Fern Cable pattern as established until 6 cable twists have been made—24 rounds.

Thumb gusset

Round 25 (row 3 of chart): Work in pattern as established to last stitch, place marker, M1R, p1, M1L, place marker—45 stitches.

Rounds 26–28: Work in pattern as established to marker, slip marker, k1, p1, k1, slip marker.

Round 29 (Increase Round): Work in pattern to marker, slip marker, M1R, knit to center stitch, p1, knit to marker, M1L, slip marker—49 stitches.

Rounds 30–38: Continue in pattern as established, working Increase Round every other round 4 times more—57 stitches.

Round 39: Work in pattern to marker, remove marker, place next 13 stitches on a holder, cast on 1 stitch to bridge the gap—45 stitches. In the next round, purl that new stitch to reestablish the rib pattern.

Rounds 40–48: Work in pattern as established.

Round 49: (K2, p2) twice, k2, ssk, k2tog, k2, p2, (k2, p2) 6 times, k2, p1—43 stitches.

Round 50: (K2, p2) twice, k1, ssk, k2tog, k1, p2, (k2, p2) 6 times, k2, p1—41 stitches.

Bind off loosely.

Work thumb as instructed below.

Thumb (work 1 on each mitt)

Place the first 7 stitches from the holder on a needle. Place the remaining 6 stitches on another needle. Join yarn, leaving a generous tail, and use a 3rd needle to pick up and knit 3 stitches across the top of the thumb opening—16 stitches. Join to work in the round.

Next round: K6, p1, k9.

Repeat this round 5 times more.

Bind off.

Weave in ends with a tapestry needle, using the tail from the thumb to close up any gaps at the base of the thumb.

Sweet Fern Cable Chart

STITCH KEY

□ = K

⊡ = P

⬚ = Slip 2 sts onto cable needle and hold in back, k2, k2 from cable needle

⬚ = Slip 2 sts onto cable needle and hold in front, k2, k2 from cable needle

10 Stitches

Risti Mittens   Designed by Nancy Bush

No book about wool would be complete without a pattern for fine-gauge colorwork mittens like the ones that were so popular in the Baltic countries, especially in Estonia. And nobody knows Estonian knitting better than author, teacher, and designer Nancy Bush. These mittens sport a popular pattern that hails from several areas of southern and western Estonia, including the village of Risti (hence the pattern name). The cuff was often the most colorful part of an Estonian mitten, and here Nancy chose a pattern known as Peacock's Tail, which gives the cuff a scalloped edge and lends itself easily to using multiple colors.

This pattern uses Vuorelma Satakieli, a durable two-ply fingering-weight wool yarn from Finland that is extremely popular for this kind of fine colorwork. We can only guess that it includes some Finnsheep wool or fibers from a similar breed. The yarn is lustrous but extremely strong, is available in a multitude of colors, and has a faint halo that helps trap still air for warmth while concealing the strands of yarn being carried on the reverse side of the fabric.

SKILL LEVEL
Experienced

SIZE
Women's M

FINISHED MEASUREMENTS
Hand circumference: 8" (20.5cm)
Length (cuff to fingertips): 10½" (26.5cm)

YARN
250 yd (229m) of fingering-weight yarn:
Vuorelma Satakieli, 100% wool, 3½ oz (100g), 350 yd (320m), 1 skein each color 199 Ochre (A), 003 Cream (B), 288 Rust (C), 631 Blue (D), and 184 Yellow (E)

NEEDLES
Set of 5 size 0 (2mm) double-pointed needles, or size to obtain gauge

NOTIONS
Small amount of smooth, thin waste yarn
Tapestry needle

GAUGE
36 stitches and 48 rows = 4" (10 cm) in stockinette stitch in Risti Mitten Chart Pattern

Notes

▸ *The front and the back of the hand are different.*

▸ *Each square on the chart represents 1 stitch. Because the mittens are worked in the round, every row of the chart is read from right to left.*

▸ *For the hand, carry colors not in use loosely along the wrong side of the work. Do not weave in the stranded yarns.*

▸ *For the cuff, break off colors not in use and rejoin them when they are needed again.*

Stitch guide

Peacock's Tail Pattern

Round 1: * K1, yo, k2, skp, p1, k2tog, k2, yo; repeat from * to the end of the round.

Round 2: * K5, p1, k4; repeat from * to the end of the round.

Repeat these 2 rounds for pattern.

Right mitten

Cuff

Using color A, cast on 70 stitches. Arrange the stitches on 4 needles, with 20 stitches on each of the first 3 needles and 10 stitches on the 4th needle. Join to work in the round, being careful not to twist the stitches around the needles. Purl 1 round.

Begin working Peacock's Tail Pattern, changing colors as follows:

Work 2 rounds with color A.

Work 4 rounds with color B.

Work 2 rounds with color C.

Work 2 rounds with color D.

Work 2 rounds with color E.

Work 2 rounds with color A.

Work 2 rounds with color B.

Work 2 rounds with color D.

Work 2 rounds with color C.

Work 2 rounds with color B.

Work 2 rounds with color A.

Work 2 rounds with color E.

Change to color B.

Next round: Knit.

Next round: Purl.

Next round: Knit.

Hand

Rearrange stitches so you have 18 stitches on the first needle, 17 stitches on the second needle, 17 stitches on the third needle, and 18 stitches on the fourth needle. Begin working from Risti Mitten Chart pattern with colors B and D.

On row 29 of chart, position the thumb opening as follows:

Work in pattern over the stitches on needles 1 and 2. On needle 3, work 2 stitches in pattern, knit the next 15 stitches with the waste yarn. Slip these 15 stitches back to the left-hand needle and work across them in pattern as established. Continue in pattern to the end of the round.

Continue working in chart pattern. Note that all the decreases at the tip of the mitten are worked in color D. At the completion of the chart, 6 stitches remain. Break yarn, thread tail through a tapestry needle and draw through the remaining stitches. Pull tight and fasten off.

Pick up and knit 2 stitches in the corner, the first with color B, the second with color D—32 stitches. Work in stockinette stitch in the round, alternating colors B and D in a checkerboard pattern, until the thumb measures 2¼" (5.5cm).

Shape top of thumb

Next round: Continuing to alternate colors (except using color D for all decreases), slip 1, k1, psso, work in pattern to the last 2 stitches on needle 2, k2tog, slip 1, k1, psso, work in pattern to the last 2 stitches on needle 3, k2tog.

Repeat this round until 12 stitches remain. With color D only, work 1 more round with decreases as established—8 stitches remain.

Break yarn and thread through a tapestry needle. Use the tapestry needle to draw the tail through the remaining stitches. Pull tight and fasten off.

Weave in ends, and block lightly.

Left mitten

Work same as for the right mitten through row 28 of the Risti Mitten Chart.

On row 29 of chart, position thumb opening as follows: Work in pattern over the stitches on needle 1. On needle 2, knit 15 stitches with the waste yarn. Slip these 15 stitches back to the left-hand needle and work across them in pattern as established. Continue in pattern to the end of the round.

Continue to the tip of the mitten same as for Right Mitten.

Work thumb as for Right Mitten.

Thumb

Carefully remove the waste yarn 1 stitch at a time. Have 2 needles ready to catch the mitten stitches as you free them, 1 for the lower edge and 1 for the upper edge. You will end up with 15 stitches for the lower edge and 14 stitches for the upper edge. Divide the stitches for the lower edge onto 2 needles—29 stitches. Attach colors B and D at the right side of the thumb opening.

Work across lower edge of thumb opening as follows: * K1 with color B, k1 with color D; repeat from * 6 times more, k1 with color B. With color D, pick up and knit 1 stitch in the corner.

Continue across upper edge of thumb opening as follows: * K1 with color B, k1 with color D; repeat from * 6 times more.

Risti Mitten Chart

COLOR AND STITCH KEY

☐ = B

■ = D

☒ = K2tog with D

☒ = Slip 1, k1, pass slip st over with D

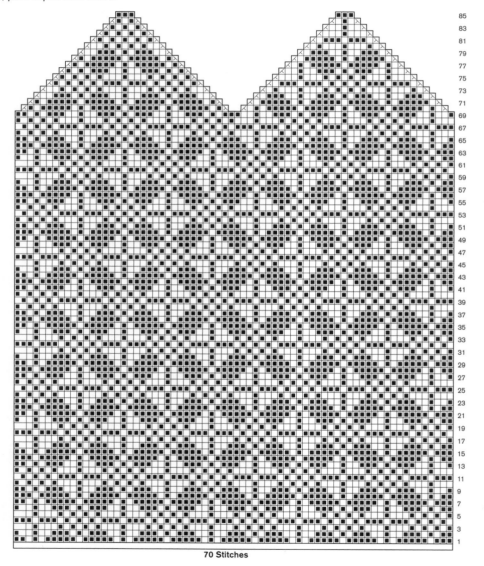

70 Stitches

Cabin Socks

Designed by Clara Parkes

The rustic, wooly nature of these socks makes them perfect to wear on those evenings when you're reading a good book with your feet propped in front of a roaring fire. The socks shown here were knit using a worsted-spun Perendale wool from New Zealand. A generous staple length and worsted preparation make this yarn durable for socks, and the lofty and resilient Perendale fibers render the Broken Rib Pattern with crisp precision. I encourage you to experiment with other breeds, such as Finn, Suffolk, or even Dorset Down and see which ones you like best. This pattern uses a small amount of yarn, and the simple stitch pattern can be easily memorized, making this an ideal on-the-go project that you can put down and pick up without getting lost.

SKILL LEVEL
Intermediate

SIZE
Women's M/Men's S (Women's L/Men's M)

FINISHED MEASUREMENTS
Calf circumference: 8 (9½)" (20.5 [24]cm)
Foot length: 9 (10½)" (23 [26]cm)

YARN
250 (300) yd (227 [274]m) of lightweight yarn:
3 skeins Naturally Perendale Yarn, 100% wool,
1¾ oz (50g), 110 yd (101m), color 71 Denim

NEEDLES
Set of 4 size 4 (3.5mm) double-pointed needles,
or size to obtain gauge

NOTIONS
Tapestry needle

GAUGE
24 stitches and 30 rows = 4" (10cm) in Broken Rib
Pattern

Stitch guide
Broken Rib Pattern
Round 1: * K1, p1; repeat from * to the end of the round.
Round 2: Knit.
Repeat these 2 rounds for pattern.

Cuff
Loosely cast on 48 (56) stitches. Arrange the stitches evenly on 3 needles, and join to work in the round, being careful not to twist the stitches around the needles.
Round 1: * K1, p1; repeat from * to the end of the round. Repeat this round until the piece measures 1" (2.5cm) from the cast-on edge.

Leg
Begin working Broken Rib Pattern. Continue in pattern until the piece measures 8" (20.5cm) from the cast-on edge, or until desired leg length has been reached, ending with round 1.

Heel flap
Row 1: K12 (14). Move the remaining stitches on the first needle to the second needle. Turn the work.
Row 2: P24 (28). Move the remaining stitches on the third needle to the second needle. Turn the work and continue working back and forth on these 24 (28) stitches. The remaining 24 (28) stitches are held on a single needle for the instep.
Row 3: * Slip 1, k1; repeat from * to the end of the row.
Row 4: Slip 1, purl to the end of the row.
Repeat these last two rows 10 (12) times more, then work row 3 once more—25 (29) rows on heel flap.

Turn heel
Row 1: Slip 1, p12 (14), p2tog, p1, turn.
Row 2: Slip 1, k3, ssk, k1, turn.
Row 3: Slip 1, p4, p2tog, p1, turn.
Row 4: Slip 1, k5, ssk, k1, turn.
Row 5: Slip 1, p6, p2tog, p1, turn.
Row 6: Slip 1, k7, ssk, k1, turn.
Row 7: Slip 1, p8, p2tog, p1, turn.
Row 8: Slip 1, k9, ssk, k1, turn.
Row 9: Slip 1, p10, p2tog, p1, turn.
Row 10: Slip 1, k11, ssk, k1—14 stitches remain.

Row 11: Slip 1, p12, p2tog, p1, turn.
Row 12: Slip 1, k13, ssk, k1—16 stitches remain.

Gussets

Continuing with the needle holding the heel stitches, pick up and knit 12 (14) stitches down the left side of the heel flap. With another needle, knit across the 24 (28) instep stitches. With another needle, pick up and knit 12 (14) stitches up the right side of the heel flap. Continuing with this needle, knit 7 (8) heel stitches—62 (72) stitches. The center of the heel is the beginning of the round.

Round 1: Knit the 19 (22) stitches on needle 1, work row 1 of Broken Rib Pattern on needle 2, and knit the 19 (22) stitches on needle 3.

Round 2: Knit to the last 3 stitches on needle 1, k2tog, k1, work row 2 of Broken Rib Pattern on needle 2, k1, ssk, knit to the end of needle 3.

Repeat these 2 rounds 6 (7) times more—48 (56) stitches.

Foot

Work even, maintaining Broken Rib Pattern as established on needle 2 and keeping needles 1 and 3 in stockinette stitch, until the foot measures 7½ (9)" (19 [23]cm) from the back of the heel, or until foot measures 1½" (3.8cm) shorter than desired foot length.

Toe

Round 1: On needle 1—knit to the last 3 stitches, k2tog, k1. On needle 2—k1, ssk, knit to the last 3 stitches, k2tog, k1. On needle 3—k1, ssk, knit to the end of the round.

Round 2: Knit.

Repeat these 2 rounds 3 (4) times more—32 (36) stitches. Discontinue the plain knit rounds and work round 1 three times more—20 (24) stitches remain.

Knit across needle 1 so the yarn is coming from the side of the toe.

Graft toe closed with Kitchener stitch.

Weave in ends.

Repeat pattern to make a matching pair.

Windjammer Socks

Designed by Jennifer Tepper Heverly

You'll find no shortage of hand-dyed, wool-based sock yarns on the market today, including those that Jennifer Heverly dyes for Spirit Trail Fiberworks. The color variegation in hand-dyed yarns presents a special challenge when choosing patterns: You want stitches that engage the colors without being overtaken by them. The Cable and Chevron motif in these socks gives the right balance of texture and undulating colors. In terms of yarns, the plump and luxurious blend of Merino, cashmere, and nylon used in sock A (pictured at left) softens the design with its hint of halo and modestly contrasting colors. But in sock B (shown above)—the perennially popular Koigu hand-painted Merino—you can see what happens when you use a finer, more tightly spun 100% Merino with more color contrast.

Because these socks have no true ribbing along the leg, you'll want to stick with a wool that has good natural bounce and elasticity to it. It could be a finewool such as Merino or Cormo, a springy Finn mediumwool, or even a Down or Down-type wool—whatever grade of fiber makes your fingers and feet happy.

SKILL LEVEL
Intermediate

SIZE
Women's S (M, L)

FINISHED MEASUREMENTS
Foot circumference: 7½ (8½, 9½)"
(19 [21.5, 24]cm)

YARN
**326 (360, 420) yd (298 [329, 384]m) of
fingering-weight yarn:**
Sock A (page 110): 2 skeins Spirit Trail Fiberworks
Paivatar, 80% superwash Merino wool, 10%
cashmere, 10% Nylon, 4 oz (115g), 253 yd
(230m), color Fiji Sunrise

Sock B (page 111): 2 (2, 3) skeins Koigu Painter's
Palette Premium Merino, 100% Merino wool, 1¾
oz (50g), 175 yd (160m), color P42246

NEEDLES
2 size 3 (3.25mm) 16" (40cm) circular needles, or
size to obtain gauge

NOTIONS
Cable needle
Stitch markers
Tapestry needle

GAUGE
24 stitches and 36 rows = 4" (10cm) in stockinette
stitch

Notes

▸ *These socks are worked on two circular needles. When working in the round on two circular needles, use only one needle at a time. Let both ends of the resting needle hang down out of the way while you work with the other needle. Each needle is used to work only the stitches on that needle.*

▸ *Slipped stitches are slipped as if to purl, with the yarn held to the wrong side of the work.*

Stitch guide

Cable and Chevron Pattern

Rounds 1, 3, 5: * K6, p1, k7 (9, 11), p1; repeat from * to the end of the round.

Rounds 2 and 4: * K6, p1, M1L, k2 (3, 4), slip 1, k2tog, psso, k2 (3, 4), M1R, p1; repeat from * to the end of the round.

Round 6: * Slip the next 3 stitches to a cable needle and hold to the front, knit next 3 stitches, k3 stitches from cable needle, p1, M1L, k2 (3, 4), slip 1, k2tog, psso, k2 (3, 4), M1R, p1; repeat from * to the end of the round. Repeat these 6 rounds for pattern.

Leg

Cast on 60 (68, 76) stitches. Divide the stitches evenly on two circular needles and join to work in the round.

Work in Cable and Chevron Pattern for 60 (60, 66) rows.

Heel flap

Knit the next 10 (11, 12) stitches, and transfer them to the other needle. Turn work; purl these stitches and the 20 (23, 26) stitches that follow. Transfer the 10 (11, 12) stitches that remain unworked on this needle to the other needle. The stitches just worked will become the heel flap and the bottom of the foot; the stitches on the other needle will become the instep.

Work back and forth on the heel stitches as follows:

Row 1: * Slip 1, k1; repeat from * to the end of the row.

Row 2: Slip 1, purl to the end of the row.

Repeat these 2 rows 14 (16, 16) times more.

Turn heel

Row 1 (RS): K15 (17, 19), ssk, k1. Turn.
Row 2: Slip 1, p5, p2tog, p1. Turn.
Row 3: Slip 1, k6, ssk, k1. Turn.
Row 4: Slip 1, p7, p2tog, p1. Turn.
Row 5: Slip 1, k8, ssk, k1. Turn.
Row 6: Slip 1, p9, p2tog, p1. Turn.
Row 7: Slip 1, k10, ssk, k1. Turn.
Row 8: Slip 1, p11, p2tog, p1. Turn.
Row 9: Slip 1, k12, ssk, k1. Turn.
Row 10: Slip 1, p13, p2tog, p1. Turn.

Size M only

Row 11: Slip 1, k14, ssk. Turn.
Row 12: Slip 1, p14, p2tog. Turn.

Size L only

Row 11: Slip 1, k14, ssk, k1. Turn.
Row 12: Slip 1, p15, p2tog, p1. Turn.

All sizes

Next row: Knit 16 (16, 18) stitches. Continuing with the heel needle, pick up and knit 15 (16, 16) stitches along left-hand side of the heel flap. With the instep needle, work 30 (34, 38) stitches in Cable and Chevron Pattern as established. With the heel needle, pick up and knit 15 (16, 16) stitches along right-hand side of heel flap—76 (80, 88) stitches.

Transfer the first 2 (3, 4) and last 2 (3, 4) stitches from the instep needle to the heel needle—26 (28, 30) stitches remain on the instep needle and 50 (52, 58) stitches are on the heel needle.

Gusset

Round 1: On heel needle—K1, ssk, knit to 3 stitches before the end of the needle, k2tog, k1. On instep needle—Work in Cable and Chevron Pattern as established, keeping the first 2 stitches and the last stitch in stockinette stitch.

Round 2: On heel needle—Knit. On instep needle—Work in Cable and Chevron Pattern as established, keeping the first 2 stitches and the last stitch in stockinette stitch.

Repeat these 2 rounds until 52 (56, 60) stitches remain.

Foot

Continue in stockinette stitch and Cable and Chevron Pattern as established until foot measures 7 (8, 9)" (18 [20.5, 23]cm) from the back of the heel (or 1½" [3.8cm] shorter than desired foot length).

Toe

Discontinue Cable and Chevron Pattern and complete the sock in stockinette stitch.

Round 1: On heel needle—K1, ssk, knit to 3 stitches before the end of the needle, k2tog, k1. On instep needle—K1, ssk, knit to 3 stitches before the end of the needle, k2tog, k1.

Round 2: Knit across both needles.

Repeat these 2 rounds until 28 stitches remain.

Work Round 1 only until 16 stitches remain.

Graft toe closed with Kitchener stitch.

Weave in ends.

Repeat pattern to make a matching pair.

Reversing Leaves Socks

Designed by Cat Bordhi

Knit on two circular needles, these intriguing socks feature a reversing leaf pattern that reveals itself when you fold down the cuff. Such "Aha!" moments are a trademark of Cat Bordhi's designs. These socks are shown in two wools: a tightly spun springy Merino (pictured near right) and a loosely spun Bluefaced Leicester (far right). Both yarns offer enough elasticity to compensate for the lack of any ribbing on the cuff and are soft enough for even the most sensitive feet. Both yarns also were dyed with natural dyes: Darlene Hayes dyed the Merino in California and The Natural Dye Studio dyed the Bluefaced Leicester in Suffolk, England. Too much color variety will obscure the stitch pattern, so I recommend that you stick with yarns that have solid to faintly variegated hues.

SKILL LEVEL
Experienced

SIZE
Women's M

FINISHED MEASUREMENTS
Foot circumference: 8" (20.5cm)
Leg length (sole to top of cuff): 9½" (24cm)

YARN
370 yd (338m) of fingering-weight yarn:
Sock A (near right): 2 skeins Hand Jive Nature's Palette Fingering-Weight Merino, 100% Merino wool, 1¾ oz (50g), 185 yd (169m), color Tuscan Ocre
Sock B (far right): 2 skeins The Natural Dye Studio Bluefaced Leicester, 100% wool, 3½ oz (100g), 360 yd (329m), color Dazzle

NEEDLES
2 size 1 (2.25 mm) 24" (60cm) circular needles, or size to obtain gauge
Size C-2 (2.75mm) crochet hook

NOTIONS
Small amount of smooth waste yarn
Tapestry needle
Stitch marker

GAUGE
30 stitches and 42 rows = 4" (10 cm) in Reversing Leaves Socks Chart Pattern

Notes

▸ *These socks are worked on two circular needles. When working in the round on two circular needles, only one needle is used at a time. Let both ends of the resting needle hang down out of the way while you work with the other needle. Each needle is used to work only the stitches on that needle.*

▸ *The stitch pattern can be worked from the written instructions or from the charts.*

▸ *The Instep Expansion Chart represents the stitches on one needle, designated as the instep needle. The stitches on the other needle are the sole, and are worked in stockinette stitch without shaping until the heel begins.*

▸ *The Leg Chart represents one repeat of the pattern; it is worked 5 times total around the leg.*

▸ *To give more room for muscular calves, you may wish to change to needles 1 size larger for the leg of the sock.*

Stitch guide

Dpi (double purl increase): P1 in loop below the next stitch, purl the next stitch, insert tip of left needle into the strand running between the 2 stitches just purled, and purl the strand.

Dpd (double purl decrease): Slip 2 stitches as if to purl, p1, pass the 2 slipped stitches over the purled stitch.

Toe

Using the crochet hook, waste yarn, and provisional cast-on (page 197), cast on 13 stitches to each of 2 circular needles—26 stitches. Knit 2 rounds.

Next round (Increase Round): * K1, M1R, knit to the last stitch on the needle, M1L, k1; repeat from * on the second needle—30 stitches.

Work in stockinette stitch, working the Increase Round every other round 8 times more—62 stitches.

Continue in stockinette stitch without shaping until piece measures 6" (15 cm) from beginning or 4" (10 cm) shorter than the desired foot length.

Instep expansion (Instep Expansion Chart)

Round 1: K15, p1, k46.
Round 2: K15, dpi, k46.

Round 3: K15, p3, k46.
Round 4: K15, p1, dpi, p1, k46.
Round 5: K15, p5, k46.
Round 6: K15, p2, dpi, p2, k46.
Round 7: K15, p7, k46.
Round 8: K15, p3, dpi, p3, k46.
Round 9: K15, p9, k46.
Round 10: K13, M1L, k1, M1R, k1, p3, dpd, p3, k1, M1L, k1, M1R, k44.
Round 11: K17, p7, K48.
Round 12: K13, M1L, k3, M1R, k1, p2, dpd, p2, k1, M1L, k3, M1R, k44.
Round 13: K19, p5, k50.
Round 14: K13, M1L, k5, M1R, k1, p1, dpd, p1, k1, M1L, k5, M1R, k44.
Round 15: K21, p3, k52.
Round 16: K13, M1L, k7, M1R, k1, dpd, k1, M1l, k7, M1R, k44.
Round 17: K11, p1, k11, p1, k11, p1, k42—78 stitches.
Round 18: K11, dpi, ssk, k7, k2tog, dpi, ssk, k7, k2tog, dpi, k42.
Round 19: K11, p3, k9, p3, k9, p3, k42.
Round 20: K11, (p1, dpi, p1, ssk, k5, k2tog) twice, p1, dpi, p1, k42.

Round 21: K11, (p5, k7) twice, p5, k42.

Round 22: K11, (p2, dpi, p2, ssk, k3, k2tog) twice, p2, dpi, p2, k42.

Round 23: K11, (p7, k5) twice, p7, k42.

Round 24: K11, (p3, dpi, p3, ssk, k1, k2tog) twice, p3, dpi, p3, k42.

Round 25: K11, (p9, k3) twice, p9, k42.

Round 26: K9, M1L, k1, M1R, k1, p3, dpd, p3, (k1, M1L, k1, M1R, k1, p3, dpd, p3) twice, k1, M1L, k1, M1R, k40.

Round 27: K13, (p7, k5) twice, p7, k44.

Round 28: K9, M1L, k3, M1R, k1, (p2, dpd, p2, k1, M1L, k3, M1R, k1) 3 times, k39.

Round 29: K15 (p5, k7) twice, p5, k46.

Round 30: K9, M1L, k5, M1R, k1, (p1, dpd, p1, k1, M1L, k5, M1R, k1) 3 times, k7. Move the final stitch on this needle to the sole needle. Do not work across the sole needle. Move the first stitch from other end of the instep needle to the adjacent end of the sole needle—59 stitches on instep needle with pattern, 33 stitches on sole needle in stockinette stitch.

Turn heel

Working on the sole needle only, work short rows as follows:

Row 1: K3, (slip 1, k1) 14 times, W&T.

Row 2: P29, W&T.

Row 3: (K1, slip 1) 14 times, W&T.

Row 4: P27, W&T.

Row 5: (Slip 1, k1) 13 times, W&T.

Row 6: P25, W&T.

Row 7: (K1, slip 1) 12 times, W&T.

Row 8: P23, W&T.

Row 9: (Slip 1, k1) 11 times, W&T.

Row 10: P21, W&T.

Row 11: (K1, slip 1) 10 times, W&T.

Row 12: P19, W&T.

Row 13: (Slip 1, k1) 9 times, W&T.

Row 14: P17, W&T.

Row 15: (K1, slip 1) 8 times, W&T.

Row 16: P15, W&T.

Row 17: (Slip 1, k1) 7 times, W&T.

Row 18: P13, W&T.

Row 19: (K1, slip 1) 6 times, W&T.

Row 20: P11, W&T.

Row 21: (Slip 1, k1) 5 times, slip 1, (lift wrap over and behind the wrapped stitch, then knit wrap and stitch together through back loops) 9 times, lift wrap over and behind the wrapped stitch, then knit wrap and next 2 stitches together through back loops, turn.

Row 22: Slip 1, p20, (lift wrap over and behind the wrapped stitch, then purl wrap and stitch together) 9 times, lift wrap over and behind the wrapped stitch, then purl wrap and next 2 stitches together, turn—31 stitches on sole.

Back of heel

Move 16 stitches from each end of the instep needle to adjacent ends of the sole needle—27 stitches on instep, 63 stitches on sole. Arrange the sole needle so the tips emerge with 16 stitches on the right and 47 stitches on the left, with the working yarn coming from the 17th stitch.

Row 1: (Slip 1, k1) 15 times, ssk, turn.

Row 2: Slip 1, p29, p2tog, turn.

Rows 3–30: Repeat rows 1 and 2 until 33 stitches remain on this needle—60 stitches total.

Leg (Leg Chart)

Resume working in the round on both needles.

Round 1: Slip 1, k31, (p3, k9) twice, p3.

Round 2: (K1, M1L, k7, M1R, k1, dpd) 5 times.

Round 3: (K11, p1) 5 times.

Round 4: (Ssk, k7, k2tog, dpi) 5 times.

Round 5: (K9, p3) 5 times.

Round 6: (Ssk, k5, k2tog, p1, dpi, p1) 5 times.

Round 7: (K7, p5) 5 times.

Round 8: (Ssk, k3, k2tog, p2, dpi, p2) 5 times.

Round 9: (K5, p7) 5 times.

Round 10: (Ssk, k1, k2tog, p3, dpi, p3) 5 times.

Round 11: (K3, p9) 5 times.

Round 12: (K1, M1L, k1, M1R, k1, p3, dpd, p3) 5 times.

Round 13: (K5, p7) 5 times.

Round 14: (K1, M1L, k3, M1R, k1, p2, dpd, p2) 5 times.

Round 15: (K7, p5) 5 times.

Round 16: (K1, M1L, k5, M1R, k1, p1, dpd, p1) 5 times.

Round 17: (K9, p3) 5 times.

Repeat rounds 2–17 twice more, then rounds 2–11 once more.

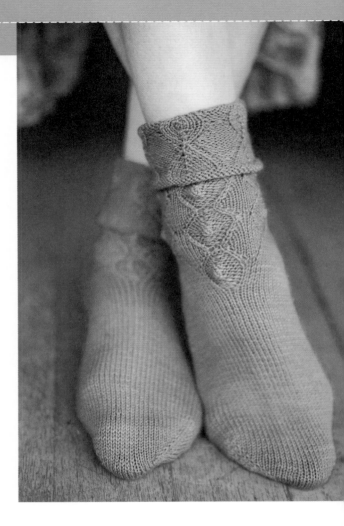

Cuff

Round 1: (K3, p4, dpi, p4) 5 times.

Round 2: (K3, p11) 5 times.

Knit 3 rounds. Bind off very loosely.

Finishing

Remove waste yarn at toes, and place those stitches from cast-on edge on needles. Graft toes closed with Kitchener stitch.

Weave in ends.

Repeat pattern to make a matching pair.

Reversing Leaves Socks Chart

STITCH KEY

□ = K

⊡ = P

◩ = K2tog

◪ = Ssk

▽ = Dpi

△ = Dpd

■ = No stitch

◨ = M1R

◧ = M1L

LEG CHART

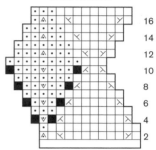

INSTEP EXPANSION CHART

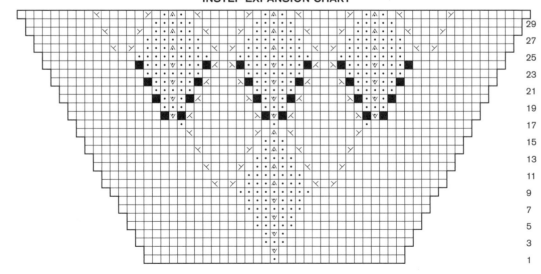

SWEATERS AND TOPS

Bella Baby Ensemble

Designed by Sandi Rosner

The yarn market is literally packed with colorful hand-dyed superwash Merino sock yarns. And, contrary to popular belief, most of us can knit only so many socks before our minds start to wander. What else can we do with these yarns? What other types of projects knit up at the same fine gauge, aren't too big, and benefit from being made from a soft machine-washable wool? Baby clothes, of course! Sized for babies aged 3–24 months, this ensemble features a simple ballet-wrap cardigan with matching bonnet and booties. For the more subdued yet variegated ensemble A (pictured at left), I turned to Dream in Color and their aptly named yarn Smooshy. For the more variegated ensemble B (pages 123–125), I chose a colorful Socks That Rock yarn from Blue Moon Fiber Arts, a leader in the hand-dyed variegated sock yarn movement. An optional crochet ruffle edging is also shown in this version.

SKILL LEVEL
Intermediate

SIZE
3–6 (9–12, 18–24) months

FINISHED MEASUREMENTS
Sweater chest circumference: 20 (22, 24)"
(51 [56, 61]cm)
Sweater length: 8 (9 10)" (20.5 [23, 25.5]cm)
Bonnet height: 4 (4½, 5)" (10 [11, 12.5]cm)
Bootie foot length (heel to toe): 4 (4½, 5)"
(10 [11, 12.5]cm)

YARN
Sweater: 400 (460, 560) yd (366 [421, 512]m) of
sportweight yarn
Bonnet: 100 (110, 120) yd (91 [101, 110]m) of
sportweight yarn
Booties: 100 (110, 120) yd (91 [101, 110]m) of
sportweight yarn
Ensemble A: 2 (2, 2) skeins Dream in Color
Smooshy, 100% superfine Merino wool, 4 oz
(114g), 450 yd (410m), color VS170 Some
Summer Sky
Ensemble B: 2 (2, 2) skeins Blue Moon Fiber Arts
Socks That Rock Mediumweight, 100% superwash
Merino wool, 5½ oz (155g), 380 yd (347m), color
Grimm's Willow-Wren

NEEDLES
Size 2 (2.75mm) and size 3 (3.25mm) needles, or
size to obtain gauge
Size C-2 (2.75mm) crochet hook

NOTIONS
Stitch holders
Tapestry needle
1 snap ½" (1.5mm) wide
2 buttons ½" (1.5mm) wide

GAUGE
25 stitches and 32 rows = 4" (10cm) in stockinette
stitch using larger needles

Sweater

Back

Using the smaller needles, cast on 62 (68, 76) stitches.

Rows 1–9: Knit.

Change to larger needles.

Next row (RS): Knit

Work in stockinette stitch until the piece measures 8 (9, 10)" (20 [22.5, 25]cm) long.

Next row: K20 (21, 24) stitches, and place them on a stitch holder. Bind off the next 22 (26, 28) stitches. Knit the remaining 20 (21, 24) stitches, and place them on another stitch holder.

Right front

Using the smaller needles, cast on 62 (68, 76) stitches.

Rows 1–5: Knit.

Row 6 (Buttonhole Row) (RS): K2, k2tog, yo, knit to the end of the row.

Rows 7–9: Knit.

Change to larger needles.

Starting with a knit row, work in stockinette stitch. At the same time, bind off 2 stitches at the beginning of every right-side row 18 (18, 19) times, then decrease 1 stitch at the beginning of every right-side row 6 (11, 14) times—20 (21, 24) stitches remain. Work even until the same length as the Back to the shoulders. Place stitches on a stitch holder.

Left front

Using the smaller needles, cast on 62 (68, 76) stitches.

Rows 1–9: Knit.

Change to larger needles.

Starting with a knit row, work in stockinette stitch. At the same time, bind off 2 stitches at the beginning of every wrong-side row 18 (18, 19) times, then decrease

1 stitch at the end of every right-side row 6 (11, 14) times—20 (21, 24) stitches remain. Work even until the same length as the Back to the shoulders. Place stitches on a stitch holder.

Sleeves (make 2)

Using the smaller needles, cast on 34 (38, 42) stitches.

Rows 1–9: Knit.

Change to larger needles.

Starting with a knit row, work in stockinette stitch, increasing 1 stitch at the beginning and the end of every 4th (6th, 6th) row 10 times—54 (58, 62) stitches.

Continue without shaping until the piece measures 7 (8½, 10)" (18 [21.5, 25.5]cm). Bind off.

Finishing

Attach the Right Front and the Left Front to the Back at the shoulders using the three-needle bind-off (page 198). Sew the Sleeves to the sides, matching the center of the bound-off edge of the Sleeve to the shoulder seam.

Neckband

Using the smaller needle, with the right side facing, pick up and knit 48 (58, 76) stitches up the Right Front, 22 (23, 26) stitches along the back neck, and 48 (58, 76) stitches down the Left Front—118 (139, 178) stitches.

Rows 1–3: Knit to the last 3 stitches, k2tog, k1.

Row 4 (Buttonhole Row): K2, k2tog, yo, knit to the last 3 stitches, k2tog, k1.

Rows 5–9: Knit to the last 3 stitches, k2tog, k1.

Bind off.

Sew side and Sleeve seams.

Sew buttons onto Left Front to correspond to buttonholes on Right Front.

Sew snap to point of Left Front and to inside of Right Front at side seam.

Weave in ends.

Optional crochet ruffle (shown above and on the following pages)

Using crochet hook, work 1 row of single crochet along bound-off row of neck edge and cast-on row of Sleeve cuff. Chain 3 for turning post, then work 2 double crochets in each stitch across the row. Fasten off.

Bella Baby Sweater Schematic

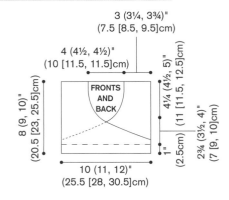

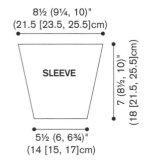

Bonnet

Back

Using the larger needle, cast on 22 (25, 28) stitches. Work in stockinette stitch until the piece measures 4 (4½, 5)" (10 [11, 12.5]cm), ending with a right-side row.

Shape crown

Row 1 (WS): P13 (16, 19), p2tog, p1, turn.
Row 2: Slip 1, k5 (8, 11), ssk, k1, turn.
Row 3: Slip 1, p6 (9, 12), p2tog, p1, turn.
Row 4: Slip 1, k7 (10, 13), ssk, k1, turn.
Row 5: Slip 1, p8 (11, 14), p2tog, p1, turn.
Row 6: Slip 1, k9 (12, 15), ssk, k1, turn.
Row 7: Slip 1, p10 (13, 16), p2tog, p1, turn.
Row 8: Slip 1, k11 (14, 17), ssk, k1—14 (17, 20) stitches remain.

Continuing in the direction of the last row, pick up and knit 25 (28, 31) stitches down the left-hand side of the piece. Turn work and purl to the end of the row, then pick up and purl 25 (28, 31) stitches down the right-hand side of the piece—64 (73, 82) stitches.

Work in stockinette stitch until the piece measures 3 (3½, 4)" (7.5 [9, 10]cm) from the point where the stitches were picked up, ending with a right-side row. Change to smaller needles.

Next 9 rows: Knit.

Bind off all stitches; this is the front edge of the bonnet.

Neckband and ties

Using the smaller needles, with right side facing, pick up and knit 24 (27, 29) stitches along the neck edge of the left side, 20 (23, 26) stitches along the cast-on edge of the Back, and 24 (27, 29) stitches along the neck edge of the right side—66 (77, 84) stitches.

Cast on 36 stitches using the cable cast-on method (page 197). Turn work and bind off those 36 stitches. Knit the remaining 66 (77, 84) stitches, and cast on 36 new stitches using the cable cast-on method. Turn work and bind off those 36 stitches, then knit the remaining 66 (77, 84) stitches.

Next row: Knit.

Bind off all stitches.

Weave in ends.

Optional crochet ruffle (page 123)

If desired, work optional crochet ruffle along the front edge of the bonnet as for the sweater.

Booties *(make 2)*

Using the smaller needle, cast on 30 (33, 36) stitches.

Rows 1–9: Knit.

Change to larger needles.

Starting with a knit row, work 5 rows in stockinette stitch.

Next row (Eyelet Row) (WS): P4 (3, 4), * yo, p2tog, p1; repeat from * to the last 2 (0, 2) stitches, end with p2 (0, 2).

Next row: Knit.

Next row: Purl.

Divide for instep

K20 (22, 24), place the remaining 10 (11, 12) stitches on a stitch holder, turn work.

Next row: P10 (11, 12), place the remaining 10 (11, 12) stitches on another stitch holder.

Work 16 (18, 20) rows in stockinette stitch. Break yarn, and put the stitches on a stitch holder.

Reattach yarn to stitches on right side and knit these stitches from the holder; pick up and knit 12 (14, 15) stitches from right side of instep, knit 10 (11, 12) instep stitches from holder, pick up and knit 12 (14, 15) stitches from left side of instep, knit 10 (11, 12) stitches from holder at left side—54 (61, 66) stitches. Beginning with a purl row, work 8 (10, 12) rows of stockinette stitch.

Shape sole

Rows 1, 3, 5 (WS): Knit.

Row 2: K2, ssk, k20 (24, 26), k2tog, k2 (1, 2), ssk, k20 (24, 26), k2tog, k2.

Row 4: K2, ssk, k18 (22, 24), k2tog, k2 (1, 2), ssk, k18 (22, 24), k2tog, k2.

Row 6: K2, ssk, k16 (20, 22), k2tog, k2 (1, 2), ssk, k16 (20, 22), k2tog, k2—42 (49, 54) stitches remain. Bind off.

Finishing

Fold bootie in half with the wrong side facing out, and sew back and sole seams.

Drawstring

Using the smaller needle, cast on 90 stitches. Bind off. Thread drawstring through the eyelets and tie in a bow. Weave in ends.

Optional crochet ruffle (page 123)

If desired, work optional crochet ruffle along the cuff of the bootie as for the sweater.

The Three Bears Pullovers

Designed by Sandi Rosner

Sometimes nothing beats a simple, fast-knitting pattern that steps aside and lets the wool do the talking, which is exactly what this trio of patterns does. All three pullovers use the same bulky weight of wool, but each has a slightly different ribbing treatment.

For the Mama Bear, Sandi and I chose a soft, luxurious kettle-dyed three-ply Merino from Uruguay. For the Papa Bear, we switched to a more rugged, hearty single-ply undyed Icelandic Lopi yarn. And for the Baby Bear (sized for ages 2–12), we chose a sturdy two-ply wool undyed wool from the Peruvian highlands that is the perfect compromise between a supersoft, ready-to-pill Merino and a rugged, "It's too scratchy, Mom!" Lopi. All three are essentially worsted-spun yarns, but you could have great fun trying a woolen yarn as well, keeping in mind that woolen-spun yarn tends to bloom and some precision in the ribbing may be lost.

Mama Bear Pullover

SKILL LEVEL
Easy

SIZE
Women's S (M, L, 1X, 2X)

FINISHED MEASUREMENTS
Bust: 36 (40, 44, 48, 52)" (91 [101.5, 112, 122, 132]cm)
Length: 22 (23, 24, 25, 26)" (56 [58.5, 61, 63.5, 66]cm)

YARN
675 (780, 900, 1,025, 1,150) yd (617 [713, 823, 937, 1,052]m) of bulky-weight yarn: 7 (8, 9, 10, 12) skeins Malabrigo Chunky, 100% Merino wool, 3½ oz (100g), 104 yd (95m), color 72 Apricot

NEEDLES
Size 7 (4.5mm) and size 9 (5.5mm) needles, or size to obtain gauge
Size 7 (4.5mm) 16" (40cm) circular needles

NOTIONS
Tapestry needle

GAUGE
16 stitches and 20 rows = 4" (10cm) in stockinette stitch using larger needles

Back

Using the smaller needles, cast on 73 (81, 89, 97, 105) stitches.

Row 1 (WS): K1, * p1, k1; repeat from * to the end of the row.

Row 2 (RS): P1, * k1, p1; repeat from * to the end of the row.

Repeat these 2 rows until the piece measures 4" (10cm), ending with a wrong-side row.

Change to larger needles.

Next row (RS): P3 (0, 3, 0, 3), k3 (2, 3, 2, 3), * p5, k3; repeat from * to the last 3 (7, 3, 7, 3) stitches, p3 (5, 3, 5, 3), k0 (2, 0, 2, 0).

Next row (WS): K3 (0, 3, 0, 3), p3 (2, 3, 2, 3), * k5, p3; repeat from * to the last 3 (7, 3, 7, 3) stitches, k3 (5, 3, 5, 3), p0 (2, 0, 2, 0).

Repeat these 2 rows until the piece measures 14 (15, 15½, 16½, 17)" (35.5 [38, 39.5, 42, 43]cm) from the beginning, ending with a wrong-side row.

Shape armholes

Maintaining the rib pattern as established, bind off 4 (5, 6, 7, 8) stitches at the beginning of the next 2 rows.

Decrease 1 stitch at the beginning and the end of every right-side row 4 (6, 8, 10, 12) times—57 (59, 61, 63, 65) stitches remain.

Continue without shaping until the armhole measures 7 (7, 7½, 7½, 8)" (18 [18, 19, 19, 20.5]cm), ending with a wrong-side row.

Shape back neck and shoulders

Next row (RS): Bind off 6 stitches, work 11 (11, 12, 12, 13) stitches in rib pattern, attach a second ball of yarn, bind off the center 23 (25, 25, 27, 27) stitches for the back neck, work in rib pattern to the end of the row. Working both sides at once, bind off 6 stitches at the beginning of the next row.

Decrease 1 stitch at the neck edge on each side. At the same time, bind off 5 (5, 6, 6, 6) stitches at the beginning of the next 2 rows, then bind off the remaining 5 (5, 5, 5, 6) stitches on each side.

Front

Work the same as for the Back until the armhole measures 5½ (5½, 6, 6, 6½)" (14 [14, 15, 15, 16.5] cm), ending with a wrong-side row.

Shape front neck

Next row (RS): Work 22 (22, 23, 23, 24) stitches in rib pattern, attach a second ball of yarn and bind off the center 13 (15, 15, 17, 17) stitches for the front neck. Work in rib pattern to the end of the row.

Working both sides at once, bind off 3 stitches at each neck edge, then bind off 2 stitches at each neck edge, then decrease 1 stitch at each neck edge—16 (16, 17, 17, 18) stitches remain on each side. At the same time, when the piece is the same length as the Back to the shoulders, bind off 6 stitches at the beginning of the next 2 rows, then bind off 5 (5, 6, 6, 6) stitches at the beginning of the following 2 rows, then bind off the remaining 5 (5, 5, 5, 6) stitches on each side.

Sleeves (make 2)

Using the smaller needles, cast on 35 (37, 39, 41, 43) stitches.

Row 1 (WS): P1 (0, 1, 0, 1), * k1, p1; repeat from * to the last 0 (1, 0, 1, 0) stitches, k0 (1, 0, 1, 0).

Row 2 (RS): K1 (0, 1, 0, 1), * p1, k1; repeat from * to the last 0 (1, 0, 1, 0) stitches, p0 (1, 0, 1, 0).

Repeat these 2 rows until the piece measures 4" (10cm), ending with a wrong-side row.

Change to larger needles.

Next row (RS): P0 (1, 2, 3, 4), * k3, p5; repeat from * to the last 3 (4, 5, 6, 7) stitches, k3, p0 (1, 2, 3, 4).

Next row (WS): K0 (1, 2, 3, 4), * p3, k5; repeat from * to the last 3 (4, 5, 6, 7) stitches, p3, k0 (1, 2, 3, 4).

Incorporating the added stitches into the established rib pattern, increase 1 stitch at the beginning and end of the next row and every following 8th row 7 (8, 7, 5, 3) times, then every 6th row 0 (0, 2, 5, 8) times—49 (53, 57, 61, 65) stitches.

Continue without shaping until the piece measures 18"
(45cm) from beginning, or desired length to armhole,
ending with a wrong-side row.

Shape sleeve cap

Bind off 4 (5, 6, 7, 8) stitches at the beginning of the
next 2 rows. Decrease 1 stitch at the beginning and
the end of every right-side row 13 times. Bind off 2
stitches at the beginning of the next 2 rows. Bind off the
remaining 11 (13, 15, 17, 19) stitches.

Finishing

Sew Front to Back at the shoulders.

Neckband

Using the circular needle, with the right side facing and
beginning at the right shoulder seam, pick up and knit 35
(37, 37, 39, 39) stitches across the back neck and 41
(43, 43, 45, 45) stitches across the front neck—76 (80,
80, 84, 84) stitches total. Join to work in the round.
Next round: K1 (0, 1, 0, 1), * p1, k1; repeat from * to
the last 1 (0, 1, 0, 1) stitch, p1 (0, 1, 0, 1).
Repeat this round until the neckband measures 3"
(7.5cm).
Bind off loosely.
Sew Sleeves into armholes. Sew side and Sleeve seams.
Weave in ends and block to finished measurements.

Mama Bear Pullover Schematic

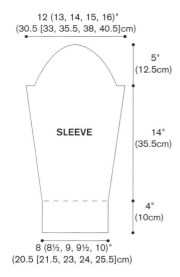

12 (13, 14, 15, 16)"
(30.5 [33, 35.5, 38, 40.5]cm)

5"
(12.5cm)

SLEEVE

14"
(35.5cm)

4"
(10cm)

8 (8½, 9, 9½, 10)"
(20.5 [21.5, 23, 24, 25.5]cm)

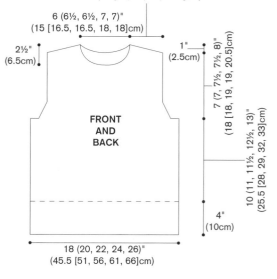

4 (4, 4¼, 4¼, 4½)"
(10 [10, 11, 11, 11.5]cm)

6 (6½, 6½, 7, 7)"
(15 [16.5, 16.5, 18, 18]cm)

2½"
(6.5cm)

1"
(2.5cm)

7 (7, 7½, 7½, 8)"
(18 [18, 19, 19, 20.5]cm)

FRONT
AND
BACK

10 (11, 11½, 12½, 13)"
(25.5 [28, 29, 32, 33]cm)

4"
(10cm)

18 (20, 22, 24, 26)"
(45.5 [51, 56, 61, 66]cm)

Papa Bear Pullover

SKILL LEVEL
Easy

SIZE
Men's S (M, L, 1X, 2X)

FINISHED MEASUREMENTS
Chest: 40 (44, 48, 52, 56)" (101.5 [112, 122, 132, 142]cm)
Length: 24 (25, 26½, 28, 29½)" (61 [63.5, 70, 71, 75]cm)

YARN
850 (960, 1,120, 1,270, 1,450) yd (777 [878, 1,024, 1,161, 1,326]m) of bulky-weight yarn: 8 (9, 11, 12, 13) skeins Reynolds Lopi, 100% Icelandic wool, 3½ oz (100g), 110 yd (101m), color 9973 Wheat Heather

NEEDLES
Size 7 (4.5mm) and size 9 (5.5mm) needles, or size to obtain gauge
Size 7 (4.5mm) 16" (40cm) circular needle

NOTIONS
Stitch marker
Tapestry needle

GAUGE
15 stitches and 20 rows = 4" (10cm) in stockinette stitch using larger needles

Back

Using the smaller needles, cast on 75 (83, 91, 99, 107) stitches.

Row 1 (WS): P1, * k1, p1; repeat from * to the end of the row.

Row 2 (RS): K1, * p1, k1; repeat from * to the end of the row.

Repeat these 2 rows until the piece measures 2" (5cm), ending with a wrong-side row.

Next row (RS): K3, * p5, k3; repeat from * to the end of the row.

Next row (WS): P3, * k5, p3; repeat from * to the end of the row.

Repeat these 2 rows until the piece measures 4" (10cm).

Change to larger needles and work in stockinette stitch until the piece measures 15 (16, 17, 18, 19)" (38 [40.5, 43, 45.5, 48.5]cm) from the beginning, ending with a wrong-side row.

Shape armholes

Bind off 3 (4, 5, 5, 6) stitches at the beginning of the next 2 rows, then bind off 0 (2, 3, 3, 3) stitches at the beginning of the following 2 rows. Decrease 1 stitch at the beginning and the end of every right-side row 3 (3, 4, 6, 7) times—63 (65, 67, 71, 75) stitches remain. Continue without shaping until the armhole measures 8 (8, 8½, 9, 9½)" (20.5 [20.5, 21.5, 23, 24]cm), ending with a wrong-side row.

Shape back neck and shoulders

Next row (RS): Bind off 6 (6, 6, 6, 7), k13 (13, 14, 15, 15), attach a second ball of yarn and bind off the center 25 (27, 27, 29, 31) stitches for back neck, knit to the end of the row.

Working both sides at once, bind off 6 (6, 6, 6, 7) stitches at the beginning of the next row.

Bind off 6 (6, 6, 7, 7) stitches at the beginning of the next 2 rows. At the same time, decrease 1 stitch on both sides at the neck edge on the next right-side row. Bind off the remaining 6 (6, 7, 7, 7) stitches on each side.

Front

Work the same as for the Back until the armhole measures 6½ (6½, 7, 7½, 8)" (16.5 [16.5, 18, 19, 20.5]cm), ending with a wrong-side row.

Shape front neck

Next row (RS): K22 (22, 23, 24, 25), attach a second ball of yarn and bind off the center 19 (21, 21, 23, 25) stitches for front neck, knit to the end of the row. Working both sides at once, decrease 1 stitch on both sides at the neck edge every right-side row 4 times—18 (18, 19, 20, 21) stitches remain on each side. At the same time, when the same length as the Back to the shoulder, bind off 6 (6, 6, 6, 7) stitches at the beginning of the next 2 rows, then bind off 6 (6, 6, 7, 7) stitches at the beginning of the following 2 rows. Bind off the remaining 6 (6, 7, 7, 7) stitches on each side.

Sleeves (make 2)

Using the smaller needles, cast on 35 (37, 39, 41, 41) stitches.

Row 1 (WS): K0 (1, 0, 1, 1) * p1, k1; repeat from * to the last 1 (0, 1, 0, 0) stitch, p1 (0, 1, 0, 0).

Row 2 (RS): P0 (1, 0, 1, 1) * k1, p1; repeat from * to the last 1 (0, 1, 0, 0) stitch, k1 (0, 1, 0, 0).

Repeat these 2 rows until the piece measures 2" (5cm), ending with a wrong-side row.

Change to larger needles.

Next row (RS): P0 (1, 2, 3, 3), * k3, p5; repeat from * to the last 3 (4, 5, 6, 6) stitches, k3, p0 (1, 2, 3, 3).

Next row (WS): K0 (1, 2, 3, 3), * p3, k5; repeat from * to the last 3 (4, 5, 6, 6) stitches, p3, k0 (1, 2, 3, 3).

Repeat these 2 rows until the piece measures 4" (10cm). Change to stockinette stitch.

At the same time, beginning with the 5th row worked with the larger needle, increase 1 stitch at the beginning and the end of every 4th row 10 (11, 12, 14, 19) times, then every 6th row 4 (4, 4, 3, 0) times—63 (67, 71, 75, 79) stitches. Continue without shaping until the piece measures 18 (18, 18½, 18½, 19)" (45.5 [45.5, 47, 47, 48.5]cm) or desired length to the armhole, ending with a wrong-side row.

Shape sleeve cap

Bind off 3 (4, 5, 5, 6) stitches at the beginning of the next 2 rows, then bind off 0 (2, 3, 3, 3) stitches at the beginning of the following 2 rows. Decrease 1 stitch at the beginning and the end of every right-side row 18 (17, 17, 19, 19) times. Bind off 2 stitches at the beginning of the next 2 rows. Bind off the remaining 17 (17, 17, 17, 19) stitches.

Finishing

Sew Front to Back at shoulders.

Neckband

Using circular needle, beginning at right shoulder seam, pick up and knit 29 (31, 31, 33, 35) stitches across back neck, 8 (10, 10, 8, 10) stitches down left front neck, 19 (21, 21, 23, 25) stitches across front neck, and 8 (10, 10, 8, 10) stitches up right front neck—64 (72, 72, 72, 80) stitches. Place a marker on the needle to indicate the beginning of the round.

Next 6 rounds: * K3, p5; repeat from * to the end of the round.

Next 6 rounds: * K1, p1; repeat from * to the end of the round.

Bind off loosely.

Sew Sleeves into armholes. Sew side and Sleeve seams. Weave in ends, and block to finished measurements.

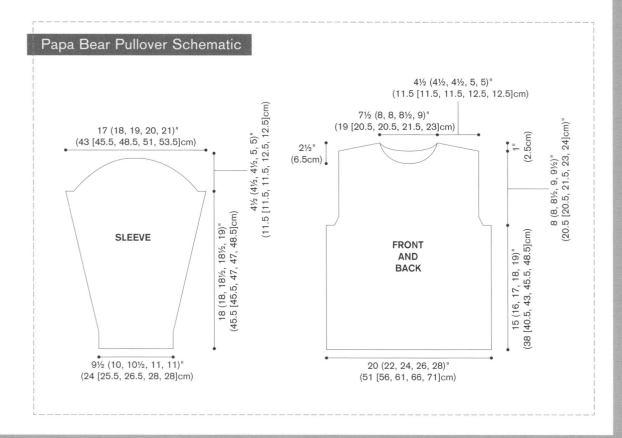

Papa Bear Pullover Schematic

SLEEVE

17 (18, 19, 20, 21)"
(43 [45.5, 48.5, 51, 53.5]cm)

4½ (4½, 4½, 5, 5)"
(11.5 [11.5, 11.5, 12.5, 12.5]cm)

18 (18, 18½, 18½, 19)"
(45.5 [45.5, 47, 47, 48.5]cm)

9½ (10, 10½, 11, 11)"
(24 [25.5, 26.5, 28, 28]cm)

FRONT
AND
BACK

4½ (4½, 4½, 5, 5)"
(11.5 [11.5, 11.5, 12.5, 12.5]cm)

7½ (8, 8, 8½, 9)"
(19 [20.5, 20.5, 21.5, 23]cm)

2½"
(6.5cm)

1"
(2.5cm)

8 (8, 8½, 9, 9½)"
(20.5 [20.5, 21.5, 23, 24]cm)

15 (16, 17, 18, 19)"
(38 [40.5, 43, 45.5, 48.5]cm)

20 (22, 24, 26, 28)"
(51 [56, 61, 66, 71]cm)

Baby Bear Pullover

SKILL LEVEL
Easy

SIZE
Children's 2–4 (6–8, 10–12)

FINISHED MEASUREMENTS
Chest circumference: 26 (30, 34)" (66 [76, 86]cm)
Length: 12 (14, 17)" (30.5 [35.5, 43]cm)

YARN
360 (485, 675) yd (329 [443, 617]m) of bulky-weight yarn: 1 (2, 2) skeins Cascade Ecological Wool, 100% Peruvian Highland wool, 8¾ oz (250g), 478 yd (437m), color 8015

NEEDLES
Size 8 (5mm) and size 10 (6mm) needles, or size to obtain gauge

NOTIONS
Tapestry needle

GAUGE
17 stitches and 22 rows = 4" (10cm) in stockinette stitch using larger needles

Note

▸ *When winding yarn for the size Small, wind off a separate ball of approximately 5 yards (4.5m), to use when shaping the front neck.*

Back

Using the smaller needles, cast on 57 (65, 73) stitches.
Row 1 (WS): K1, * p1, k1; repeat from * to the end of the row.
Row 2 (RS): P1, * k1, p1; repeat from * to the end of the row.
Repeat these 2 rows until the piece measures 2" (5cm), ending with a wrong-side row.
Change to larger needles.
Next row (RS): K2 (0, 2), p5, (3, 5), * k3, p5; repeat from * to the last 2 (6, 2) stitches, k2 (3, 2), p0 (3, 0).
Next row (WS): P2 (0, 2), k5 (3, 5), * p3, k5; repeat

from * to the last 2 (6, 2) stitches, p2 (3, 2), k0 (3, 0).
Repeat these 2 rows until the piece measures 6½ (7, 9)" (16.5, [18, 23]cm) from the beginning, ending with a wrong-side row.

Shape armholes

Maintaining the rib pattern as established, bind off 3 stitches at the beginning of the next 4 rows.
Decrease 1 stitch at the beginning and the end of every right-side row 1 (2, 3) times—43 (49, 55) stitches remain.
Continue without shaping until the armhole measures

4½ (6, 7)" (11.5 [15, 17.5]cm), ending with a wrong-side row.

Shape shoulders

Maintaining the rib pattern as established, bind off 6 (7, 8) stitches at the beginning of the next 2 rows. Bind off 5 (6, 7) stitches at the beginning of the following 2 rows. Bind off the remaining 21 (23, 25) stitches for the back neck.

Front

Work the same as for the Back until the armhole measures 3½ (5, 6)" (9 [12.5, 15]cm), ending with a wrong-side row.

Shape front neck

Next row (RS): Work 16 (18, 20) stitches in rib pattern, attach a second ball of yarn and bind off the center 11 (13, 15) stitches for the front neck, work in rib pattern to the end of the row.

Working both sides at once, bind off 2 stitches at each neck edge 2 times, then decrease 1 stitch at each neck edge once—11 (13, 15) stitches remain on each side. Continue without shaping until the same length as the Back to the shoulders.

Shape shoulders

Bind off 6 (7, 8) stitches at the beginning of the next 2 rows. Bind off the remaining 5 (6, 7) stitches on each side.

Sleeves (make 2)

Using the smaller needles, cast on 29 (31, 33) stitches.

Row 1 (WS): K1 (0, 1), * p1, k1; repeat from * to the last 0 (1, 0) stitch, p0 (1, 0).

Row 2 (RS): P1 (0, 1), * k1, p1; repeat from * to the last 0 (1, 0) stitch, k0 (1, 0).

Repeat these 2 rows until the piece measures 2" (5cm), ending with a wrong-side row.

Change to larger needles.

Next row (RS): K0 (1, 2), * p5, k3; repeat from * to the last 5 (6, 7) stitches, p5, k0 (1, 2).

Next row (WS): P0 (1, 2), * k5, p3; repeat from * to the last 5 (6, 7) stitches, k5, p0 (1, 2).

Repeat these 2 rows for rib pattern.

Increase 1 stitch at the beginning and end of the next and every following 6th row 6 (8, 11) times, incorporating the added stitches into the rib pattern—41 (47, 55) stitches.

Continue without shaping until the piece measures 11 (13, 15)" (28 [33, 38]cm) from beginning, ending with a wrong-side row.

Shape sleeve cap

Bind off 3 stitches at the beginning of the next 4 rows. Decrease 1 stitch at the beginning and the end of every right-side row 1 (2, 3) times, then decrease 1 stitch at the beginning and the end of every 4th row 3 (4, 4) times, then decrease 1 stitch at the beginning and the end of every right-side row 1 (1, 3) times. Bind off 2 stitches at the beginning of the next 4 rows. Bind off the remaining 11 (13, 15) stitches.

Finishing

Sew Front to Back at the left shoulder.

Neckband

Using the smaller needle and with the right side facing, pick up and knit 21 (23, 25) stitches across the back neck, 11 stitches down the left front neck, 11 (13, 15) stitches across the front neck, and 11 stitches up the right front neck—54 (58, 62) stitches.

Next 7 rows: * K1, p1; repeat from * to the end of the row. Bind off loosely.

Sew right shoulder and neckband seam. Sew Sleeves into armholes. Sew side and Sleeve seams.

Weave in ends, and block to finished measurements.

Baby Bear Pullover Schematic

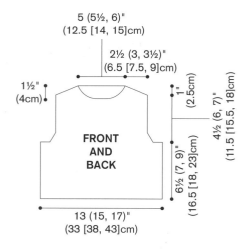

5 (5½, 6)"
(12.5 [14, 15]cm)

2½ (3, 3½)"
(6.5 [7.5, 9]cm)

1½"
(4cm)

1"
(2.5cm)

4½ (6, 7)"
(11.5 [15.5, 18]cm)

FRONT
AND
BACK

6½ (7, 9)"
(16.5 [18, 23]cm)

13 (15, 17)"
(33 [38, 43]cm)

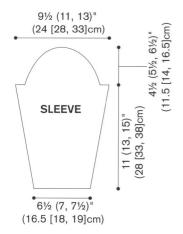

9½ (11, 13)"
(24 [28, 33]cm)

4½ (5½, 6½)"
(11.5 [14, 16.5]cm)

SLEEVE

11 (13, 15)"
(28 [33, 38]cm)

6½ (7, 7½)"
(16.5 [18, 19]cm)

Comfy Cardigan

Designed by Pam Allen

Wool is as much a part of my daily routine as my first cup of tea, perhaps because I always don a wool sweater in the morning before I go downstairs and start the kettle. Pam Allen—my friend and the creative director of Classic Elite Yarns—is the same way, and she jumped at the chance to design the ultimate first-thing-in-the-morning cardigan. It is the perfect warm and comfortable everyday project for lightweight, lofty, fine to midrange wool yarns.

The yarn chosen for this project is a plump two-ply, worsted-weight blend of organic Columbia wool with a small amount of mohair. Columbia is a cross between Rambouillet and Lincoln, and the mohair only enhances the long staple and slight sheen that the Lincoln genes already lend the Columbia fiber. This yarn is mule spun in Canada using old, slower equipment that closely mimics the motions of a handspinner, producing a lofty yarn that retains much of the fiber's natural elasticity. Finally, the yarn is hand-dyed by Darlene Hayes of Hand Jive Knits using natural dyestuffs and environmentally friendly practices.

Easy

SIZE
Women's XS (S, M, L, XL)

FINISHED MEASUREMENTS
Bust: 33 (37, 41, 45, 49)" (84 [94, 104, 114, 124]cm)
Length: 25 (25, 25, 27, 27)" (63.5 [63.5, 63.5, 69, 69]cm)

YARN
920 (1,030, 1,140, 1,360, 1,480) yd (841 [942, 1,042, 1,244, 1,353]m) of mediumweight yarn:
4 (5, 5, 6, 7) skeins Hand Jive Organic Worsted Weight Columbia, 90% organic Columbia wool, 10% mohair, 4 oz (114g), 230 yd (209m), color Spring Grass

NEEDLES
Size 7 (4.5mm) and size 8 (5mm) needles
Size G-6 (4mm) crochet hook

NOTIONS
Several yards (meters) of smooth waste yarn
Stitch markers
Tapestry needle
Stitch holder
5 (5, 5, 6, 6) buttons ¾" (2cm) wide

GAUGE
17 stitches and 25 rows = 4" (10cm) in stockinette stitch using larger needles

Notes

▸ *This cardigan begins at the center back bodice. The right back starts from a provisional cast-on at the center and is worked sideways to the shoulder, and then the right front is worked to the same place. The pieces are joined and the right bodice continues down the Sleeve to the cuff. Stitches for the left back are picked up from the provisional cast-on at the center back edge. The left side of the bodice is worked to mirror the right side.*

▸ *When the bodice is complete, the skirt is worked in one piece from stitches picked up at the lower edge down to the hem.*

Right side

Right back

Using crochet hook, waste yarn, and provisional cast-on (page 197), cast on 51 (51, 51, 61, 61) stitches.

With main yarn and larger needles, knit 4 rows.

Next row (row 1 of Beehive Stitch Chart) (RS): Work stitches 1–11 from chart, then repeat stitches 2–11 four (4, 4, 5, 5) times.

Continue working from chart for 25 more rows.

Shape right back neck

Row 27 (Increase Row) (RS): Work in chart pattern as established to the last stitch, m1, k1.

Next 5 rows: Work even.

Row 33: Repeat Increase Row.

Row 34: Work even.

Row 35: Repeat Increase Row—54 (54, 54, 64, 64) stitches.

Row 36: Work even. Place all stitches on a holder.

Right front

Using smaller needles, cast on 43 (43, 43, 53, 53) stitches. Knit 2 rows.

Next row (Buttonhole Row): K3, * yo twice, k2tog, k8; repeat from * 3 (3, 3, 4, 4) times more, yo twice, k2tog, k7.

Next row: Knit, dropping the extra yo.

Next row (RS): * Knit to buttonhole, knit next stitch into buttonhole; repeat from * 4 (4, 4, 5, 5) times more, knit to the end of the row.

Next row: Knit.

Change to larger needles.

Next row (RS): Work stitches 6–11 from chart, repeat stitches 2–11 3 (3, 3, 4, 4) times, then work stitches 2–8. Continue working from chart as established for 9 more rows.

Shape right front neck

Row 11 (Increase Row) (RS): K1, m1, work in pattern to the end of the row.

Next 3 rows: Work even.

Row 15: Repeat Increase Row.

Next 3 rows: Work even.

Row 19: Repeat Increase Row.

Next 16 rows: Continue in pattern as established, repeating Increase Row every right-side row 8 times more—54 (54, 54, 64, 64) stitches.

Row 36 (WS): Work even. Break yarn.

Join right front and right back

Next row (RS): Join yarn to Right Back stitches on holder and work these stitches in established pattern, then, continuing in pattern, work across Front stitches—108 (108, 108, 128, 128) stitches. Continue in chart pattern until 3 repeats of the 16 rows of the chart have been worked.

Change to stockinette stitch and work even until the piece measures 8½ (9½, 10½, 11½, 12½)" (21.5 [24, 26.5, 29, 32]cm) from cast-on edge of Back, ending with a wrong-side row.

Begin sleeve

Continuing in stockinette stitch, bind off 18 (17, 16, 25, 24) stitches at the beginning of the next 2 rows—72 (74, 76, 78, 80) stitches remain.

Next 4 rows: Work even.

Next row (Decrease Row) (RS): K2, k2tog, knit to the last 4 stitches, ssk, k2.

Continue in stockinette stitch, working Decrease Row every 8th row 6 (7, 7, 8, 8) times more—58 (58, 60, 60, 62) stitches remain.

Work even until the piece measures 14½ (14, 13½, 13, 12½)" (37 [35.5, 34.5, 33, 32]cm) from bound-off stitches, ending with a wrong-side row.

Change to smaller needles.

Next row (RS): K1 (1, 3, 3, 5), * k2tog, k1; repeat from * to the end of the row—39 (39, 41, 41, 43) stitches.

Next 6 rows: Knit.

Bind off all stitches.

Left side

Left back

Remove waste yarn from provisional cast-on and recover the stitches at the center back—50 (50, 50, 60, 60) stitches.

First row (RS): Knit to the last stitch, kfb in the last stitch—51 (51, 51, 61, 61) stitches.

Next 3 rows: Knit.

Next row (row 1 of Beehive Stitch Chart) (RS): Work stitches 8–11 from chart, then repeat stitches 2–11 four (4, 4, 5, 5) times, then work stitches 2–8.

Continue working from chart for 25 more rows.

Shape left back neck

Row 27 (Increase Row) (RS): K1, m1, work in chart pattern as established to the end of the row.

Next 5 rows: Work even.

Row 33: Repeat Increase Row.

Row 34: Work even.

Row 35: Repeat Increase Row—54 (54, 54, 64, 64) stitches.

Row 36: Work even. Place all stitches on a holder.

Left front

Using smaller needles, cast on 43 (43, 43, 53, 53) stitches. Knit 6 rows.

Change to larger needles.

Next row (RS): Work stitches 1–11 from chart, then repeat stitches 2–11 three (3, 3, 4, 4) times. Continue working from chart as established for 9 more rows.

Shape left front neck

Row 11 (Increase Row) (RS): Work in pattern as established to the last stitch, m1, k1.

Next 3 rows: Work even.

Row 15: Repeat Increase Row.

Next 3 rows: Work even.

Row 19: Repeat Increase Row.

Next 16 rows: Continue as established, repeating Increase Row every right-side row 8 times more—54 (54, 54, 64, 64) stitches.

Row 36 (WS): Work even.

Join left front and left back

Next row (RS): Work across Left Front stitches in established pattern, then, continuing in pattern, work across Back stitches from holder—108 (108, 108, 128, 128) stitches. Continue in chart pattern until 3 of the 16-row repeats of chart are complete.

Change to stockinette stitch and work even until piece measures 8½ (9½, 10½, 11½, 12½)" (21.5 [24, 26.5, 29, 32]cm) from cast-on edge of Back, ending with a wrong-side row.

Begin Sleeve

Shape the sleeve as for the Left Side.

Sew side seams of bodice.

Skirt

Using the larger needles, with the right side facing and starting at Left Front center edge, pick up and knit 38 (42, 48, 52, 56) stitches along lower edge of Left Front to side seam, 35 (39, 45, 49, 53) stitches along the bottom edge of Left Back to center, 35 (39, 45, 49, 53) stitches along lower edge of Right Back to side seam, and 34 (38, 44, 48, 52) stitches along lower edge of Right Front to 4 stitches before Right Front center edge, cast on 2 stitches for buttonhole, then pick up and knit 2

final stitches—146 (162, 186, 202, 218) stitches. Place a marker on the needle at the beginning and the end of each patterned section on Front and Back.

Next row (WS): K4; purl to marker, increasing 9 stitches evenly across patterned section; purl across stockinette stitch section to next marker; purl, increasing 18 stitches evenly across patterned section of the Back; purl across stockinette stitch section to next marker; purl to last 4 stitches, increasing 9 stitches evenly across patterned section; k4—182 (198, 222, 238, 254) stitches.

Continue in stockinette stitch, keeping the first 4 and last 4 stitches in garter stitch for Front borders, until the piece measures 13" (33cm) from bodice edge, ending with a wrong-side row.

Change to smaller needles.

Next row (RS): K4, * k1, p1; repeat from * to the last 4 stitches, k4.

Next 3 rows: Continue to work in k1, p1 ribbing with garter stitch borders as established.

Bind off loosely in pattern.

Neckband

Using the smaller needle and with the right side facing, starting at the Right Front edge, pick up and knit 29 stitches along Right Front neck edge to shoulder seam, place marker, pick up and knit 26 stitches along Right Back neck edge to center back, pick up and knit 26 stitches along Left Back neck edge to shoulder seam, place marker, and pick up and knit 29 stitches along Left Front neck edge to center front edge—110 stitches.

Next row (WS): * Knit to 2 stitches before marker, k2tog, slip marker, ssk; repeat from * once more, knit to the end of the row.

Next row (RS): * Bind off to 1 stitch before marker, slip 1, remove marker, return slipped stitch to left-hand

needle, k2tog; repeat from * once more, and bind off remaining stitches.

Finishing

Sew Sleeve seams. Weave in ends.

Sew buttons to Left Front border to line up with buttonholes on Right Front border.

Block to finished measurements.

Beehive Stitch Chart

STITCH KEY

☐ = K on RS, p on WS

⊡ = P on RS, k on WS

⊞ = Slip st as if to purl with yarn in back on right side, slip st as if to purl with yarn in front on wrong side

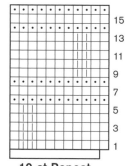

10-st Repeat

Comfy Cardigan Schematic

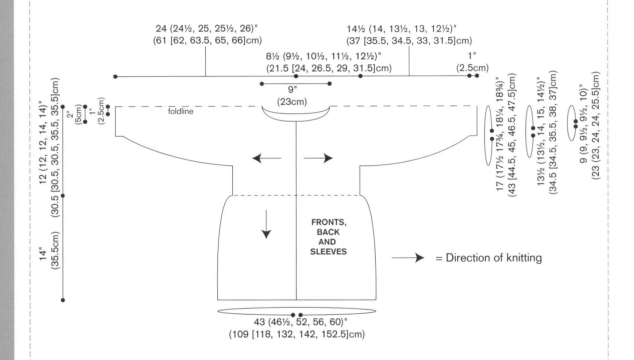

24 (24½, 25, 25½, 26)"
(61 [62, 63.5, 65, 66]cm)

14½ (14, 13½, 13, 12½)"
(37 [35.5, 34.5, 33, 31.5]cm)

8½ (9½, 10½, 11½, 12½)"
(21.5 [24, 26.5, 29, 31.5]cm)

1"
(2.5cm)

9"
(23cm)

foldline

12 (12, 12, 14, 14)"
(30.5 [30.5, 30.5, 35.5, 35.5]cm)

2"
(5cm)

1"
(2.5cm)

14"
(35.5cm)

17 (17½, 17¾, 18¼, 18¾)"
(43 [44.5, 45, 46.5, 47.5]cm)

13½ (13½, 14, 15, 14½)"
(34.5 [34.5, 35.5, 38, 37]cm)

9 (9, 9½, 9½, 10)"
(23 [23, 24, 24, 25.5]cm)

**FRONTS,
BACK
AND
SLEEVES**

= Direction of knitting

43 (46½, 52, 56, 60)"
(109 [118, 132, 142, 152.5]cm)

Allegan Cardigan

Designed by Sandi Rosner

This cardigan gets its name from the Michigan town where Marr Haven Wool Farm has been raising Merino/Rambouillet-cross sheep for decades. The mule-spun Marr Haven yarn has an incredibly soft hand and an elastic, doughy composition (thanks to those plush finewool fibers) that gets even better after the first wash. While I confess that this sweater was conceived expressly with Marr Haven yarn in mind (cardigan A, pictured far left and above), I discovered that it works equally well with other lofty and slightly finer woolen-spun yarns, such

as the Rowan Scottish Tweed Aran (cardigan B, near left). The natural elasticity of woolen-spun yarns is further magnified by the Farrow Rib patterning. It's the closest thing yet to a "wool hug."

Because the fabric is so thick and because you're likely to wear something underneath, this cardigan is also an excellent midrange-to-outerwear project for some of the "crunchier" wools.

SKILL LEVEL
Easy

SIZE
Women's S (M, L, 1X, 2X)

FINISHED MEASUREMENTS
Bust: 36 (40, 44, 48, 52)" (91 [101.5, 112, 122, 132]cm)
Length: 22 (22½, 23, 23½, 24)" (56 [57, 58.5, 59.5, 61]cm)

YARN
1,000 (1,100, 1,250, 1,400, 1,600) yd (914 [1,006, 1,143, 1,280, 1,463]m) of worsted-weight yarn:
Cardigan A: 5 (6, 6, 7, 8) skeins Marr Haven Fine Wool, 100% Merino–Rambouillet wool, 4 oz (115g), 210 yd (192m), color Burgundy Heather

Cardigan B: 6 (6, 7, 8, 9) skeins Rowan Scottish Tweed Aran, 100% wool, 3½ oz (100g), 186 yd (179m), color 009 (**4** MEDIUM)

NEEDLES
Size 6 (4mm) and size 8 (5mm) 32" (80cm) circular needles, or size to obtain gauge
Size 8 (5mm) 16" (40cm) circular needle
Sets of 4 size 6 (4mm) and size 8 (5mm) double-pointed needles

NOTIONS
Tapestry needle
Stitch markers
Stitch holders
7 buttons ¾" (2cm) wide

GAUGE
16 stitches and 24 rows = 4" (10cm) in Farrow Rib Pattern using larger needles

Notes

▸ *Cardigan Body is worked in one piece, from the bottom up to the armholes.*
▸ *Sleeves are worked separately in the round and then joined with Body, and the yoke is knit in one piece to the collar. The only seams are at the underarms.*

Stitch guide

Farrow Rib Pattern

Round 1: K2, * p1, k3; repeat from * to the last 2 stitches, p1, k1.

Round 2: * K1, p3; repeat from * to the end of the round. Repeat these 2 rows for pattern.

Sleeves (make 2)

Using smaller double-pointed needles, cast on 32 (36, 36, 40, 40) stitches. Join to work in the round, being careful not to twist the stitches. Place marker to indicate the beginning of the round.

Round 1: * K1, p1; repeat from * to the end of the round. Repeat this round until piece measures 2" (5cm).

Change to larger double-pointed needles and work in Farrow Rib Pattern.

Next round (Increase Round): Kfb, work in pattern to the last stitch, kfb.

Work an Increase Round every 8th round 7 (7, 9, 9, 11) times more, incorporating increased stitches into Farrow Rib Pattern—48 (52, 56, 60, 64) stitches.

Change to 16" (40cm) circular needle when you have enough stitches to do so.

Continue in Farrow Rib Pattern until Sleeve measures 17 (17½, 17½, 18, 18)" (43 [44.5, 44.5, 45.5, 45.5]cm) from beginning or desired length to underarm, ending with Round 2.

Next round: Work 45 (49, 51, 55, 57) stitches in pattern as established, bind off the last 3 (3, 5, 5, 7) stitches.

Next round: Bind off the first 4 (4, 6, 6, 8) stitches. Break yarn, leaving a 12" (30.5cm) tail, and place all stitches on a stitch holder.

Body

Using smaller 32" (80cm) circular needle, cast on 147 (163, 179, 195, 211) stitches.

Row 1 (WS): * K1, p1; repeat from * to the last stitch, k1.

Row 2 (RS): * P1, k1; repeat from * to the last stitch, p1. Repeat these 2 rows until piece measures 2" (5cm) from the beginning, ending with a wrong-side row.

Change to larger 32" (80cm) circular needle and work Farrow Rib Pattern as follows:

Row 1 (RS): * K3, p1; repeat from * to the last 3 stitches, k3.

Row 2 (WS): K1, *p1, k3; repeat from * to last 2 stitches, p1, k1.

Repeat these 2 rows until piece measures 14 (14, 14½, 14½, 15)" (35.5 [35.5, 37, 37, 38]cm), or desired length to underarm, ending with a right-side row.

Next row (WS): Work 34 (38, 40, 44, 46) stitches in pattern as established, bind off 7 (7, 11, 11, 15) stitches for left armhole, work 65 (73, 77, 85, 89) stitches in pattern, bind off 7 (7, 11, 11, 13) stitches for right armhole, work in pattern to the end of the row.

Join sleeves

Transfer 1 Sleeve to the 16" (40cm) circular needle.

Next row (RS): Work 33 (37, 39, 43, 45) of the right front Body stitches in pattern; work the last right front stitch together with the first stitch of the Sleeve. Work in pattern across the Sleeve to the last stitch, and work it together with the first stitch of the back of the Body. Transfer the other Sleeve to the 16" (40cm) circular needle. Work 63 (71, 75, 83, 87) stitches in pattern across the back of the Body; work the last back stitch together with the first stitch of the Sleeve. Work in pattern across the Sleeve stitches to the last stitch, working it together with the first stitch of the left front of the Body. Work in pattern to the end of the row—211 (235, 243, 267, 275) stitches.

Yoke

Continue in Farrow Rib Pattern for 2 (2½, 2½, 3, 3)" (5 [6.5, 6.5, 7.5, 7.5]cm), ending with a wrong-side row.

Next row (RS): P1, *k1, p3; repeat from * to the last 2 stitches, k1, p1.

Next row (WS): K1, * p1, k3; repeat from * to the last 2 stitches, p1, k1.

Repeat the last 2 rows twice more.

Next row (RS): P1, * k1, p1, p2tog; repeat from * to the last 2 stitches, k1, p1—159 (177, 183, 201, 207) stitches remain.

Next row (WS): K1 * p1, k2; repeat from * to the last 2 stitches, end with p1, k1.

Next row (RS): P1, * k1, p2; repeat from * to the last 2 stitches, k1, p1.

Repeat the last 2 rows 4 times more, then work the wrong-side row again.

Next row (RS): P1, * k1, p2tog; repeat from * to the last 2 stitches, k1, p1—107 (119, 123, 135, 139) stitches remain.

Next row (WS): K1, *p1, k1; repeat from * to the end of the row.

Next row (RS): P1 *k1, p1; repeat from * to the end of the row.

Repeat the last 2 rows once more, then work the wrong-side row again.

Shape neckline

Next row (RS): Work 91 (101, 103, 113, 117) stitches in p1, k1 ribbing as established, W&T.

Next row (WS): Work 75 (83, 83, 91, 95) stitches in ribbing as established, W&T.

Next row (RS): Work 73 (81, 81, 89, 93) stitches in ribbing as established, W&T.

Next row (WS): Work 71 (79, 79, 87, 91) stitches in ribbing as established, W&T.

Next row (RS): Work 69 (77, 77, 85, 89) stitches in ribbing as established, W&T.

Next row (WS): Work 67 (75, 75, 83, 87) stitches in ribbing as established, W&T.

Next row (RS): Work the entire row in ribbing as established, picking up the wraps and knitting them together with the wrapped stitches as you come to them.

Next row (WS): Work the entire row in ribbing as established, picking up the wraps and purling them together with the wrapped stitches as you come to them.

Next row (RS): Work 11 (11, 11, 11, 13) stitches in ribbing as established, * k3tog, work 13 (9, 9, 7, 7) stitches in ribbing; repeat from * 5 (8, 8, 11, 11) times more, work 0 (0, 4, 4, 6) stitches in ribbing—95 (101, 105, 111, 115) stitches remain.

Work the next 3 rows in ribbing as established.

Next row (RS): Work 11 (11, 11, 11, 13) stitches in ribbing as established, * k3tog, work 11 (7, 7, 5, 5) stitches in ribbing; repeat from * 5 (8, 8, 11, 11) times more, work 0 (0, 4, 4, 6) stitches in ribbing—83 (83, 87, 87, 91) stitches remain.

Collar

Change to smaller 32" (80cm) circular needle and work in p1, k1 ribbing as established for 6 rows.

Change to larger 32" (80cm) circular needle and work in p1, k1 ribbing as established for 12 rows.

Bind off loosely in ribbing.

Finishing

Sew underarm seams.

Button band

Using smaller 32" (80cm) circular needle and beginning at the bound-off edge of the collar, pick up and knit 101 (103, 107, 109, 111) stitches along the edge of the left front.

Row 1: K1, *p1, k1; repeat from * to the end of the row.

Repeat this row 4 times more.

Bind off all stitches in pattern.

Buttonhole band

Using smaller 32" (80cm) circular needle and beginning at the cast-on edge, pick up and knit 101 (103, 107, 109, 111) stitches along the edge of the right front.

Row 1: K1, * p1, k1; repeat from * to the end of the row.

Repeat this row once more.

Next row (Buttonhole Row) (WS): K1, [p1, k1] 8 (9, 11, 12, 13) times, k2tog, yo, * k1, [p1, k1] 5 times, k2tog, yo; repeat from * 5 times more, [p1, k1] twice.

Next row (RS): K1, * p1, k1; repeat from * to the end of the row.

Repeat this row once more.

Bind off all stitches in pattern.

Sew buttons to button band opposite buttonholes.

Weave in ends.

Block gently to finished measurements.

Allegan Cardigan Schematic

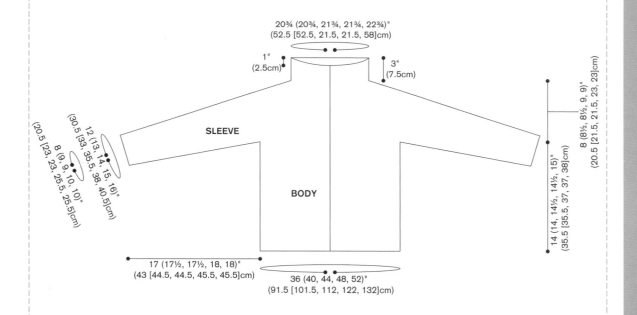

20¾ (20¾, 21¾, 21¾, 22¾)"
(52.5 [52.5, 21.5, 21.5, 58]cm)

1"
(2.5cm)

3"
(7.5cm)

8 (8½, 8½, 9, 9)"
(20.5 [21.5, 21.5, 23, 23]cm)

SLEEVE

12 (13, 14, 15, 16)"
(30.5 [33, 35.5, 38, 40.5]cm)

8 (9, 9, 10, 10)"
(20.5 [23, 23, 25.5, 25.5]cm)

BODY

14 (14, 14½, 14½, 15)"
(35.5 [35.5, 37, 37, 38]cm)

17 (17½, 17½, 18, 18)"
(43 [44.5, 44.5, 45.5, 45.5]cm)

36 (40, 44, 48, 52)"
(91.5 [101.5, 112, 122, 132]cm)

Leafy Glen Shell   Designed by Ilga Leja

In case you thought wool was only for winter, let this lacy shell prove otherwise. Shell A (pictured at left) is worked in the lightweight Fleece Artist Sea Wool, a plump and succulent summer blend that combines 70 percent Merino and 30 percent SeaCell. A second, even warmer-weather shell B (detail shown on page 155) is knit in Louet MerLin, which combines a fine strand of Merino with a fine strand of linen. The leafy design follows the natural shape of the feminine form. Demure with its high square neckline, it still offers allure with its openwork patterning.

SKILL LEVEL
Intermediate

SIZE
Women's XS (S, M, L, 1X, 2X)

FINISHED MEASUREMENTS
Bust: 30 (34, 38½, 43, 48, 52)" (76 [86, 98, 109, 122, 132]cm)
Length: 21 (21, 21, 23¼, 23¼, 25¼)" (53.5 [53.5, 53.5, 59, 59, 64]cm)

YARN
440 (500, 550, 685, 775, 850) yd (402 [457, 503, 626, 709, 777]m) of lightweight yarn:
Shell A: 2 (2, 2, 2, 3, 3) skeins Fleece Artist Sea Wool, 70% Merino wool, 30% SeaCell, 4 oz (115g), 385 yd (350m), color Periwinkle
Shell B: 2 (2, 3, 3, 4, 4) skeins Louet MerLin, 60% linen, 40% Merino wool, 3½ oz (100g), 250 yd (229m), color Lemon Grass

NEEDLES
Size 6 (4mm) needles, or size to obtain gauge
Size 3 (3.25mm) needles

NOTIONS
Stitch markers
Stitch holder
Rustproof pins for blocking
Tapestry needle

GAUGE
18 stitches and 26 rows = 4" (10cm) in Chart A Pattern using larger needles, after blocking

Notes

▸ *Charts show right-side rows only; purl all wrong-side rows in charted patterns.*

▸ *When working the neckline shaping, be sure every yarn over (yo) has an accompanying decrease. If there are not enough stitches to work both the yarn over and the decrease at the edges of the piece, keep the edge stitches in stockinette stitch.*

▸ *The borders at the armhole and neck edges add 1 stitch with a yarn over at the beginning of each row, and then decrease 1 stitch at the end of each row. Although the border is 3 stitches on each side, it requires 7 stitches to produce, with the extra stitch changing side on each row.*

Back

With larger needles, cast on 67 (77, 87, 97, 107, 117) stitches.

Set up row (WS): Knit.

Work the lower border according to Chart A (B, A, B, A, B) twice—40 rows.

Work the Central Panel using Chart C as follows:

Next row (RS): K23 (28, 33, 38, 43, 48), place marker, work the next 21 stitches as shown in Chart C, place marker, knit to the end of the row.

Next row (and all WS rows): Purl.

Keeping the stitches on either side of the central panel in stockinette stitch, work rows 1–4 of Chart C.

Change to smaller needles.

Work rows 5–20 of Chart C.

Work rows 1–14 of Chart C once more.

Change to larger needles.

Continue to work in stockinette stitch and Chart C pattern as established until row 20 has been completed, removing markers on final row.

Shape yoke and armholes

Next row (RS): K13 (18, 23, 28, 33, 38), place marker, work the next 41 stitches as shown in Chart D, place marker, knit to the end of the row.

Continue to work in stockinette stitch and Chart D pattern as established. **At the same time**, beginning with row 1 (1, 1, 7, 7, 11) of Chart D, work armhole shaping as follows:

Row 1 (1, 1, 7, 7, 11): Knit to first marker, work Chart D, knit to the end of the row.

Row 2 (2, 2, 8, 8, 12): K7, purl to last 7 stitches, k7.

Row 3 (3, 3, 9, 9, 13): Knit to first marker, work Chart D, knit to the end of the row.

Row 4 (4, 4, 10, 10, 14): K8, purl to last 8 stitches, k8.

Row 5 (5, 5, 11, 11, 15): Knit to first marker, work Chart D, knit to the end of the row.

Row 6 (6, 6, 12, 12, 16): K9, purl to last 9 stitches, k9.

Row 7 (7, 7, 13, 13, 17): Bind off 4 stitches, knit to first marker, work Chart D, knit to the end of the row.

Row 8 (8, 8, 14, 14, 18): Bind off 4 stitches, k7, purl to last 7 stitches, k7.

Row 9 (9, 9, 15, 15, 19): Bind off 4 stitches, knit to first marker, work Chart D, knit to the end of the row.

Row 10 (10, 10, 16, 16, 20): Bind off 4 stitches, k3, purl to last 3 stitches, k3.

Row 11 (11, 11, 17, 17, 21): Yo, k3, ssk, knit to first marker, work Chart D, knit to last 5 stitches, k2tog, k3.

Row 12 (12, 12, 18, 18, 22): Yo, k3, purl to last 4 stitches, k2, k2tog.

Row 13 (13, 13, 19, 19, 23): Yo, k3, ssk, knit to first marker, work Chart D, knit to last 6 stitches, k2tog, k2, k2tog.

Row 14 (14, 14, 20, 20, 24): Yo, k3, purl to last 4 stitches, k2, k2tog.

Row 15 (15, 15, 21, 21, 25): Yo, k3, ssk, knit to first marker, work Chart D, knit to last 6 stitches, k2tog, k2, k2tog.

Row 16 (16, 16, 22, 22, 26): Yo, k3, purl to last 4 stitches, k2, k2tog.

46 (56, 66, 76, 86, 96) stitches remain.

Continue working as established, with a three-stitch border at each armhole edge and keeping the stitches on either side of Chart D pattern in stockinette stitch, until 40 (40, 40, 50, 50, 60) rows of yoke pattern have been worked.

Shape neck

Row 1 (RS): Yo, k3, work 4 (8, 11, 15, 18, 21) stitches in pattern as established, k31 (33, 37, 39, 43, 47), work 4 (8, 11, 15, 18, 21) stitches in pattern as established, k2, k2tog.

Row 2 (WS): Yo, k3, p7 (11, 14, 18, 22, 24), k25 (27, 31, 33, 37, 43), purl to last 4 stitches, k2, k2tog.

Row 3: Work same as row 1.

Row 4: Yo, k3, p5 (9, 12, 16, 19, 22), k29 (31, 35, 37, 41, 45), purl to last 4 stitches, k2, k2tog.

Row 5: Yo, k3, work 4 (8, 11, 15, 18, 21) in pattern as established, k3, place stitches just worked on a stitch holder, loosely bind off 25 (27, 31, 33, 37, 41) stitches, k3, work 4 (8, 11, 15, 18, 21) in pattern as established, k2, k2tog.

Row 6: Yo, k3, purl to last 3 stitches, k3.

Row 7: Yo, k3, work in established pattern to last 4 stitches, k2, k2tog.

Row 8: Yo, k3, purl to last 4 stitches, k2, k2tog.

Row 9: Work same as row 7.

Row 10: Work same as row 8.

Shape shoulder

Row 1 (RS): Yo, k3, knit to last 4 stitches, W&T.

Row 2: Purl to last 4 stitches, k2, k2tog.

Row 3: Yo, k3, knit to last 9 stitches, W&T.

Row 4: Purl to last 4 stitches, k2, k2tog.

Sizes L, 1X, and 2X only

Row 5: Yo, k3, knit to last 14 stitches, W&T.

Row 6: Purl to last 4 stitches, k2, k2tog.

All sizes

Next row: Yo, k3, knit to last 4 stitches, knitting the wraps together with their stitches as you come to them, k2, k2tog.

Next row: K3, purl to last 4 stitches, k2, k2tog.

Transfer stitches to a stitch holder.

Rejoin yarn to held stitches of other shoulder with the wrong side facing for the next row.

Row 1 (WS): K3, purl to last 4 stitches, k2, k2tog.

Row 2 (RS): Yo, k3, work in established pattern to last 4 stitches, k2, k2tog.

Row 3: Yo, k3, purl to last 4 stitches, k2, k2tog.

Row 4: Work same as row 2.

Row 5: Work same as row 3.

Row 6: Work same as row 2.

Shape other shoulder

Row 1 (WS): Yo, k3, purl to last 4 stitches, W&T.

Row 2: Knit to last 4 stitches, k2, k2tog.

Row 3: Yo, k3, purl to last 9 stitches, W&T.

Row 4: Knit to last 4 stitches, k2, k2tog.

Sizes L, 1X and 2X only

Row 5: Yo, k3, purl to last 14 stitches, W&T.

Row 6: Knit to last 4 stitches, k2, k2tog.

All sizes

Next row: K3, purl to last 4 stitches, purling the wraps together with their stitches as you come to them, k2, k2tog.

Transfer stitches to a stitch holder.

Front

Work the same as for the Back.

Finishing

Block pieces to finished measurements, stretching gently and pinning edges to open up the lace pattern. Allow to dry completely.

Join Front and Back at shoulders using a three-needle bind-off (page 198).

Sew side seams.

Weave in ends.

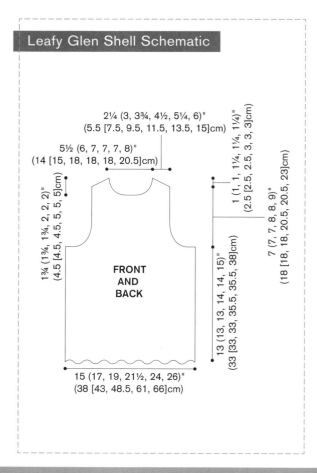

Leafy Glen Shell Schematic

2¼ (3, 3¾, 4½, 5¼, 6)"
(5.5 [7.5, 9.5, 11.5, 13.5, 15]cm)

5½ (6, 7, 7, 7, 8)"
(14 [15, 18, 18, 18, 20.5]cm)

1 (1, 1, 1¼, 1¼, 1¼)"
(2.5 [2.5, 2.5, 3, 3, 3]cm)

1¾ (1¾, 1¾, 2, 2, 2)"
(4.5 [4.5, 4.5, 5, 5, 5]cm)

7 (7, 7, 8, 8, 9)"
(18 [18, 18, 20.5, 20.5, 23]cm)

13 (13, 13, 14, 14, 15)"
(33 [33, 33, 35.5, 35.5, 38]cm)

FRONT
AND
BACK

15 (17, 19, 21½, 24, 26)"
(38 [43, 48.5, 61, 66]cm)

Leafy Glen Shell Charts

STITCH KEY

- ☐ = K on RS, p on WS
- ⋀ = Central Double Decrease
- ⟋ = K2tog
- ⟍ = Ssk
- ☉ = Yarn over (yo)

CHART C CENTER PANEL

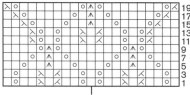

Center Stitch

CHART A LOWER BORDER SIZES XS, M AND 1X

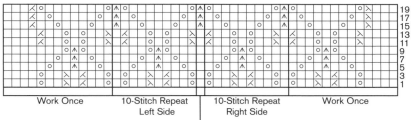

Work Once   10-Stitch Repeat   10-Stitch Repeat   Work Once
Left Side   Right Side

Center Stitch

CHART B LOWER BORDER SIZES S, L AND 2X

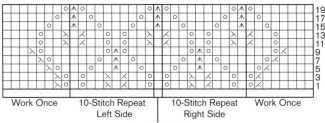

Work Once   10-Stitch Repeat   10-Stitch Repeat   Work Once
Left Side   Right Side

Center Stitch

CHART D YOKE

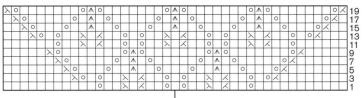

Center Stitch

SCARVES, SHAWLS, AND STOLES

Nara Scarf   Designed by Shelia January

So soft and squishy, lightweight finewools beg to be knit into something you'll wear close to your skin. A scarf can be the easiest and best answer. You'll know you've found the right yarn for this project when you can't put the skein down, can't stop squeezing it, and can't fight the urge to rub it against your cheek. That's how I felt when I touched the luscious Cormo / silk / alpaca blend from artisan farm Foxfire Fiber that Shelia chose for this project. When contemplating yarns for your own scarf, seek fibers from finewool breeds, don't be afraid of blends, and, above all, have fun.

Shelia devised the selvage edge pattern in this scarf to solve the common problem of rolling edges on stockinette or stockinette-based fabrics. The end borders are both knitted on, the first beginning at the cast-on edge and the final worked in reverse directly from the scarf body.

SKILL LEVEL
Intermediate

FINISHED MEASUREMENTS
6½" (16.5cm) wide x 70" (178cm) long

YARN
450 yd (412m) of lightweight yarn:
2 skeins Foxfire Fiber and Designs Farm Yarn Collection Cormo Silk Alpaca, 55% Cormo wool, 25% silk, 20% alpaca, 2¾ oz (75g), 225 yd (205m), color Blue Storm

NEEDLES
Size 7 (4.5 mm), or size to obtain gauge

NOTIONS
Stitch markers
Tapestry needle
Rustproof pins for blocking

GAUGE
21 stitches and 23 rows = 4" (10cm) in Chart B pattern

Notes

▸ *Charts show both right- and wrong-side rows.*

▸ *The stitch count does not remain the same on every row of the border pattern. On the beginning border, stitches are added on rows 1, 3, and 5, and then decreased away on row 7. On the ending border, stitches are added on row 1 and decreased away on rows 5 and 7.*

▸ *The first and last 5 stitches of every row form a double-knit border pattern. Be sure to work these stitches loosely; otherwise, the scarf will draw up at the sides.*

Cast on 35 stitches.

Work rows 1–8 of Chart A for beginning border.

Next row (RS): K1, slip 1 wyif, k1, slip 1 wyif, knit to last 4 stitches, slip 1 wyif, k1, slip 1 wyif, k1.

Next row (WS): Slip 1 wyif, k1, slip 1 wyif, k1, slip 1 wyif, purl to last 5 stitches, slip 1 wyif, k1, slip 1 wyif, k1, slip 1 wyif.

Repeat these 2 rows once more.

Work rows 1–6 of Chart B. Repeat these 6 rows until the piece measures approximately 68" (172.5cm), ending with Row 4.

Next row (RS): K1, slip 1 wyif, k1, slip 1 wyif, knit to last 4 stitches, slip 1 wyif, k1, slip 1 wyif, k1.

Next row (WS): Slip 1 wyif, k1, slip 1 wyif, k1, slip 1 wyif, purl to last 5 stitches, slip 1 wyif, k1, slip 1 wyif, k1, slip 1 wyif.

Repeat these 2 rows once more.

Work rows 1–7 of Chart C for ending border.

Bind off the first 5 stitches in p1, k1 ribbing, bind off next 25 stitches knitwise, and bind off final 5 stitches in p1, k1 ribbing.

Weave in ends.

Block to finished measurements.

Nara Scarf Charts

STITCH KEY

☐ = K on RS, p on WS

· = P on RS, k on WS

⋀ = Central Double Decrease

⋁ = (K1, p1, k1) in same st

⟋ = K2tog

Ⓜ = Make 1 stitch

■ = No stitch

⟋ = P2tog

— = Slip 1 wyif

⟍ = Ssk

○ = Yarn over (yo)

CHART A BEGINNING BORDER

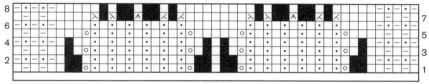

47 Stitches

CHART B

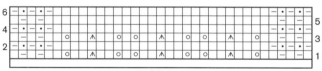

35 Stitches

CHART C ENDING BORDER

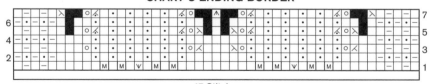

47 Stitches

Prairie Rose Lace Shawl

Designed by Evelyn A. Clark

I have long admired Evelyn Clark's triangle shawls, whose construction is always both completely engaging and technically foolproof. They offer a perfect way to experiment with different types of wools, from the fuzzy woolen-spun to the smooth worsted-spun yarns, from airy Shetland to lustrous Leicester. But why stick to wool alone?

I asked Evelyn to design a shawl that would make good use of a laceweight yarn that combines fine wool and other even more luxurious fibers: lustrous silk and qiviut, the precious downy undercoat of the Arctic musk ox (Shawl A, pictured at near left). The silk adds drape and shimmer, while the qiviut fiber gives incredible warmth and a delicate halo that grows over time.

I realize that qiviut is not in everybody's budget, even in this less-expensive blended form. Fortunately, the shawl is equally beautiful in a laceweight Shetland blend (Shawl B, far left and above). The Shetland compensates for the lack of shimmer and drape with a delicate fuzz and great warmth.

Although both versions shown here were knit in finer yarns, you can easily substitute any yarn you'd like, up to worsted weight, to create a larger, more substantial shawl. You'll just need to increase the amount of yarn as well as the needle size to keep the fabric open and loose.

SKILL LEVEL
Experienced

FINISHED MEASUREMENTS
Approx 48" (122cm) wide x 24" (61cm) long at center point

YARN
370 yd (338m) of fingering-weight yarn:
Shawl A: 2 skeins Jacques Cartier Clothier Qiviuk Silk Merino, 45% qiviut, 45% extra fine Merino, 10% silk, 1 oz (28g), 217 yd (198m), color 2020
Shawl B: 2 skeins Jamieson & Smith 2-Ply Blended Shetland Lace Yarn, 100% wool, 0.9 oz (25g), 185 yd (169m), color L203

NEEDLES
Size 4 (3.5 mm) 24" (60 cm) circular needle, or size to obtain gauge

NOTIONS
3 stitch markers
Tapestry needle
Rustproof pins for blocking

GAUGE
20 stitches and 28 rows = 4" (10cm) in stockinette stitch

Notes

▶ *The Shawl is knit from the top down and increases 4 stitches every other row until the Scalloped Lace Edging.*

▶ *The lace can be knit from written instructions or charts.*

▶ *Shawl is formed by two triangles joined by a center stitch. Work the pattern as follows: Work 2 border stitches (shown at the beginning of the chart), work chart pattern to center stitch, work center stitch (shown at the end of the chart), work chart pattern again, work final 2 border stitches.*

▶ *You may find it helpful to place a marker after the first 2 stitches, before the center stitch, and before the last 2 border stitches.*

Stitch guide

Elastic bind-off: K2, * slip those 2 stitches back onto left-hand needle, and knit them together through the back loops (1 stitch bound off), k1, * and repeat between * until all stitches are bound off.

Cast on 2 stitches.
Rows 1–6: Knit.
Row 7: K2, pick up and knit 3 stitches along side edge, pick up and knit 2 stitches in cast-on stitches—7 stitches.

Prairie Rose Lace Beginning (Chart A)

Row 1 (RS): K2, place marker, yo, k1, yo, place marker, k1, yo, k1, yo, place marker, k2—11 stitches.

All even rows (WS): K2, purl to last 2 stitches, k2.

Row 3: K2, * yo, k3, yo, k1; repeat from * once, k1—15 stitches.

Row 5: K2, * yo, k2tog, yo, k1, yo, ssk, yo, k1; repeat from * once, k1—19 stitches.

Row 7: K2, * yo, k2tog, yo, k3, yo, ssk, yo, k1; repeat from * once, k1—23 stitches.

Row 9: K2, * yo, k2tog, yo, k2, yo, k2tog, k1, yo, ssk, yo, k1; repeat from * once, k1—27 stitches.

Row 11: K2, * yo, k3, yo, ssk, k1, k2tog, yo, k3, yo, k1; repeat from * once, k1—31 stitches.

Row 13: K2, * yo, k2, yo, k2tog, k1, yo, sk2p, yo, k2, yo, k2tog, k1, yo, k1; repeat from * once, k1—35 stitches.

Row 15: K2, * yo, k1, yo, ssk, k1, k2tog, yo, k3, yo, ssk, k1, k2tog, yo, k1, yo, k1; repeat from * once, k1—39 stitches.

Row 17: K2, * yo, k1, (yo, ssk, yo, sk2p, yo, k2tog, yo, k1) 2 times, yo, k1; repeat from * once, k1—43 stitches.

Row 19: K2, * yo, k3, (yo, ssk, k1, k2tog, yo, k3) 2 times, yo, k1; repeat from * once, k1—47 stitches.

Row 21: K2, * yo, k5, (yo, sk2p, yo, k5) 2 times, yo, k1; repeat from * once, k1—51 stitches.

Start Prairie Rose Lace Repeat.

Prairie Rose Lace Repeat (Chart B)

Note: Work Rows 1–24 for pattern. Stitch count is given only for first repeat.

Row 1 (RS): K2, * yo, k3, k2tog, k2, yo, k1, yo, k2, (sk2p, k2, yo, k1, yo, k2) to 5 stitches before marker, ssk, k3, yo, k1; repeat from * once, k1—55 stitches.

All even rows (WS): K2, purl to last 2 stitches, k2.

Row 3: K2, * yo, k1, (yo, k2, sk2p, k2, yo, k1) to marker, yo, k1; repeat from * once, k1—59 stitches.

Row 5: K2, * yo, k3, (yo, k1, sk2p, k1, yo, k3) to marker, yo, k1; repeat from * once, k1—63 stitches.

Row 7: K2, * yo, k2tog, yo, k1, yo, ssk, (yo, sk2p, yo, k2tog, yo, k1, yo, ssk) to marker, yo, k1; repeat from * once, k1—67 stitches.

Row 9: K2, * yo, k2tog, yo, k3, yo, ssk, (k1, k2tog, yo, k3, yo, ssk) to marker, yo, k1; repeat from * once, k1—71 stitches.

Row 11: K2, * yo, k2tog, yo, k2, yo, k2tog, k1, yo, (sk2p, yo, k2, yo, k2tog, k1, yo) to 2 stitches before marker, ssk, yo, k1; repeat from * once, k1—75 stitches.

Row 13: K2, * yo, k3, (yo, ssk, k1, k2tog, yo, k3) to marker, yo, k1; repeat from * once, k1—79 stitches.

Row 15: K2, * yo, k2, yo, k2tog, k1, (yo, sk2p, yo, k2, yo, k2tog, k1) to marker, yo, k1; repeat from * once, k1—83 stitches.

Row 17: K2, * yo, k1, yo, ssk, k1, k2tog, yo, (k3, yo, ssk, k1, k2tog, yo) to 1 stitch before marker, k1, yo, k1, repeat from * once, k1—87 stitches.

Row 19: K2, * yo, k1, (yo, ssk, yo, sk2p, yo, k2tog, yo, k1) to marker, yo, k1; repeat from * once, k1—91 stitches.

Row 21: K2, * yo, k3, (yo, ssk, k1, k2tog, yo, k3) to marker, yo, k1; repeat from * once, k1—95 stitches.

Row 23: K2, * yo, k5, (yo, sk2p, yo, k5) to marker, yo, k1; repeat from * once, k1—99 stitches.

Work Rows 1–24 a total of 4 times, or to desired length, ending with Row 24—243 stitches. Start Leaf Lace Border.

Leaf Lace Border (Chart C)

Row 1 (RS): K2, * yo, k3, k2tog, k2, yo, k1, yo, k2, (sk2p, k2, yo, k1, yo, k2) to 5 stitches before marker, ssk, k3, yo, k1; repeat from * once, k1—247 stitches.

All even rows (WS): K2, purl to last 2 stitches, k2.

Row 3: K2, * yo, k1, (yo, k2, sk2p, k2, yo, k1) to marker, yo, k1; repeat from * once, k1—251 stitches.

Row 5: K2, * yo, k3, (yo, k1, sk2p, k1, yo, k3) to marker, yo, k1; repeat from * once, k1—255 stitches.

Row 7: K2, * yo, k5, (yo, sk2p, yo, k5) to marker, yo, k1; repeat from * once, k1—259 stitches. Start Scalloped Lace Edging.

Scalloped Lace Edging (Chart D)

Note: Stitch count does not change until Row 7.

Rows 1, 3, 5 (RS): K2, (yo, k2, sk2p, k2, yo, k1) to last stitch, k1.

Rows 2, 4, 6 (WS): K2, purl to last 2 stitches, k2.

Row 7: K2, (yo, k7, yo, k1) to last stitch, k1—323 stitches.

Row 8: Knit.

Row 9 (RS): Work elastic bind-off.

Finishing

Weave in yarn ends, but don't trim ends until after blocking.

Blocking

Soak shawl in water—adding soap if desired—for at least 20 minutes to relax the fibers. Rinse and wrap in a towel to blot out water. If using blocking wires, weave them through eyelets along top edge of shawl. Lay the shawl flat, smooth into shape, and pin each scallop.

Leave shawl in place until thoroughly dry. Trim yarn ends.

Prairie Rose Lace Shawl Charts

STITCH KEY

☐ = K on RS, p on WS

⊡ = P on RS, k on WS

⊙ = Yarn over (yo)

⊠ = K2tog

◩ = Ssk

◪ = Sk2p

Charts A–C show RS rows only.
On WS rows: K2, purl to last 2 stitches, k2

Prairie Rose Lace Beginning (Chart A)

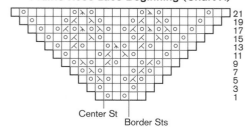

Center St
Border Sts

Prairie Rose Lace Repeat (Chart B)

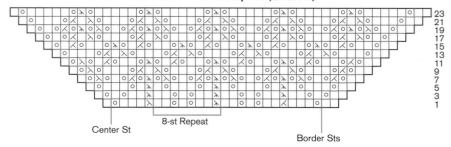

Center St

8-st Repeat

Border Sts

Leaf Lace Border (Chart C)

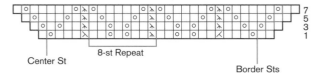

Center St

8-st Repeat

Border Sts

Scalloped Lace Edging (Chart D)

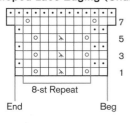

8-st Repeat

End

Beg

Falling Waters Shawl

Designed by Jane Cochran

How do you tame the color variegation in hand-dyed yarns so that it becomes an integral part of a pattern instead of distracting from it? Jane has tamed Gina Wilde's gorgeous Alchemy Yarns colors by putting them in a large rectangular fabric through which streams of modified tilting blocks flow, seemingly at random. The combination of bold architectural blocks and perpetually flowing water made me think of Fallingwater, Frank Lloyd Wright's architectural masterpiece, hence the name of this pattern.

This shawl also serves as an example of what is possible when a lofty matte finewool like Merino is blended with a shimmery, flowing fiber such as silk. Although wool is the predominant fiber, the silk gives the fabric a luminous quality that enhances the feeling of movement.

This pattern works best with smooth, worsted-spun, multiple-ply yarns in semisolid and somewhat variegated colorways whose variegation stays within the same color family. Contrasting colors may overpower the stitch pattern. When in doubt, swatch first.

SKILL LEVEL
Intermediate

FINISHED MEASUREMENTS
24" (61cm) wide x 76" (193cm) long

YARN
1,350 yd (1,234m) of lightweight yarn: 11 skeins Alchemy Yarns of Transformation Sanctuary, 70% Merino wool, 30% silk, 1¾ oz (50g), 125 yd (114m), color 112c Secret Agent Blues

NEEDLES
Size 7 (4.5 mm) 24" (60cm) circular needle, or size to obtain gauge

NOTIONS
Stitch markers (optional)
Tapestry needle
Rustproof pins for blocking

GAUGE
18 stitches and 28 rows = 4" (10cm) in chart pattern

Notes

▸ *The lace pattern can be knit from the written instructions or from the charts.*

▸ *The charts and stitch patterns detail right-side rows only. All wrong-side rows are worked as follows: K2, purl to last 2 stitches, k2.*

▸ *The first 2 stitches and last 2 stitches of every row are knit. These border stitches are not shown in the charts or written in the Stitch Guide, but they are detailed in the pattern instructions.*

▸ *You may find it helpful to place a marker after first 2 border stitches, at the center of the row (after the 50th stitch), and before the last 2 border stitches.*

▸ *Be sure to cast on and bind off loosely. These edges should be as flexible as the rest of the shawl.*

Stitch guide

Border Pattern (Chart A; multiple of 16 stitches)

Rows 1, 3, 5, 7 (RS): * (Yo, k2tog) 4 times, p8; repeat from * to the end of the row.

Row 2 (WS) and all even-numbered rows: Purl.

Rows 9, 11, 13, 15: * P8, (ssk, yo) 4 times; repeat from * to the end of the row.

Left Leaning Pattern (Chart B; multiple of 48 stitches)

Rows 1, 3, 5, 7 (RS): K8, p8, (yo, k2tog) 4 times, p8, (yo, k2tog) 4 times, k8.

Row 2 (WS) and all even-numbered rows: Purl.

Rows 9, 11, 13, 15: K16, p8, (ssk, yo) 4 times, p8, (ssk, yo) 4 times.

Rows 17, 19, 21, 23: (Yo, k2tog) 4 times, k16, p8, (yo, k2tog) 4 times, p8.

Rows 25, 27, 29, 31: P8, (ssk, yo) 4 times, k16, p8, (ssk, yo) 4 times.

Rows 33, 35, 37, 39: (Yo, k2tog) 4 times, p8, (yo, k2tog) 4 times, k16, p8.

Rows 41, 43, 45, 47: P8, (ssk, yo) 4 times, p8, (ssk, yo) 4 times), k16.

Right Leaning Pattern (Chart C; multiple of 48 stitches)

Rows 1, 3, 5, 7 (RS): (Yo, k2tog) 4 times, p8, (yo, k2tog) 4 times, p8, k16.

Row 2 (WS) and all even-numbered rows: Purl.

Rows 9, 11, 13, 15: P8, (ssk, yo) 4 times, p8, k16, (ssk, yo) 4 times.

Rows 17, 19, 21, 23: (Yo, k2tog) 4 times, p8, k16, (yo, k2tog) 4 times, p8.

Rows 25, 27, 29, 31: P8, k16, (ssk, yo) 4 times, p8, (ssk, yo) 4 times.

Rows 33, 35, 37, 39: K16, (yo, k2tog) 4 times, p8, (yo, k2tog) 4 times p8.

Rows 41, 43, 45, 47: K8, (ssk, yo) 4 times, p8, (ssk, yo) 4 times, p8, k8.

Loosely cast on 100 stitches.

Knit 2 rows.

Work 16 rows of Border Pattern as follows: K2, work the 16 stitches of Border Pattern 6 times, k2.

Work 48 rows of Left Leaning Pattern as follows: K2, work the 48 stitches of Left Leaning Pattern twice, k2.

Work 48 rows of Right Leaning Pattern as follows: K2, work 48 stitches of Right Leaning Pattern twice, k2.

Work 48 rows of Left Leaning Pattern as follows: K2, work 48 stitches of Left Leaning Pattern twice, k2.

Repeat the Left Leaning Pattern twice more.

Work 48 rows of Right Leaning Pattern as follows: K2, work 48 stitches of Right Leaning Pattern twice, k2.

Repeat the Right Leaning Pattern twice more.

Work the 48 rows of Left Leaning Pattern as follows: K2, work 48 stitches of Left Leaning Pattern twice, k2.

Work the 48 rows of Right Leaning Pattern as follows: K2, work 48 stitches of Right Leaning Pattern twice, k2.

Work the 16 rows of Border Pattern as follows: K2, work 16 stitches of Border Pattern 6 times, k2.

Knit 2 rows.

Bind off loosely.

Finishing

Weave in yarn ends.

Blocking

Hand wash the shawl carefully in warm water with gentle soap. Remove excess water by rolling the shawl in a bath towel without wringing or stretching.

On a flat, absorbent surface, gently stretch the shawl to 24 x 76" (61 x 193cm) and pin it to dry. If desired, you can also accentuate the points at each end by pinning them. Leave undisturbed until shawl is thoroughly dry.

Falling Waters Shawl Charts

STITCH KEY

☐ = K on RS, p on WS

⊡ = P on RS, k on WS

⊠ = K2tog

⊠ = Ssk

⊙ = Yarn over (yo)

BORDER PATTERN (CHART A)

16 Stitches

LEFT LEANING PATTERN (CHART B)

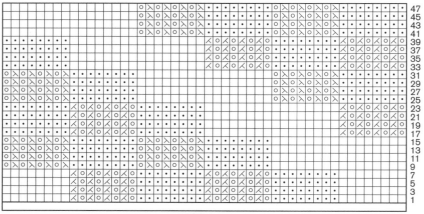

48 Stitches

RIGHT LEANING PATTERN (CHART C)

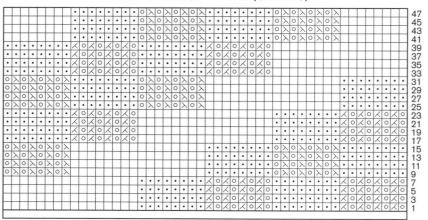

48 Stitches

Tibetan Clouds Beaded Stole

Designed by Sivia Harding

With a little fiber blending, wool can become just as ethereal as it is substantial. To give this stole the kind of luminous shimmer and regal drape that it deserves, I chose a worsted-spun two-ply fingering-weight yarn that blends equal parts silk and Merino for a luxurious finish. This type of yarn is readily available from a multitude of large yarn companies and smaller hand-dyers, which makes color the key adventure. A solid will perform beautifully, but also consider a semisolid built upon varying saturations of one color. The shadows and highlights lend a sense of depth to the lace patterning, while the consistent hue holds it all together.

For this stole, Sivia Harding—a genius with lace—used a subtly shaded but still clear and vibrant ochre hue from Sundara Yarn. She chose lace patterns reminiscent of cultural and spiritual images found in Tibetan Buddhist art: a mandala-like center and wings of beaded brocade and cloudlike feather and fan (pictured in detail above).

SKILL LEVEL
Experienced

FINISHED MEASUREMENTS
21" (53.5cm) wide x 74" (188cm) long

YARN
1,000 yd (914m) of fingering-weight yarn:
2 skeins Sundara Yarn Fingering Silky Merino, 50% Merino wool, 50% silk, 5¼ oz (150g), 500 yd (457m), color Spiced

NEEDLES
Size 5 (3.75 mm) 24" (60cm) circular needle, or size to obtain gauge
Set of 5 size 5 (3.75mm) double-pointed needles
0.6mm crochet hook or short length of beading wire for placing beads

NOTIONS
Stitch markers (optional)
732 size 6/0 silver lined topaz seed beads
Tapestry needle
Rustproof pins for blocking

GAUGE
21 stitches and 37 rows = 4" (10cm) over center lace pattern after blocking

Notes

▸ *The stole begins with a square center panel that is worked in the round from the center outward, and then two side panels are worked outward from this center.*

▸ *The center charts (A, B, and C) represent one-quarter of the pattern. Repeat the pattern 4 times around the square to complete the center panel. Placing a stitch marker after each repeat will help you keep track of the pattern.*

▸ *The charts show both right- and wrong-side rows.*

▸ *Purchase a few extra beads to allow for the inevitable broken or misshapen ones.*

▸ *When a stitch is to be beaded, work the stitch or decrease as indicated on the chart before placing the bead on the stitch. To place a bead, insert a fine crochet hook through the bead and use the hook to draw the stitch through the bead. Replace the beaded stitch on the right-hand needle. (Or bend a short length of fine beading wire to use in lieu of a crochet hook. There's no need to place the stitch back on the needle, just push the bead off the wire and onto the stitch.)*

Center panel

With double-pointed needles, cast on 8 stitches. Join to work in the round, being careful not to twist your stitches around the needles. Place a marker to indicate the beginning of the round.

Knit 1 round.

Work Chart A. Repeat the chart pattern 4 times around the square, placing a marker after each pattern repeat. Change to circular needle.

Work Chart B, repeating the chart pattern 4 times around the square.

Work Chart C, repeating the chart pattern 4 times around the square—396 stitches.

Next round: Loosely bind off 99 stitches to the first marker, knit 99 stitches to the second marker and place these stitches on a stitch holder, loosely bind off 99 stitches to the third marker, and knit the remaining 99 stitches.

First side panel

Next row (WS): K3, place marker, p31, m1, p31, m1, p31, place marker, k3—101 stitches.

Next 9 rows: Slip 1 stitch with yarn in front, k2, slip marker, work Chart D to marker, slip marker, k3.

Next row (row 10 of Chart D): Slip 1 stitch with yarn in front, k2, slip marker, p19, * M1P, p19; repeat from * 3 times more, slip marker, k3—105 stitches.

Maintaining 3-stitch borders as established, begin working from Chart E. Work rows 1–20 of chart 8 times, then work rows 1–10 once more.

Maintaining 3-stitch borders as established, begin working from Chart F. Work rows 1–6 once, then work rows 3–6 twice, then work row 3 once more—117 stitches.

Next row (WS): Knit.

Next row (RS): P2, * p1 and bead this stitch, p3; repeat from * to the last 3 stitches, p1 and bead this stitch, p2.

Bind off loosely.

Second side panel

Slip held stitches onto a needle, and work the second side panel the same as the first.

Finishing

Weave in ends.

Block to finished measurements.

Tibetan Clouds Beaded Stole Chart

STITCH KEY

- □ = K on RS, p on WS
- ⊡ = P on RS, k on WS
- ■ = Bead
- ⋀ = Central Double Decrease
- ⟋ = K2tog
- ℓ = Knit in back loop
- B = Make purl bobble: K1, yo, k1, yo, k1 in stitch. Turn. k5. Turn. Pass 2nd, 3rd, 4th and 5th stitch over first stitch.
- ⋏ = Sk2p
- ⟍ = Ssk
- ○ = Yarn over (yo)

CHART A

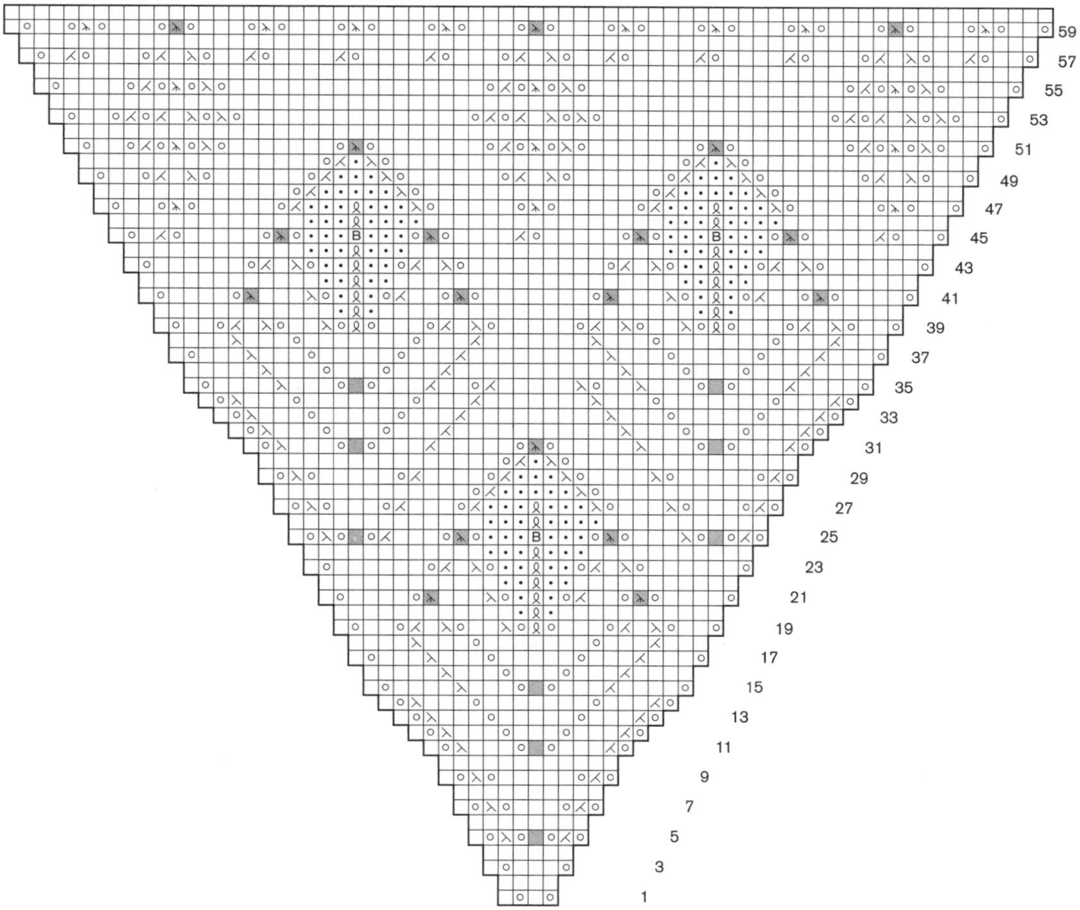

Tibetan Clouds Beaded Stole Charts

STITCH KEY

☐ = K on RS, p on WS   ⅄ = Sk2p
⊡ = P on RS, k on WS   ⊠ = Ssk
▩ = Bead   ⊙ = Yarn over (yo)
⊼ = Central Double Decrease
⊠ = K2tog
⅋ = Knit in back loop

CHART B

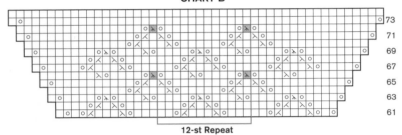

73
71
69
67
65
63
61

12-st Repeat

CHART C

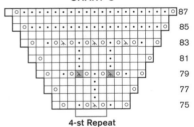

87
85
83
81
79
77
75

4-st Repeat

CHART E

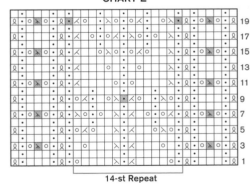

19
17
15
13
11
9
7
5
3
1

14-st Repeat

CHART D

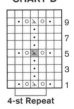

9
7
5
3
1

4-st Repeat

CHART F

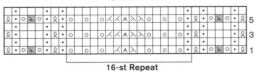

5
3
1

16-st Repeat

Lillia Hyrna Shawl   Designed by Shelia January

While most people may think of bulky Lopi-style yarn when they think of Icelandic wool, it also makes a beautiful yarn for dramatic lace. Because the yarn is spun from the sheep's long outercoat (tog) and its soft, short undercoat (thel) together, the yarn blooms little but it provides a lovely three-dimensional texture and depth to textured stitches such as eyelet and garter.

Although I chose two natural colors for this shawl, it would also be beautiful in solid or complementary dyed colors—picture, for example, a solid black shawl accented with charcoal or deep rose.

This project is a striking example of how the sheep breed can impact the finished garment. Knit in a bouncy Merino or a bloomy Shetland, the shawl would lose much of the open, architectural structure but it would gain the qualities of the other fibers (which you may prefer). If you're not sure how a particular wool is going to perform, swatch first and see if you like the results.

SKILL LEVEL
Intermediate

FINISHED MEASUREMENTS
70" wide (178cm) x 38" (96.5cm) long at center point

YARN
850 yd (777m) of 2-ply laceweight yarn:
Schoolhouse Press Icelandic Laceweight, 100% Icelandic wool, 1¾ oz (50g), 250 yd (229m), 2 skeins each of color 0851 cream (A) and color 1038 tan (B)

NEEDLES
Size 5 (3.75 mm) 32" (80 cm) circular needle, or size to obtain gauge
Size F-5 (3.75mm) crochet hook

NOTIONS
Stitch markers
Rustproof pins for blocking
Tapestry needle

GAUGE
18 stitches and 30 rows = 4" (10cm) in stockinette stitch

Notes

▸ *This shawl is knit from the center neck down.*

▸ *The charts show right-side rows only; purl all wrong-side rows.*

▸ *Two triangles joined by a center stitch form this shawl. Charts A and B show only the right-hand triangle. Work the pattern for Charts A and B as follows: Knit the border stitch (not shown in the charts), work the chart pattern to the center stitch, knit the center stitch (not shown in the charts), work the chart pattern to the last stitch, work the final border stitch (not shown in the charts).*

▸ *Chart C is the bottom border of the shawl. It is repeated 33 times across the row. There are no border or center stitches.*

▸ *All shaping and patterning happen before and after the markers around the center stitch; the center stitch should remain alone between the markers.*

Stitch guide

Crochet bind-off: Insert crochet hook into the first 3 stitches as if to knit them together. Draw a loop through these stitches. * Chain 5, work 1 single crochet in the next 3 stitches; repeat from * until all stitches have been bound off.

Garter stitch: Knit all rows.

With color A, loosely cast on 5 stitches.

Row 1 (RS): K1, yo, k1, yo, place marker, k1, place marker, yo, k1, yo, k1—9 stitches.

Row 2 (WS) and all even-numbered rows through row 30: Purl.

Row 3: K1, yo, knit to marker, yo, slip marker, k1, slip marker, yo, knit to last stitch, yo, k1—13 stitches.

Row 5 and all odd rows through row 29: Work same as row 3, increasing after first stitch, before and after center stitch, and before final stitch—65 stitches.

Rows 31–34: Work in garter stitch (knit every row), continuing to increase 4 stitches on every right-side row as established.

Row 35 (Eyelet Row): K1, yo, k1, * yo, k2tog; repeat from * to marker, yo, slip marker, k1 (center stitch),

slip marker, yo, k1, * yo, k2tog; repeat from * to last 2 stitches, k1, yo, k1—77 stitches.

Row 36: Knit.

Rows 37–38: Work in garter stitch, continuing to increase 4 stitches on every right-side row as established.

Rows 39–58: Work in stockinette stitch, continuing to increase 4 stitches on every right-side row as established—121 stitches.

Rows 59–62: Change to color B and work in garter stitch, continuing to increase 4 stitches on every right-side row as established.

Row 63: Change to color A and work Eyelet Row, same as for row 35.

Row 64: Knit.

Rows 65 and 66: Change to color B and work in garter stitch, continuing to increase 4 stitches on every right-side row as established—137 stitches.

Rows 67–88: Change to color A and work in stockinette stitch, continuing to increase 4 stitches on every right-side row as established—181 stitches.

Rows 89–92: Change to color B and work in garter stitch, continuing to increase 4 stitches on every right-side row as established.

Row 93: Change to color A and work Eyelet Row, same as for row 35.

Row 94: Knit.

Rows 95–98: Change to color B and work in garter stitch, continuing to increase 4 stitches on every right-side row as established.

Row 99: Change to color A and work Eyelet Row, same as for row 35.

Row 100: Knit.

Rows 101–104: Change to color B and work in garter stitch, continuing to increase 4 stitches on every right-side row as established—213 stitches.

Rows 105–116: Change to color A and work in stockinette stitch, continuing to increase 4 stitches on every right-side row as established—237 stitches.

Rows 117–120: Change to color B and work in garter stitch, continuing to increase 4 stitches on every right-side row as established.

Row 121: Work Eyelet Row, same as for row 35.

Rows 122–124: Work in garter stitch, continuing to increase 4 stitches on every right-side row as established—253 stitches.

Rows 125–136: Change to color A and work Chart A—277 stitches.

Rows 137–140: Change to color B and work in garter stitch, continuing to increase 4 stitches on every right-side row as established.

Row 141: Work Eyelet Row, same as for row 35.

Rows 142–144: Work in garter stitch, continuing to increase 4 stitches on every right-side row as established.

Row 145: Work Eyelet Row, same as for row 35.

Rows 146–148: Work in garter stitch, continuing to increase 4 stitches on every right-side row as established.

Row 149: Work Eyelet Row, same as for row 35.

Rows 150–152: Work in garter stitch, continuing

to increase 4 stitches on every right-side row as established—309 stitches.

Rows 153–192: Change to color A and work Chart B—389 stitches.

Row 193–195: Change to color B and work in garter stitch, continuing to increase 4 stitches on every right-side row as established.

Row 196: Knit, decreasing 1 stitch in the center of the row—396 stitches.

Rows 197–212: Discontinuing border stitches and center stitch, work Chart C, repeating 33 times across the row—693 stitches.

Work Crochet Bind-Off. Break yarn and pull it through the last loop.

Soak the shawl in warm soapy water, rinse, blot excess moisture, and block it to shape on a large flat surface until completely dry.

Weave in ends.

Lillia Hyrna Shawl Charts

STITCH KEY

☐ = K on RS, p on WS

⊡ = P on RS, k on WS

⚠ = Central Double Decrease

╱ = K2tog

╱ = K3tog

⊼ = Sk2p

╲ = Ssk

⊙ = Yarn over (yo)

CHART A

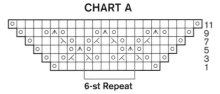

11
9
7
5
3
1

6-st Repeat

CHART B

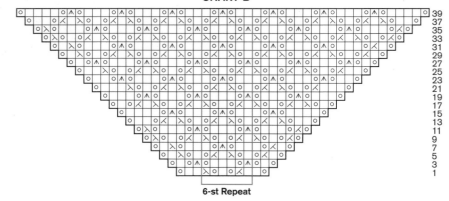

39
37
35
33
31
29
27
25
23
21
19
17
15
13
11
9
7
5
3
1

6-st Repeat

CHART C

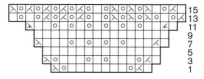

15
13
11
9
7
5
3
1

Frida Pillow

Designed by M. Diane Brown

*This pillow and the Reflecting Pools Bag
(page 186) were conceived as a creative pair
to showcase worsted- and woolen-spun wool
yarns in colorwork, because the difference can
be dramatic. The Frida Pillow begs to be knit in
a finewool, such as the scrumptious Shelridge
Farm Soft Touch Merino yarn we used here. Although the three-ply DK-weight yarn is spun worsted,
the Merino fibers still give the finished fabric a delicate bloom, helping conceal the colors being
stranded on the back side of the otherwise smooth and detailed fabric.*

*With its simple shaping and generous gauge, this project is a perfect and speedy introduction to Fair
Isle colorwork. The bold, happy colors remind me of Frida Kahlo's studio, where I'd like to think this
pillow would have been a welcome addition—hence the pattern's name.*

SKILL LEVEL
Intermediate

FINISHED MEASUREMENTS
14" (35.5cm) square

YARN
650 yd (594m) of DK-weight yarn:
Shelridge Farm Soft Touch DK, 100% wool,
3½ oz (100g), 250 yd (229m), 1 skein each
Navy (A), Heath (B), Cardinal (C), Pussywillow (D),
and Straw (E)

NEEDLES
2 size 6 (4mm) 24" (60cm) circular needles, or size
to obtain gauge
Size 7 (4.5mm) 24" (60cm) circular needle
1 size 6 (4mm) double-pointed needle
Size C-2 (2.75mm) crochet hook

NOTIONS
Stitch markers
Tapestry needle
9 buttons ⅝" (1.5cm) wide
14" (35.5cm) square pillow form

GAUGE
22 stitches and 32 = 4" (10cm) in color pattern on
smaller needles

Note

▶ *This pillow is knit in the Fair Isle colorwork style. Carry colors not in use loosely across the back side of the work, and do not weave them in among your working stitches.*

Bottom

With smaller circular needle and color A, cast on 160 stitches. Join to work in the round, being careful not to twist the stitches around the needles.

Knit 2 rounds.

Change to color B, and knit 17 rounds.

Change to color C, and knit 2 rounds.

Change to larger needles, and begin working pattern from the Frida Pillow Chart.

Repeat the 16 stitches of the chart pattern 10 times around.

After completing the 55 rows of the chart, change to smaller needles and color C. Knit 2 rounds.

Change to color B, and knit 17 rounds.

Change to color A, and knit 1 round.

Next round: K80, place marker, * k2tog, k6; repeat from * 9 times more—150 stitches.

Remove the marker at the beginning of the round, and turn the work.

With the wrong side facing, bind off 70 stitches as if to knit. Break yarn. Remove the remaining marker.

With the right side facing, attach color C to 80 remaining stitches and knit 1 row. Set aside.

Buttonhole band

With color B and smaller circular needle, cast on 80 stitches.

Row 1 (WS): Knit.

Row 2 (RS): Knit.

Row 3: Purl.

Repeat the last 2 rows 3 times more.

Change to color A and work 2 more rows in stockinette stitch.

Change to color C and knit 1 row.

Join band to pillow

With the wrong sides of the pillow together, hold the 2 needles parallel in the left hand. Using the double-pointed needle and a double strand of color C, join the pieces using a three-needle bind-off (page 198)

Finishing

At the cast-on edge of the pillow, use one smaller circular needle and color C to pick up and knit the first 80 stitches, then use the other smaller circular needle and color C to pick up and knit the remaining 80 stitches. Using the double-pointed needle and a double strand of color C, join the two sides together using a three-needle bind-off.

Button loops

Using color B and the crochet hook, with the right side of the buttonhole band facing, work 1 single crochet in each of the first 6 stitches along the free edge, chain 4, skip the next 3 stitches, * work 1 single crochet in each of the next 5 stitches, chain 4, skip the next 3 stitches; repeat from * 8 times more, work 1 single crochet in each remaining stitch. Fasten off.

Sew sides of buttonhole band to pillow. Sew buttons opposite button loops.

Weave in ends.

Block to finished measurements.

Insert pillow form, and close the pillow with the buttons.

Frida Pillow Chart

COLOR KEY
◼ = A Navy
◻ = B Heath
◼ = C Cardinal
◻ = D Pussywillow
◻ = E Straw

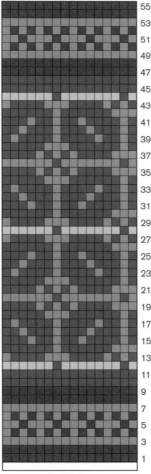

55
53
51
49
47
45
43
41
39
37
35
33
31
29
27
25
23
21
19
17
15
13
11
9
7
5
3
1

16 Stitches

Reflecting Pools Bag

Designed by M. Diane Brown

Our bodies and homes aren't the only things that deserve knitterly adornment; what about our knitting? This project was conceived for two reasons: first, to give knitters a beautiful bag in which we can carry our knitting out into the world, and second—perhaps more important—to show just how beautifully a woolen-spun Shetland wool yarn renders colorwork. It provides a decidedly fuzzy and muted contrast to its Frida Pillow sibling (page 183), which was made from worsted-spun Merino. The springy, woolen-spun Shetland fibers nestle comfortably into one another, and the colors flow in a calm, contemplative fashion that reminded me of a traditional reflecting pool. Adding to the project's organic nature is the fact that all the colors were obtained straight from the sheep without dyeing or bleaching. This project is a great showcase for any natural-colored woolen-spun fibers, especially those from dual-coated, primitive, Down, or Down-type breeds.

SKILL LEVEL
Intermediate

FINISHED MEASUREMENTS
14" (35.5cm) wide x 14" (35.5 cm) tall x 2½" (6.5cm) deep

YARN
920 yd (841m) of fingering-weight yarn:
Elemental Affects Shetland Fingering, 100% Shetland wool, 1 oz (28g), 115 yd (105m), 4 skeins Natural Black (A), 1 skein each Natural Fawn (B), Natural Emsket (C), Natural Musket (D), and Natural White (E)

NEEDLES
Set of 4 size 3 (3.25mm) double-pointed needles
3 size 3 (3.25mm) 24" (60cm) circular needles, or size to obtain gauge
Size 2 (2.75mm) 24" (60cm) circular needle

NOTIONS
Stitch markers
Tapestry needle

GAUGE
28 stitches and 32 rows = 4" (10cm) in color pattern on larger needles

Notes

▸ *For a sturdy bag, the bottom is made with a double layer of knitting. This is done by knitting a tube, which is flattened into a rectangle. Stitches for the body of the bag are picked up around the edges of the rectangle.*

▸ *For ease in working around the corners, the stitches for the body of the bag are picked up with two circular needles, and a third needle is used to knit around. You can work all the stitches on one needle after the first 4 rows, if desired.*

▸ *This bag is knit in the Fair Isle colorwork style. Carry colors not in use loosely across the back side of the work, and do not weave them in among your working stitches.*

▸ *The pattern includes instructions for knitted handles, as shown. If you prefer, you can substitute purchased purse handles instead.*

Bottom

With double-pointed needles and color A, cast on 42 stitches. Arrange the stitches on 3 needles and join to work in the round, being careful not to twist the stitches around the needles.

Round 1: Knit.

Round 2: * K20, slip 1 with yarn in back; repeat from * to the end of the round.

Repeat these 2 rounds until the piece measures 14" (35.5cm), ending with round 1. Bind off loosely.

Flatten the tube, allowing it to fold along the lines of slipped stitches. Steam lightly to hold this shape.

Body

With a larger circular needle and color A, starting at the center of the bound-off edge of the bottom and working through both layers of the piece, pick up and knit 9 stitches to the corner, place a marker, pick up and knit 73 stitches along the long side of the rectangle, place a marker at the corner, use another larger circular needle to pick up and knit 18 stitches across the cast-on edge (again, being sure to work through both layers), place a marker at the corner, pick up and knit 73 stitches along the other long side of the rectangle, place a marker at the final corner, and pick up and knit 9 stitches along

remaining bound-off edge—182 stitches.

Place a marker to indicate the beginning of the round. Use the third circular needle to knit 1 round, removing corner markers as you come to them.

Next round: * K18, m1; repeat from * 9 times more, end with k2—192 stitches.

Next 4 rounds: Knit.

Move all the stitches to single circular needle if desired.

Next 5 rounds: Work Chart A, using color A as the background and color B for the pattern.

Next 3 rounds: With color A, knit.

Next round: With color A, * k48, m1; repeat from * 3 times more—196 stitches.

Begin working from Chart B, changing colors as follows:

First 14-row repeat: Work background with color B, work pattern with color A.

Second 14-row repeat: Work background with color C, work pattern with color D.

Third 14-row repeat: Work background with color E, work pattern with color B.

Fourth 14-row repeat: Work background with color C, work pattern with color D.

Fifth 14-row repeat: Work background with color B, work pattern with color A.

Next 3 rounds: With color A, knit.

Next round: With A, * k47, k2tog; repeat from * 3 times more—192 stitches.

Next 5 rounds: Work Chart A, using color A as the background and B for the pattern.

Next 4 rounds: With color A, knit.

Next round (turning ridge): With color A, purl.

Change to smaller circular needle.

Next round: Knit.

Next round: * K17, k2tog; repeat from * 9 times more, end with k2—182 stitches.

Continue in stockinette stitch until the hem measures 2" (5cm) from the turning ridge.

Bind off.

Handles

With double-pointed needles and color A, cast on 4 stitches. * Do not turn the work. Slide the stitches to the right-hand end of the needle, bring the yarn behind the stitches and knit them; repeat from * until the resulting cord measures 60" (152.5cm). Bind off.

Fold the cord in half, and tie the ends together. Have a friend hold the knot while you insert a pencil or knitting needle in the fold and twist the doubled cord. When you think you have twisted enough, twist some more. Fold the doubled cord in half again and allow it to twist back on itself, forming a tidy knitted rope. The finished handle should measure about 15" (38cm).

Make a second handle the same way.

Finishing

Weave in ends.

Fold the hem to the inside of the Bag and sew in place. Position one handle on each side of the Bag, with the ends about 4" (10cm) in from the sides. Sew handles securely to the inside of the hem.

Block to finished measurements.

Reflecting Pools Bag Charts

COLOR KEY

☐ = Background color

■ = Pattern color

CHART A

5
3
1

6 Stitches

CHART B

13
11
9
7
5
3
1

14 Stitches

Washing Wool

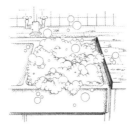

Whether you buy a skein straight from the sheep farm or have a raw fleece spun to your own specifications, chances are the yarn won't come with a care label. Which is fine, because sheep don't come with one either. Their coats survive wind, sleet, rain, and snow without the benefit of fancy soaps and solvents, so their spun fibers certainly don't need to be sent to the dry cleaner.

Unless there's a compelling reason not to (say, a sweater is adorned with bird feathers and confetti), I wash all my woolens by hand in a bubbly bath of lukewarm water. It's as easy and instinctive as washing your hair. Easier, really, because only your hands get wet. Here's what you do.

First, the soap. Choose a gentle soap that has a pH somewhere near neutral. This means no laundry detergents, which may strip wool fibers of their natural moisture and luster. Instead, consider a gentle dishwashing liquid (such as Ivory or Dawn) or any of the many wool washes that are marketed to knitters (like Eucalan, Soak, Kookaburra, and Unicorn Fibre Wash). They all do a fine job and are so concentrated that you need only a capful or two per gallon of water. In a pinch you also can use a gentle shampoo.

Second, the water. Although a very hot water is used to scour the lanolin and suint out of raw wool, the ideal washing temperature for a dyed wool yarn is approximately 100 degrees Fahrenheit (38 degrees Celsius), which translates roughly as "lukewarm." The hotter the water, the greater your chances of losing dye colorfastness. It also may cause white yarns to yellow over time.

When your sink is full of soapy water, drop your garment into its bath. Use your fingertips to gently tap it down, then use the palms of your hands to submerge the entire garment and get rid of any air pockets. You want that warm soapy water to reach every single fiber. (It feels nice on your hands, too.) Give the garment a few gentle squeezes, then let it rest for a couple of minutes. Pull the garment together and lift it out of the water, and let the wash water drain from the sink. Wool is weaker when wet, so be sure to hold the entire garment to avoid stretching or stressing the fibers.

Now it's time to rinse. It's important that you fill the sink with the same temperature water you used in the wash—that is, unless you want to shock the wool fibers into a semifelted state (yarn manufacturers often do this to finish a multiple-ply yarn because it helps the plies adhere to one another). Slip the garment back in the water, tap it gently, squeeze it a few times, gather it together, lift it up, and drain the rinse water. Repeat this process until any residual soap bubbles are gone.

By the way, don't be alarmed if you see some color in the wash and rinse water. This color is simply excess dye that wasn't absorbed or sufficiently rinsed after dyeing. If you continue rinsing until the water runs clear, then you run very little risk of that same color showing up elsewhere later.

After you've rinsed your garment for the last time, give it a good squeeze, but be careful not to wring it. Lay it out on a large clean towel, place another towel on top of it, roll it all up, and gently press out the excess water. You also can use the spin cycle on your washing machine for 5–10 seconds; more than that and you'll run the risk of stretching or creasing the fabric. Then it's simply a matter of laying the garment flat on a towel or mesh-covered sweater rack, patting it back into shape, and letting it dry. Avoid heat or direct sunlight.

Once dry, woolens are happiest when gently folded and stored flat. Nothing terrifies a wool sweater like the sight of an approaching coat hanger.

Keeping Moths at Bay

Wool's number-one enemy is the common clothes moth, which seems to take great pleasure in seeking out our most cherished hand-knits—not to mention yarn stashes—and laying its eggs in them. There the eggs sit for days, these silent, pin-sized time-bombs, until they hatch and the real damage begins. The hungry larvae start munching away on the tasty, keratin-laden wool fibers around them.

If the fibers happen to have traces of perspiration or food stains and crumbs, those pesky larvae eat even more voraciously. Usually, this whole process occurs in a dark corner of a closet, undiscovered, until it's too late. But there is hope. The easiest way to lower the odds of moth damage is by regularly washing and airing your woolens. It's that simple.

If you suspect a moth infestation, the first thing to do (after screaming, sobbing, and pouring yourself a stiff drink) is to take all your woolens outside and vacuum the storage area thoroughly. You want to remove any remaining stray eggs or larvae. Next, wash the woolens and let them dry outside in a brightly lit, well-ventilated area. (Eggs and larvae thrive in dark areas and dislike bright, breezy ones immensely.) Another option is to place the yarn or garments in the freezer for about a week, although I still recommend washing your woolens afterward and setting them outside to dry, preferably in a bright area. If you're worried about direct sunlight causing fading or fiber damage, simply place the items in an area with strong indirect light.

> *The easiest way to* **lower the odds** *of moth damage is by* **regularly washing** *and airing your woolens. It's that simple.*

While I confess a strange nostalgia for the smell of mothballs, which makes me think of my grandma, I do not use these products today with my own woolens—especially not mothballs containing naphthalene or paradichlorobenzene. Even though both products have been proven effective against moths, they are now known to carry potential health risks. Naphthalene vapors have been found potentially carcinogenic to both humans and pets; its more recent replacement, paradichlorobenzene, is also used in toilet deodorizers and is a registered pesticide (by the U.S. Environmental Protection Agency). According to the U.S. Department of Health and Human Services, it may also reasonably be anticipated to be a carcinogenic at high exposures. I don't know about you, but I don't find the idea of fumigating my hand-knits with a carcinogenic toilet deodorizer all that appealing.

A more indirect but eco-friendly alternative is to store woolens with sachets of highly aromatic spices or herbs (such as cloves, lavender, mint, pennyroyal, rosemary, rue, and thyme—alone or in combination) or a small amount of camphor. The idea is that these strong odors cloak wool's attractive scent and steer moths away from its tasty fibers. But herb sachets do not actively stifle eggs or larvae, so you'll still need to keep your garments clean and well aired.

Resource List

I've listed many yarns, organizations, and fiber-related products throughout this book. The yarns mentioned come from large yarn companies, small artisan mills, and even smaller fiber farms.

What follows is a comprehensive list of each source, followed by a link to its most direct online presence. I've also included a few of my favorite sources for breed-specific wools that your LYS may not yet carry.

Some sources provide online ordering or details on how to contact them directly for more information; others will direct you to retailers that carry their yarns. LYS owners, let these links guide you toward new and potentially exciting additions to your shop.

Alchemy Yarns of Transformation
www.alchemyyarns.com

American Sheep Industry Association
www.sheepusa.org

Australian Wool Innovation Limited
www.wool.com.au

Blue Moon Fiber Arts
www.bluemoonfiberarts.com

British Wool Marketing Board
www.britishwool.org.uk

Cascade Yarns
www.cascadeyarns.com

Celestial Yarns
www.tradewindknits.com

Classic Elite Yarns
www.classiceliteyarns.com

Dream in Color
www.dreamincoloryarn.com

Elemental Affects
www.elementalaffects.com

Elsa Wool Company
www.wool-clothing.com

Eucalan
www.eucalan.com

Fleece Artist
www.fleeceartist.com

Foxfire Fiber and Designs
www.foxfirefiber.com

Garthenor Organic Pure Wool
www.organicpurewool.co.uk

Green Mountain Spinnery
www.spinnery.com

Hand Jive Knits
www.handjiveknits.com

Iriss of Penzance
www.iriss.co.uk

Jacques Cartier Clothier
www.qiviuk.com

Jamieson & Smith
www.jamiesonandsmith.co.uk

Koigu
www.koigu.com

Kookaburra
www.kookaburraco.com

Louet North America
www.louet.com

Malabrigo Yarn
www.malabrigoyarn.com

Marr Haven Wool Farm
www.marrhaven.com

Naturally Yarns
www.naturallyyarnsnz.com

Peace Fleece
www.peacefleece.com

Reynolds
www.jcacrafts.com

Riihivilla
www.riihivilla.com

Romney Ridge Farm
www.romneyridgefarm.com

Rowan Yarn
www.knitrowan.com

Schoeller & Stahl Edelweiss
www.naturesongyarns.com

Schoolhouse Press
www.schoolhousepress.com

Shelridge Farm
www.shelridge.com

Soak
www.soakwash.com

Spirit Trail Fiberworks
www.spirit-trail.net

Sundara Yarn
www.sundarayarn.com

Sweet Grass Wool
www.sweetgrasswool.com

The Natural Dye Studio
www.thenaturaldyestudio.com

Unicorn Fibre Wash
www.unicornfibre.com

Vuorelma Satakieli
Distributed in U.S. by
The Wooly West (www.woolywest.com)
and Schoolhouse Press
(www.schoolhousepress.com)

Processors

Have you found your dream fleece? If you're a handspinner, you have the advantage of knowing how to transform that fleece into yarn. And if you aren't, in an ideal world you would learn how to spin so that you could turn this fleece into your dream yarn.

But let's admit it: Not everybody has the time or inclination. You can still pick a gorgeous fleece from a farm or festival and have it transformed into a special yarn. The following are just a few of the folks who will take your raw fleece, scour it clean, card the fibers, and spin them into yarn for you. Some also will do custom dye work. Minimum runs vary; some processors will accept even one fleece, whereas others may require more fiber. And I won't lie: This yarn probably will cost a little more than what you could buy at your LYS, and the processing will take a while. But you'll end up with a unique and special yarn. Consider going in on several fleeces with some friends to split the costs and share the rewards.

Yarn store owners, I encourage you to seek out sheep farms in your area and create your own truly local yarn. You'd be promoting sustainable agriculture and providing something your customers won't be able to find anywhere else. This list will help get you started.

BELFAST MINI-MILLS LTD.

Belfast, Prince Edward Island, Canada
www.minimills.net
These folks launched the cottage artisan spinning industry and still provide some of the finest cottage-scale equipment on the market. Although Belfast Mini-Mills' growth has been fueled by the exotic fiber market, its equipment also works well with wool fibers. The mill also provides custom fiber processing and spinning services.

BLACKBERRY RIDGE WOOLEN MILL

Mt. Horeb, WI
www.blackberry-ridge.com
If your wool fibers have a staple length of five inches (12.5cm) or less when stretched, Blackberry Ridge will custom spin them into beautiful yarn of various weights, twists, and plies. Note that some high-crimp wool will be added to any "slippery" longwool fibers, such as those from Romney, Lincoln, Border Leicester, Cotswold, or Coopworth breeds.

CUSTOM WOOLEN MILLS

Carstairs, Alberta, Canada
www.customwoolenmills.com
An institution among many artisan farms, Custom Woolen Mills is one of the few remaining mule spinners in North America. Mule spinning is a much slower process that closely replicates the movements of a hand-spinner, producing a loftier yarn that retains more of the fiber's natural elasticity. The mill provides custom processing and spinning in the true woolen style in singles, two-, and three-ply yarns as well as Lopi-style and unspun pencil roving.

DONE ROVING FARM & CARDING MILL

Charlotte, ME
www.doneroving.com
Providing custom processing and spinning, Done Roving Farm & Carding Mill accepts small orders and will try to provide whatever custom variations or novelties you may desire.

FINGERLAKES CUSTOM MILL

Genoa, NY
www.fingerlakes-yarns.com
Fingerlakes Custom Mill provides custom processing and woolen spinning of fibers whose staple length is at least 2 inches (5cm) and no longer than 5 inches (12.5cm). Singles, two-, and three-ply yarns are spun in weights from light worsted to bulky.

GREEN MOUNTAIN SPINNERY

Putney, VT
www.spinnery.com
In addition to its own line of Green Mountain Spinnery yarns, this Vermont-

based community spinnery also offers custom processing and spinning services. All scouring is done with vegetable oil-based soap, and no chemicals are used during processing. Weights range from sport to worsted, with singles, two, and three or more plies, depending on what you need and what the fiber will allow.

GULF ISLANDS' SPINNING MILL

Salt Spring Island, British Columbia, Canada

www.gulfislandsspinningmill.com

Offering custom processing and spinning for small to medium-sized batches, Gulf Islands Spinning Mill primarily offers semi-worsted fiber preparation, with some flexibility depending on what you need. The mill can accommodate shorter fibers (3–4 inches [7.5–10cm]) as well as longer ones (7–8 inches [18–20.5cm]) and will also custom dye finished yarn. Biodegradable detergents are used for scouring, and no harsh acids or chemicals are used in processing. The yarns are primarily two-ply, but the mill can also create soft-spun singles as well as three- and four-ply yarns.

HOPE SPINNERY

Hope, ME

www.hopespinnery.com

This wind-powered fiber processing mill in midcoast Maine provides chemical-free processing and natural dyeing services. Hope Spinnery can spin fibers with a staple length of 2½–7 inches (6.5–18cm) into singles and two- or three-ply yarns in weights ranging from fingering to bulky.

MORA VALLEY SPINNING MILL

Mora, NM

www.tapetesdelana.com

The Taos Valley Wool Mill moved to Mora, New Mexico, and now operates under the umbrella of the Mora Valley Spinning Mill, but still under the expert consultation of Robert Donnelly. Here's where to send your longwools for some of the best semiworsted spinning in the United States, from bulky to laceweight.

OHIO VALLEY NATURAL FIBERS

Sardinia, OH

www.ovnf.com

One of the largest custom processing mills in North America, Ohio Valley Natural Fibers provides woolen spinning services for a wide range of yarns from singles up to eight plies.

STILL RIVER MILL

Eastford, CT

www.stillrivermill.com

Specializing in working with fine, delicate fibers that have short staple lengths, Still River Mill can spin singles to multiple-ply yarns in weights from fingering to bulky. The mill also provides dye services using nonhazardous, metal-free dyes.

STONEHEDGE FARM AND FIBER MILL

East Jordan, MI

www.stonehedgefibermill.com

A good choice for longer-staple wools, Stonehedge Farm and Fiber Mill provides custom processing and worsted spinning for fibers with staple lengths of 4–10 inches (10–25.5cm). The mill can spin singles, two-, and three-ply yarns in weights ranging from fingering to sport, worsted, and bulky.

TEXAS FIBER MILL

McDade, TX

www.txfibermill.com

When The Fibre Co. stopped spinning its own yarns, the equipment was quickly bought by Jim and Deborah Sharp, who now operate their own mill in Texas. Texas Fiber Mill provides custom fiber processing and spinning of singles, two-, three-, and four-ply yarns in various weights.

ZEILINGER'S

Frankenmuth, MI

www.zwool.com

A favorite place for handspinners to send their prized fleeces for processing, Zeilinger's provides custom spinning services for fibers with a staple length of 2–5 inches (5–12.5cm). The mill can provide singles, two-, or three-ply yarns in fingering, sport, worsted, and bulky weights.

Recommended Reading

If you want to learn more about the sheep breeds listed in this book, the best place to begin is with the people who raise them. At the end of each breed description in Chapter 3, you'll find the name and URL of that breed's official association. When more than one such organization exists, I included the associations in the breed's country of origin as well as in the United States.

Breed associations are responsible for maintaining the breed standard and, in many ways, keeping the breeds alive. They offer a wealth of information about that breed's history, qualities, characteristics, and genetics. They can also put you in touch with nearby farms to help you get your hands on some fiber. These people love their animals and are eager to share them with you.

Many sheep breeds exist beyond those listed in this book. To meet more of them, look no further than Nola Fournier and Jane Fournier's classic reference, *In Sheep's Clothing: A Handspinner's Guide to Wool*. This book describes 100 sheep breeds in detail, with a primary focus on wool as it relates to handspinners—which means that the rugged and exotic are intermingled with the finewools and mediumwools. The authors also offer extensive advice on how to choose a fleece, scour it, and prepare it for spinning.

The consolidation of sheep breeds across the commercial wool industry

has put many on the brink of extinction. Several years ago, *Spin-Off* magazine sponsored a "Save The Sheep" project that included a touring exhibit of exquisite textile pieces created from the wools of these rare breeds. In *Handspun Treasures from Rare Wools*, editor Deborah Robson pulled together articles, essays, and photographs detailing the garments in that exhibit and highlighting what makes the fibers so special. It's a wonderful book that will make you look twice at many breeds.

As of this writing, Carol Ekarius and Deborah Robson have been hard at work completing an encyclopedic fiber reference book for Storey Publishing. It will become a classic as soon as it hits the shelves, and I'm saving a spot on my own desk for it.

Two magazines chronicle the ever-changing fiber landscape particularly well: *Spin-Off* (www.interweave. com/spin) and *Wild Fibers* (www. wildfibersmagazine.com). *Spin-Off* taps into the very pulse of the fiber arts

world, with solid editorial on technique and history and a focus on spinning, knitting, weaving, and felting. *Wild Fibers* takes a broader, exquisitely beautiful and culturally sensitive look at fiber-producing animals and the people around the world who raise them. Both magazines bring wool to life, and I urge you to add them to your collection.

You can also learn a lot about wool by studying the life cycle of the animals, and Paula Simmons's *Raising Sheep the Modern Way* is a great place to start. This book gives the background and technical foundation you'll need in order to make sense of the rather dense yet extremely informative *Sheep Production Handbook* published by the American Sheep Industry Association.

We've covered a lot of territory here, but the journey has just begun. I invite you to pack your virtual bags and join me online each week in *Knitter's Review* (www. knittersreview.com), where I highlight new and intriguing yarns, books, tools, and events from around the world. We have much more to discover.

Abbreviations and Techniques

Cable cast-on: Make a slip-knot and place it on the left-hand needle. With the working yarn, knit a stitch into the slip-knot—but do not remove the slip-knot from the needle. Instead, place the newly worked stitch back on the left-hand needle. Once these two stitches are in place, you'll cast on all remaining stitches by knitting into the space between the two most recent stitches on the left-hand needle and then placing the newly worked stitch back on the left-hand needle.

Cdd (centered double decrease): Slip the next 2 stitches together as if to knit them together. Knit the next stitch. Pass the 2 slipped stitches over the stitch just knit.

Crochet chain: Form a slip knot on the crochet hook, then wrap the yarn around the hook and pull a loop through the slip knot. This forms 1 chain.

Double crochet: Wrap yarn around crochet hook and then insert the hook into the stitch indicated in pattern, wrap yarn around the hook again and pull a loop through, wrap yarn around hook again and pull it through the 2 closest loops on the hook, then wrap yarn around hook again to pull through the remaining 2 loops on the hook.

Garter stitch: Knit all rows.

K: Knit.

Kfb (knit front and back—to create 2 stitches from 1): Knit through the front loop of a stitch but do not take it off the left-hand needle; knit through the back loop of the same stitch, then slip both stitches off of the left-hand needle.

Ktbl: Knit through the back loop of the stitch.

K2tog: Knit 2 stitches together.

K3tog: Knit 3 stitches together.

M1 (make 1): Pick up the strand between the stitch just worked and the next stitch on the left-hand needle, place it on the left-hand needle, and knit it through the back loop.

M1L (make 1 left): Make a left-leaning increase by picking up the bar between stitches from front to back and knitting into the back of the picked-up stitch.

M1P (make 1 purl stitch): Pick up the strand between the stitch just worked and the next stitch on the left-hand needle, placing it on the left-hand needle, and purling it through the back loop.

M1R (make 1 right): Make a right-leaning increase by picking up the bar between stitches from back to front and knitting into the front of the picked-up stitch.

P: Purl.

Pm: Place marker.

Provisional cast-on: Use this cast-on when you will want to access your cast-on stitches later (e.g., to create a hemmed cuff on a pair of socks). My favorite provisional cast-on is a crochet provisional cast-on, which comes to us from Lucy Neatby (who walks you through it in her *Knitting Essentials 2* DVD).

Take a knitting needle that's the size required for your project, plus a crochet hook and a length of scrap yarn that's the same thickness as your project yarn but, ideally, in a different color so you can see it clearly. Be sure you have enough yarn to cast on all the stitches required.

Create a slipknot on the crochet hook, and hold the crochet hook in your right hand. Place the knitting needle to the left of the crochet hook so that they are parallel to one another, with the working yarn running from the crochet hook and behind the knitting needle and held in your left hand. With the crochet hook, reach over the top of your knitting needle and wrap the yarn around the hook, then pull it through the slipknot. You have now created one stitch on the knitting needle.

Before you can repeat this step, you'll need to move your working yarn around your knitting needle and to the back again. Now you're ready to reach the crochet hook over the top of the knitting needle, wrap the yarn around the hook again, and pull it through the loop on your hook.

When your total number of desired stitches is on the knitting needle, make an emergency crochet chain with a few more stitches just using the crochet hook and not catching the stitches around the knitting needle. Your provisional cast-on is complete. When you're ready to unravel your provisional cast-on, simply find that emergency crochet chain and tug the end to unravel the whole chain and release those cast-on stitches.

Psso: Pass the slipped stitch over the stitch just worked.

RS (right side): Generally, the side of the garment that will face away from the skin when it is worn; the "public" side.

Single crochet: Insert crochet hook into the stitch indicated in the pattern, wrap yarn around the hook and pull a loop through, then wrap yarn around the hook again and pull through both loops on the hook.

Skp: Slip 1 stitch as if to knit, knit the next 1 stitch, then pass the slipped stitch over the stitch you just worked.

Sk2p: Slip 1 stitch as if to knit, knit the next 2 stitches together, and then pass the slipped stitch over the k2tog.

Ssk (slip, slip, knit): Slip 1 stitch as if to knit, slip another stitch as if to knit, replace both stitches on left-hand needle, and then knit them together through the back loops.

Stockinette stitch: Knit all right-side rows, and purl all wrong-side rows.

Three-needle bind-off: Arrange the stitches to be joined on 2 needles. Hold both needles parallel in the left hand, with the right sides together, unless your pattern specifies otherwise. Insert the right-hand needle through the first stitch on the front needle, then through the first stitch on the back needle; knit these stitches together. Insert the right-hand needle through the next stitch on the front needle, then through the next stitch on the back needle; knit these stitches together. Pass the first new stitch over the stitch just made. Continue in this manner, knitting the pieces together and binding them off as you go.

W&T (wrap and turn): Use this technique to prevent holes when working short rows. On knit rows, hold yarn to the back, slip the next stitch purlwise, and bring the yarn to the front. Slip the slipped stitch back to the left-hand needle and turn the work to proceed with the next row. On purl rows, slip the next stitch purlwise, then bring the yarn to the back of the work. Pass the slipped stitch back onto the left-hand needle and turn the work.

Wyif (with yarn in front): Work the indicated stitch with the yarn held to the front (or right side) of the work.

WS (wrong side): Generally, the side that will face toward the skin when the garment is worn; the "private" side.

Yo (yarn over): Wrap the yarn around the right-hand needle in the same manner that you would wrap it while knitting a stitch—only do so without touching any stitches on your left-hand needle.

About the Designers

PAM ALLEN (PAGE 138)

Pam Allen spends her days designing projects and dreaming up new yarn ideas for Classic Elite Yarns, where she serves as creative director. Pam routinely dons a beloved gray wool cardigan to keep warm in her sunny Portland, Maine, studio. She is the former editor of *Interweave Knits* magazine; author of *Knitting for Dummies* and *Scarf Style*; and co-author of *Lace Style*, *Color Style*, and *Bag Style*.

CAT BORDHI (PAGE 114)

According to Stephanie Pearl-McPhee, "Cat Bordhi's mission is to make you a more creative, free-thinking knitter who problem-solves and experiments with vigor and fearlessness. The best part? She can." Cat teaches and inspires more than 1,000 knitters a year in her classes and retreats all over North America. Her YouTube knitting tutorials reach many thousands more, and her innovative books—*Socks Soar on Two Circular Needles*, *A Treasury of Magical Knitting*, *A Second Treasury of Magical Knitting*, and *New Pathways for Sock Knitters*—have reached more than 100,000 knitters. Coming next: a book on Houdini socks! Visit her website at www.catbordhi.com.

M. DIANE BROWN (PAGES 183, 186)

A native Canadian transplanted to the United States long ago, M. Diane Brown has been a knitter since she was 5 years old. Fair Isle is her preferred

style of knitting, stemming from a long association with Shetland yarns, British designers, and a preference for fine yarns in general. She now designs and teaches in Santa Rosa, California.

NANCY BUSH (PAGE 100)

Nancy Bush found her way to traditional knitting techniques and uses of ethnic patterns via a degree in art history and postgraduate studies in color design and weaving in San Francisco and Sweden.

She has published articles and designs in *PieceWork*, *Knitter's*, *Interweave Knits*, *Spin-Off*, *Vogue Knitting*, and *Threads*. She teaches workshops in the United States and abroad and owns The Wooly West, a mail order yarn business in Salt Lake City, Utah. She is the author of *Folk Socks*, *Folk Knitting in Estonia*, *Knitting on the Road*, *Knitting Vintage Socks*, and *Knitted Lace of Estonia: Techniques, Patterns, and Traditions*.

EVELYN A. CLARK (PAGE 162)

Evelyn A. Clark lives in the Pacific Northwest, where she enjoys a quiet life that includes spinning and knitting. She specializes in lace designs and is the author of *Knitting Lace Triangles*, published by Fiber Trends. For more information about her designs, visit her website, www.evelynclarkdesigns.com.

JANE COCHRAN (PAGE 168)

Jane Cochran knits, spins, and runs a bookstore on the East End of Long Island, New York. She'll knit with most any fiber, but wool makes her hands and heart sing. Texture, color, twist, and luster on the needles are pure heaven, and she considers each new yarn and project a journey that she looks forward to taking. Jane blogs at www .notplainjane.blogspot.com.

SIVIA HARDING (PAGE 173)

A designer who dabbles in lace, beads, and, most recently, socks, Sivia Harding has been self-publishing her knitting patterns for several years. Her work can be found in the online magazine *Knitty*; the print magazine *Yarn*; and the books *Knitgrrl 2*, *Big Girl Knits*, *More Big Girl Knits*, and *No Sheep for You*. Follow her knitting adventures on her blog, www. siviaharding.blogspot.com. Her patterns are for sale at www.siviaharding.com and numerous yarn stores.

JENNIFER TEPPER HEVERLY (PAGE 110)

Jennifer Tepper Heverly owns Spirit Trail Fiberworks (www.spirit-trail.net), a company specializing in one-of-a-kind hand-painted yarns and luxury/rare breed spinning fibers. Her work has allowed her to join her love of color, fiber, and artistic expression in a vocation that is also an avocation. She knits and spins in Rappahannock County, Virginia, in a hand-made house in the woods with her husband, children, and numerous pets. Visit her blog at www.thespirittrail .blogspot.com.

SHELIA JANUARY (PAGES 92, 158, 178)

Shelia January has been a knitter since she was 8 years old. Knitting saved her sanity while attending college, while working for 28 years in the financial services industry, and, finally, while preparing to retire to a farm in Oregon, where she now lives. She knits and designs with her homespun yarn as well as with commercial yarn, and she teaches spinning and knitting at retreats, festivals, and shops across the country. Visit her blog at www.letstalkstash .blogspot.com.

ILGA LEJA (PAGE 152)

Nova Scotia–based designer Ilga Leja specializes in classic, elegant hand-knit designs featuring intriguing stitch patterns and unusual construction. Her theme-based collections include shawls, wraps, and sweaters. To see more of her designs, visit her website at www .ilgaleja.com.

SANDI ROSNER (PAGES 120, 126, 146)

Sandi Rosner taught herself to knit from the instructions in the back of a magazine in the late 1970s. She is the author of *Not Just Socks*, *Not Just More Socks*, and *Not Just Socks for Kids*. A former yarn store owner, Sandi is in demand as a knitting teacher, freelance designer, writer, and technical editor. She lives with her teenaged son in Sonoma County, California.

Author Acknowledgments

I remain ever grateful to the readers of Knitter's Review who brought me here and who continue to care about yarn as much as I do. You inspire me with your intelligence, your curiosity, and your eagerness for adventure, and I so enjoy our time together each week. May this book help you see even more creative possibilities for wool.

This book owes a great deal to Deborah Robson and Judith MacKenzie McCuin, both of whom have long served as my esteemed wool mentors. I sincerely thank them for so tirelessly working to raise breed awareness, and I especially thank them for patiently and generously sharing their knowledge with me.

The next debt of gratitude goes to the yarn companies, farms, and spinneries, without which we would have no yarn and no projects whatsoever—thank you.

I am equally grateful to the designers—trusted friends and colleagues—who helped me translate history and science into beautiful, wearable garments. Pam Allen, Cat Bordhi, Diane Brown, Nancy Bush, Evelyn Clark, Jane Cochran, Sivia Harding, Jennifer Heverly, Shelia January, Ilga Leja, and Sandi Rosner—it is an honor to share these pages with you. The swift and gifted fingers of knitters Cindy Grosch, Pat Hellhake, and Lindsey-Brooke Hessa brought many of these garments to life, and I thank them for taking such care with each stitch. Sandi Rosner did valiant double duty as both designer and technical editor, making sure all the patterns were as foolproof and intuitive as possible, while Peggy Greig transformed the charts and schematics into works of art.

At Potter Craft, I thank Jenny Frost for creating the hallowed halls in which I was allowed to walk, Lauren Shakely for keeping them so brightly lit, Rosy Ngo for opening the doors to me, and Rebecca Behan for guiding me inside—and I also give special thanks to my agent Linda Roghaar for staying by my side and making sure I never got lost.

What you see on the pages was greatly influenced by Chi Ling Moy, whose gifted eye brought true beauty and cohesion to each page. I also thank Alexandra Grablewski for capturing the essence of wool garments in her photographs, and Kate McKeon for capturing that same spirit in her illustrations.

Writing this book required a degree of focus that, at times, pulled me away from the rest of the world—even from those I hold nearest and dearest. I owe my family and loved ones an immense debt of gratitude for understanding and for willingly (though sometimes reluctantly) sacrificing their time with me so that I could realize this project. My cat Casey never quite figured out why my lap was unable to accommodate him and a computer. My dear friends Don and Robert, Joan and Marie, Stephanie, Mark, Cat, and Jane all helped me stay on course, with Clare serving as my beacon, my compass, and my North Star, reading every word and keeping the tea coming.

To my family's next generation of wool-wearers—Hannah and Emma, William and Henry, Jacob and Kaitlyn—may wool protect and warm you as you grow up, leave your nests, and venture out into the world.

Glossary

Bradford count A system for determining the quality of a particular wool sample on the basis of the theoretical number of 560-yard (512-m) hanks that can be spun from 1 pound (2.2kg) of clean wool roving. Established by English wool handlers in the city of Bradford, it is also called the English worsted yarn count system or spinning count system. The numbers are listed with an "s" at the end, such as "56s."

Breed A working principle that, like animals themselves, is constantly evolving. In its simplest form, a breed breeds true. One could also say that a breed exists when multiple generations of offspring consistently resemble their parents, physically and behaviorally. When used as a verb in this book, breed refers to the act of mating a ram and a ewe to produce offspring.

Carding The process of loosening up scoured fibers, opening the natural lock formation, and removing any dirt and unsuitable debris from fleece in preparation for spinning. On a commercial scale, carding is done on huge machines that consist of several series of large, opposing cylinders covered with tiny teeth. As the cylinders rotate, the fibers move through the carder and the teeth catch the fibers, stripping them from one cylinder and pulling them onto the next.

Combing A second step in the worsted fiber preparation process, whereby carded fibers are pulled through a series of fine metal combs to align all the fibers in the same direction and remove any shorter or irregular fibers. Combing tends to produce a lot of waste fiber that is saved and used in specialty yarns.

Crimp The natural curl and wave structure in a wool fiber.

Cross-breed When sheep of different breeds are mated with the intent of producing new results in the offspring. Breeders usually choose a ewe from the breed they wish to improve, then mate it with a ram from another breed whose desirable qualities they wish to pass on to the original breed.

Demiluster A category of fibers with some luster, but less than in the high-luster breeds.

Down The fine insulating fibers that grow close to the skin on dual-coated animals—the best known of which include cashmere, qiviut, and American bison. When capitalized, Down refers to the native shortwool sheep that originated in the Downs of England. Down-type wools exhibit similar characteristics to Down wools but come from sheep that originated elsewhere.

Dual-coated Also called double-coated, this term refers to those sheep breeds—usually the older so-called primitive ones—that grow an outercoat containing a mix of long, sturdy protective hairs and an undercoat of short, soft insulating fibers. Depending on the animal and the climate in which it lives, the fleece also may have some kemp intermingled among the fibers. In most cases, the fibers must be separated before spinning, but in Icelandic wool, both coats are considered wool and can be spun together into yarn.

Elasticity One of the most marvelous traits of wool is its elasticity. Wool fiber can stretch by 30 percent—up to 60 percent when wet—and still return to its original length. In yarn, elasticity allows garments to hug the body and maintain their shape.

Ewe A female sheep.

Felt / full What happens when you submerge wool fibers in hot soapy water and agitate them for a sustained period of time. The fibers swell as they absorb the water, causing the surface scales to pop out like umbrellas. The scales soon enmesh with one another, pulling together and becoming irretrievably tangled. When this process happens to fibers, it is called felting. When done to finished fabrics, it often is called fulling; it is a popular technique in the woven woolens industry. Fulling is also a common finishing technique for multiple-ply yarns, especially woolen-spun ones. The process gently felts the inside fibers together, anchoring the plies together and bringing the fiber ends to the surface to make a soft and fuzzy but cohesive yarn.

Fleece The mass of fiber shorn from a sheep. A fleece will contain everything on the sheep at the moment it was shorn, including dirt, grease (lanolin), suint, and stray vegetable matter.

Grease A raw, waxy substance that the sebaceous gland secretes onto a wool fiber as it emerges from the follicle. Grease can be extracted during scouring and later purified to create lanolin.

Guard hairs Long, coarse hairs that can grow among the finer wool fibers of many sheep. They protect the animal's softer insulating undercoat and are found most commonly among primitive sheep breeds. The trait to grow guard hairs has been essentially bred out of most modern finewool breeds.

Hand / handle How a fiber, yarn, or fabric responds to human touch.

Hank A skein of yarn wound on a reel.

Kemp Short, white prickly fibers that sheep can sometimes grow in their fleece, especially among primitive and dual-coated sheep breeds that have not been genetically "improved" over the centuries. Kemp is designed to pull moisture away from the sheep's skin, and the wetter the climate, the greater the chances that a sheep will grow kemp.

Lambswool The finest and softest fibers a sheep will ever grow: its very first coat. Lambswool comes from the first shearing, which usually takes place when the lamb is 7–8 months old.

Lanolin The waxy substance secreted onto the wool follicle by the sebaceous gland as the fiber emerges from the skin. In its raw form, it's often called grease. But when extracted through scouring and then purified, this material becomes lanolin. (Note: Many people, myself included, also call the raw, unpurified material "lanolin.")

Linebreeding A technique that involves mating sheep from two breeds, then breeding successive generations of that initial cross to further refine the genetic results. This term often is used in relation to new sheep breeds.

Lock A cluster of fibers that grow adjacent to one another on a fleece and usually share the same crimp pattern.

Loft The open, bulky quality that a fine, well-developed crimp can give to wool. Because crimp also contributes greatly to a yarn's elasticity, you'll often hear loft and elasticity used in the same sentence.

Loft also contributes greatly to insulation, because the loftier the fibers, the more still air they can trap, and the warmer the fabric will be.

Longwool A category of sheep breeds that originated in England. They grow long locks of curly fibers that often gather together into ringlets. These fibers tend to be smoother and more lustrous than their shorter finewool counterparts.

Luster A term used to describe how light reflects off the surface of a fiber. It can range from dull and chalky to matte and pearlescent to bright and silky, depending on the breed.

Micron A common unit for the measurement of fiber diameter. One micron is 1 millionth (0.000001) of a meter, or 1/25,400 inch, and is often represented with the Greek letter mu (μ). The smaller the fiber diameter (or micron count), the finer and generally more desirable the fiber. The larger the fiber diameter, the rougher the wool.

Nep Small tangled or matted clumps of fibers that can occur during carding and usually are removed later, during the combing process. The higher the crimp in wool and the finer its fiber diameter, the greater its tendency to form neps and the more careful a processor must be. Neps also can occur in long fibers that break during carding, as well as in fibers from fleeces that had natural breaks or multiple second cuts.

Noil The term for neps that have been combed out of a fiber. Noils are often saved and used for special effect in other yarns and textiles.

Polled Any variety of hornless sheep.

Primitive Although this term may carry negative connotations in other realms, it signifies wonderful things in the world of wool. Primitive breeds represent strains of animals—sheep and otherwise—that have not been genetically modified through crossbreeding. More hearty and independent than their improved counterparts, primitive sheep usually thrive with minimal human intervention.

Ram A male sheep.

Roving The continuous sheet of blended fibers produced by a carding machine. (Also may be called sliver or slubbing.)

Rooing The process of plucking hair from a sheep that is naturally shedding, which usually occurs in spring. The tendency to shed, or molt, has been largely bred out of the modern sheep breeds.

Scour To wash raw fleece to remove grease, suint, dirt, and any other impurities. Scouring is the first step in the process of turning fleece into yarn.

Shear To remove a sheep's fleece.

Shoddy Recycled or remanufactured wool. In 1813, a British man named Benjamin Law was credited with inventing the shoddy process, whereby used wool clothing and rags were shredded and regenerated into yarn and fabric. Shoddy was especially popular during World War II, when raw wool became extremely difficult to obtain.

Sliver The term that mills tend to use for a continuous sheet of blended fibers produced by the carding machine; also may be called slubbing or roving. The sliver is usually split into narrow ribbons that are fed into tall cylindrical bins for storage before being spun woolen or combed for worsted spinning.

Spinning count See Bradford count (page 202).

Staple The average length of fiber in an animal's fleece, usually after one year's growth.

Suint A salty residue of evaporated sheep perspiration on raw fiber. It is easily removed with water.

Thel The short, delicate undercoat that grows on the Icelandic sheep. It is soft, warm, and elastic.

Tog The long, strong, protective outercoat of fibers that grow on the Icelandic sheep. While most outercoats are considered hair, tog is also wool and usually is blended with thel to give the yarn strength, durability, and structure.

Top An industry term for fibers that are carded, combed, pulled into thin ribbons of fiber, and ready to be spun worsted.

Undercoat In dual-coated breeds, the undercoat tends to have the softest, finest fibers. They are protected by a more rugged outercoat that usually needs to be removed before spinning into yarn for hand-knitting.

USDA Wool Grades Micron-based fineness ratings that the U.S. Department of Agriculture assigned to the Bradford wool grades in an attempt to bring objectivity to the Bradford system.

Virgin Wool Wool that is making its debut into the yarn and textile world. Most contemporary wool hand-knitting yarns can be considered virgin.

Woolen Yarn from fibers that have been only minimally aligned before spinning, resulting in a lofty jumble of different-length fibers moving in every direction—even perpendicular to the yarn itself. Woolen-spun yarns lend themselves to crimpy fibers that are 2½ inches (6.5cm) or shorter. The yarns tend to be lofty and warm, but often at the expense of durability, especially with finer wools.

Worsted Yarn from fibers that have been carded and then fully combed so that they lie parallel to one another and are all of a uniform length. Better suited to wools that have a generous staple length, the worsted preparation tends to produce smooth and durable yarns. The term "worsted" also is used in the context of yarn thickness or weight. Worsted-weight yarn knits up at approximately 16–20 stitches per 4 inches (10cm).

Yolk The combined substances that are on raw fiber before it is scoured. They can include suint, dirt, and grease (which is later extracted and purified into lanolin).

CYCA Standard Yarn Weight System

YARN WEIGHT SYMBOL + CATEGORY NAMES	0 LACE	1 SUPER FINE	2 FINE	3 LIGHT	4 MEDIUM	5 BULKY	6 SUPER BULKY
TYPE OF YARNS IN CATEGORY	Fingering 10-count crochet thread	Sock, Fingering, Baby	Sport, Baby	DK, Light Worsted	Worsted, Afghan, Aran	Chunky, Craft, Rug	Bulky, Roving
KNIT GAUGE RANGE* IN STOCKINETTE STITCH TO 4 INCHES	33–40**sts	27–32 sts	23–26 sts	21–24 st	16–20 sts	12–15 sts	6–11 sts
RECOMMENDED NEEDLE IN METRIC SIZE RANGE	1.5–2.25 mm	2.25–3.25 mm	3.25–3.75 mm	3.75–4.5 mm	4.5–5.5 mm	5.5–8 mm	8 mm and larger
RECOMMENDED NEEDLE U.S. SIZE RANGE	000–1	1 to 3	3 to 5	5 to 7	7 to 9	9 to 11	11 and larger

Please note that these are GUIDELINES ONLY based on the most commonly used gauges and needle or hook sizes for specific yarn categories.

** *Lace weight yarns are usually worked on larger needles to create lacy, openwork patterns. Accordingly, a gauge range is difficult to determine. Always follow the gauge stated in your pattern.*

Index

Copyright © 2009 by Clara Parkes

Photography © 2009 by Potter Craft

Published in the United States by Potter Craft, an imprint of the Crown Publishing Group,
a division of Random House, Inc., New York.

www.crownpublishing.com

wwww.pottercraft.com

POTTER CRAFT and colophon is a registered trademark of Random House, Inc.

Library of Congress Cataloging-in-Publication Data
Parkes, Clara.
  The knitter's book of wool the ultimate guide to understanding, using, and loving this most
fabulous fiber / by Clara Parkes. -- 1st ed.
      p. cm.
Includes index.
ISBN 978-0-307-35217-0
1. Knitting--Patterns. 2. Wool. I. Title.
TT825.P365 2009
746.43'2--dc22

                              2009013787

Printed in China

Design by Tara Long/Dotted Line Design
Photography by Alexandra Grablewski
Illustrations by Kate McKeon
Photography page 4 by Frans Lemmons/Getty Images
Photography page 36 by Jorgen Larsson/Nordic Photos/Getty Images

Thanks to the Craft Yarn Council of America (www.yarnstandards.com)
for their Standard Yarn Weight System chart, which appears on page 204.

10 9 8 7 6 5 4 3 2 1

First Edition